RESPONSIBLE RESEARCH

A Systems Approach to Protecting Research Participants

Daniel D. Federman, Kathi E. Hanna, and
Laura Lyman Rodriguez, Editors

Committee on Assessing the System for Protecting
Human Research Participants

INSTITUTE OF MEDICINE
OF THE NATIONAL ACADEMIES

THE NATIONAL ACADEMIES PRESS
Washington, D.C.
www.nap.edu

THE NATIONAL ACADEMIES PRESS • 500 Fifth Street, N.W. • **Washington, DC 20001**

NOTICE: The project that is the subject of this report was approved by the Governing Board of the National Research Council, whose members are drawn from the councils of the National Academy of Sciences, the National Academy of Engineering, and the Institute of Medicine. The members of the committee responsible for the report were chosen for their special competences and with regard for appropriate balance.

Support for this project was provided by N01-OD-4-2139, Task Order No. 80, received support from the evaluation of set-aside Section 513, Public Health Service Act. The views presented in this report are those of the Institute of Medicine Committee on Assessing the System for Protecting Human Research Participants and are not necessarily those of the funding agencies.

Library of Congress Cataloging-in-Publication Data

Responsible research : a systems approach to protecting research
participants / Daniel D. Federman, Kathi E. Hanna, and Laura Lyman
Rodriguez, editors ; Committee on Assessing the System for Protecting
Human Research Participants.
　　p. ; cm.
Includes bibliographical references and index.
　ISBN 0-309-08488-1 (hardcover)
　1. Human experimentation in medicine—Moral and ethical aspects. 2.
Medical ethics. 3. Medical protocols. 4. Patients—Legal status, laws,
etc.
　[DNLM: 1. Clinical Protocols. 2. Human Experimentation. 3. Patient
Rights. 4. Safety. W 20.55.H9 R475 2002] I. Federman, Daniel D.,
1928- II. Hanna, Kathi E. III. Rodriguez, Laura Lyman. IV. Institute of
Medicine (U.S.). Committee on Assessing the System for Protecting Human
Research Participants.
　R853.H8 R476 2002
　　174'.28—dc21
　　　　　　　　　　　　　2002015090

Additional copies of this report are available for sale from the National Academies Press, 500 Fifth Street, N.W., Lockbox 285, Washington, DC 20055; call (800) 624-6242 or (202) 334-3313 (in the Washington metropolitan area); Internet, **www.nap.edu**.

For more information about the Institute of Medicine, visit the IOM home page at: **www.iom.edu**.

The serpent has been a symbol of long life, healing, and knowledge among almost all cultures and religions since the beginning of recorded history. The serpent adopted as a logotype by the Institute of Medicine is a relief carving from ancient Greece, now held by the Staatliche Museen in Berlin.

"Knowing is not enough; we must apply.
Willing is not enough; we must do."

—Goethe

INSTITUTE OF MEDICINE
OF THE NATIONAL ACADEMIES

Shaping the Future for Health

THE NATIONAL ACADEMIES
Advisers to the Nation on Science, Engineering, and Medicine

The **National Academy of Sciences** is a private, nonprofit, self-perpetuating society of distinguished scholars engaged in scientific and engineering research, dedicated to the furtherance of science and technology and to their use for the general welfare. Upon the authority of the charter granted to it by the Congress in 1863, the Academy has a mandate that requires it to advise the federal government on scientific and technical matters. Dr. Bruce M. Alberts is president of the National Academy of Sciences.

The **National Academy of Engineering** was established in 1964, under the charter of the National Academy of Sciences, as a parallel organization of outstanding engineers. It is autonomous in its administration and in the selection of its members, sharing with the National Academy of Sciences the responsibility for advising the federal government. The National Academy of Engineering also sponsors engineering programs aimed at meeting national needs, encourages education and research, and recognizes the superior achievements of engineers. Dr. Wm. A. Wulf is president of the National Academy of Engineering.

The **Institute of Medicine** was established in 1970 by the National Academy of Sciences to secure the services of eminent members of appropriate professions in the examination of policy matters pertaining to the health of the public. The Institute acts under the responsibility given to the National Academy of Sciences by its congressional charter to be an adviser to the federal government and, upon its own initiative, to identify issues of medical care, research, and education. Dr. Harvey V. Fineberg is president of the Institute of Medicine.

The **National Research Council** was organized by the National Academy of Sciences in 1916 to associate the broad community of science and technology with the Academy's purposes of furthering knowledge and advising the federal government. Functioning in accordance with general policies determined by the Academy, the Council has become the principal operating agency of both the National Academy of Sciences and the National Academy of Engineering in providing services to the government, the public, and the scientific and engineering communities. The Council is administered jointly by both Academies and the Institute of Medicine. Dr. Bruce M. Alberts and Dr. Wm. A. Wulf are chair and vice chair, respectively, of the National Research Council.

www.national-academies.org

COMMITTEE ON ASSESSING THE SYSTEM FOR PROTECTING HUMAN RESEARCH PARTICIPANTS

DENNIS TOLSMA, Associate Director, Clinical Affairs and Director of Research, Kaiser Permanente, Atlanta, GA

Liaisons

RICHARD J. BONNIE, John S. Battle Professor of Law and Director, Institute of Law, Psychiatry, and Public Policy, Charlottesville, VA

NANCY NEVELOFF DUBLER, Director, Division of Bioethics, Montefiore Medical Center; Professor of Epidemiology & Social Medicine, Albert Einstein College of Medicine, Bronx, NY

ELENA OTTOLENGHI NIGHTINGALE, Scholar-in-Residence, Institute of Medicine and National Research Council, Washington, DC

PILAR OSSORIO, Assistant Professor of Law and Bioethics, Associate Director of the Center for the Study of Race and Ethnicity in Medicine, University of Wisconsin, Madison Law School, Madison, WI

Study Staff

LAURA LYMAN RODRIGUEZ, Study Director
ROBERT COOK-DEEGAN, Senior Program Officer
JESSICA AUNGST, Research Assistant
NATASHA DICKSON, Senior Project Assistant

IOM Board on Health Sciences Policy Staff

ANDREW M. POPE, Board Director
CHARLES H. EVANS, JR., Scholar-in-Residence
ALDEN CHANG, Administrative Assistant
CARLOS GABRIEL, Financial Associate

Consultant

KATHI E. HANNA

Copy Editors

JILL SHUMAN
SARA MADDOX

Preface

The current extraordinary advances in basic biomedical and social sciences have unprecedented potential to improve the human condition. These insights, together with the human genome project and its successor proteomics, will require an enormous commitment to translational research to harvest their applications for medicine and public health. The progress in political and social theory, linguistics, statistics, psychology, and behavioral sciences generally deserves a similarly broad application of human research to reach full expression. These endeavors will require individuals to accept possible risk to themselves, benefiting the greater good with uncertain (or no) benefit accrued in return. Thus, those performing and overseeing research are obligated to provide the most reasonable assurances of safety possible.

Events in recent years have evoked considerable public concern about the safety of human studies and the measures in place to protect subject-participants. Isolated cases of unknown representativeness capture enormous public attention. The death of a subject during bronchoscopy, the death of a patient in a gene transfer experiment, the death of a healthy volunteer in an asthma study—these and similar occurrences are stridently announced and exhaustively analyzed for their heuristic guidance. As individual human tragedies they deserve all the attention they receive, including minute analysis as sentinel events from which to draw preventive guidance for future studies. But at this time, there is no way to know how representative these terrible events are and therefore no way to know what general lessons to infer from them for the uniquely human endeavor of studying some humans for the possible benefit of others. And, without quantification of the problem, there is no way to assess the appropriateness of new protections and their inevitable costs.

I believe any thinking person could be forgiven for assuming that there exists a reliable quantitative picture of the number of people harmed or injured each year as a result of their participation in research (let us call it the numerator)—and for assuming that there must similarly exist a comprehensive if not exhaustive registry of all individuals participating as "subjects" in biomedical or social science research (the denominator). Relating these to each other, society could reckon both the absolute magnitude of the problem and the fractional risk of harm confronting individuals considering participation. Frustratingly, neither figure is available, nor, without considerable effort, will they be forthcoming in the near future. This collective uncertainty has huge consequences.

An awareness of these problems led the Secretary of the Department of Health and Human Services to engage the Institute of Medicine for this study. We were asked to conduct an expeditious analysis of the possible value of accreditation of human research protection programs, which was published in April 2001. In addition, we were asked for a more comprehensive review of the present system for protecting human participants and to make suggestions for strengthening it. The latter is now offered.

Given the paradox of both the enormous potential and the uncertain reality in this area, what do we propose? We suggest that we address our current uncertainty by national data collection that in a few years should quantify and delimit the problem. However, until evidence is available, we believe it is necessary to pursue every promising mechanism to maximize the protection of individuals participating in research.

In order to accomplish this goal, we recommend that all research involving humans take place in settings or through organizational affiliations where the culture, announced and exemplified by the leadership, emphasizes the highest ethical standards and dedication to the welfare of every study participant. We further urge that all individuals responsible for the conceptualization and conduct of research be specifically trained in research ethics as well as techniques. We believe that the complexity of current science and, in the instance of clinical trials, the biological high stakes, require a review that begins with the scientific quality of the proposed research and a parallel examination of potential conflict of interest. These results would then lead into an explicit review of the ethical dimensions of the study. We urge a new approach to informed consent, one in which legal disclaimer and institutional self-protection are second to clear, simple, unclouded, unhurried, and sensitive disclosure that gives the potential participant all the information a reasonable person would need to make a well-informed decision, and the time to do so. Financial conflicts of interest at any stage or level of the process must be disclosed and managed so that the objectivity of research is preserved and the public trust is upheld.

We believe that the necessary efforts to accomplish these tasks are currently under-resourced, and we urge that that need for sufficient support be recognized and provided as a cost of the responsible conduct of research. And we believe that accreditation of programs should be explored as a means of achieving excellence, for it anneals two core mechanisms for improvement: self-assessment and the sharing of best practices.

We do not, however, urge a permanent accretion of new regulations and bureaucracy. Rather, we believe the protection system should be reexamined at a time when the steps described above can be accomplished, probably about five years from now. We strongly urge that a new look be taken when the magnitude of the problems and challenges facing the system can be appreciated and the appropriateness of protective mechanisms assessed. To do no harm is impossible. But to minimize harm while enabling the benefits of progress to emerge should be an attainable ideal.

Daniel D. Federman, M.D., *Chair*

Reviewers

This report has been reviewed in draft form by individuals chosen for their diverse perspectives and technical expertise, in accordance with procedures approved by the NRC's Report Review Committee. The purpose of this independent review is to provide candid and critical comments that will assist the institution in making its published report as sound as possible and to ensure that the report meets institutional standards for objectivity, evidence, and responsiveness to the study charge. The review comments and draft manuscript remain confidential to protect the integrity of the deliberative process. We wish to thank the following individuals for their review of this report:

Steven Black, Kaiser Permanente
Richard T. Campbell, University of Illinois at Chicago
Gary T. Chiodo, Oregon Health & Science University
Evan Gaines DeRenzo, The Johns Hopkins University
Gary Ellis, Silver Spring, Maryland
Michael Friedman, Pharmacia Corporation
John Gallin, National Institutes of Health
Paul L. Gelsinger, Citizens for Responsible Care and Research
Paul W. Goebel, Chesapeake Research Review, Inc.
Shirley M. Tilghman, Princeton University
Kathy Zeitz, Methodist Health System

Although the reviewers listed above have provided many constructive comments and suggestions, they were not asked to endorse the conclusions or recommendations nor did they see the final draft of the report before its release. The review of this report was overseen by Daniel R. Masys of the University of California, San Diego, and Mary Osborn, University of Connecticut Health Center. Appointed by the National Research Council and Institute of Medicine, they were responsible for making certain that an independent examination of this report was carried out in accordance with institutional procedures and that all review comments were carefully considered. Responsibility for the final content of this report rests entirely with the authoring committee and the institution.

Acknowledgments

The committee is grateful to the many administrators, investigators, policy makers, professional societies, and in particular, the research participants, their representatives, and their families that contributed their time, energy, and insight to the work and deliberations of this group throughout its two-year course (see Appendix A for listing of contributors to phase 2 activities).

Many thanks to Jeffrey Kahn and Robert J. Levine for their technical review of sections within the report and to Paul S. Appelbaum for his input to the committee's discussion regarding the informed consent process.

The committee also wishes to thank Lee Zwanziger, formerly of the Institute of Medicine, for her assistance and contribution to this project during the transition between Phases 1 and 2. Special gratitude is extended to Virginia deWolf, Constance Citro, and Andrew White of the Committee on National Statistics at the National Research Council and the entire CNSTAT/BBCSS Panel on IRBs, Surveys, and Social Science Research for their efforts to provide specialized insight into the questions facing this committee from the perspective of the social and behavioral sciences. Thanks also to Kenneth Shine, former President of the Institute of Medicine; Susanne Stoiber, Executive Officer of the Institute of Medicine; Clyde Behney, Deputy Director of the Institute of Medicine; and Andrew Pope, Director of the Institute of Medicine Board on Health Sciences Policy, for ongoing advice and guidance as this project progressed.

This report was made possible by the support of the U.S. Department of Health and Human Services (including the National Institutes of Health, the Office for Human Research Protections, the Food and Drug Administration, the Agency for Healthcare Research and Quality and the Centers for Disease Control) and The Greenwall Foundation. Special thanks to Greg Koski, Belinda Seto, and Irene Stith-Coleman for their extra efforts and repeated attention to the ongoing information needs and support of this study.

Acronyms

AAHRPP	Association for the Accreditation of Human Research Protection Programs, Inc.
AAMC	Association of American Medical Colleges
AAU	Association of American Universities
ACHRE	Advisory Committee on Human Radiation Experiments
ARENA	Applied Research Ethics National Association
BLA	Biologic License Application
CBER	Center for Biologics Evaluation and Research (FDA)
CDER	Center for Drug Evaluation and Research (FDA)
CEO	Chief Executive Officer
CIOMS	Council for International Organizations of Medical Sciences
CQI	continuous quality improvement
CRO	contract research organization
DHEW	(former) U.S. Department of Health, Education, and Welfare
DHHS	U.S. Department of Health and Human Services
DRB	Drug Research Board (NRC)
DSMB/DMC	data and safety monitoring board/data monitoring committee
DSMP	data and safety monitoring plan
FDA	Food and Drug Administration
FWA	Federalwide Assurance document (OHRP)
GAO	General Accounting Office

GCP	Good Clinical Practice (ICH)
HIPAA	Health Insurance Portability and Accountability Act of 1996
HRPPP	human research participant protection program
ICH	International Conference on Harmonisation
IND	Investigational New Drug Application (FDA)
IOM	Institute of Medicine
IRB	Institutional Review Board
MPA	Multiple Project Assurance document
NBAC	National Bioethics Advisory Commission
NCQA	National Committee for Quality Assurance
NDA	New Drug Application (FDA)
NHRPAC	National Human Research Protections Advisory Committee
NHS	National Health Service (Britain)
NIH	National Institutes of Health
NSF	National Science Foundation
OHRP	Office for Human Research Protections
OIG	Office of the Inspector General (DHHS)
OPRR	(former) Office for Protection from Research Risks
ORCA	Office of Research Compliance and Assurance (VA)
ORI	Office of Research Integrity (DHHS)
PHS	U.S. Public Health Service
PI	Principal Investigator
PLA	Product License Application (FDA)
PMA	Premarket Approval (FDA)
PRIM&R	Public Responsibility in Medicine & Research
QA	quality assurance
QI	quality improvement
Research ERB	Research Ethics Review Board
RFA	Request for Applications
SOP	standard operating procedure
SPA	Single Project Assurance document
SRC	Scientific Review Committee
VA	U.S. Department of Veterans Affairs

Contents

List of Tables, Figures, and Boxes

Tables

Figures

Boxes

RESPONSIBLE
RESEARCH

Executive Summary

ABSTRACT

The protection of individuals who volunteer to participate in research is essential to the ethical conduct of human research. In response to mounting concerns about the well-being of research participants and the ability of current approaches to ensure their protection, the Department of Health and Human Services commissioned the Institute of Medicine to perform a comprehensive assessment of the national system for providing research participant protection. The resulting analysis emphasizes the responsibilities and functions of human research participant protection programs (HRPPPs), providing substantive descriptions of the activities intrinsic to a robust protection program. In its work, the committee suggests a systems approach to providing protection, offers several broad recommendations for reform, and proposes practical suggestions to improve the oversight of human research at the institutional level.

In the committee's framework, the HRPPP is a system composed of interdependent elements that come together to implement policies and practices that ensure appropriate protection of research participants. The exact structure of an HRPPP will vary among research organizations and protocols according to the protection needs intrinsic to a particular study. Despite this flexibility, however, there are basic protection functions necessary to ensure the safety of participants and it is essential that all be met. These functions include: comprehensive review

1

of protocols (including scientific, financial conflict of interest, and ethical reviews); ethically sound participant-investigator interactions; ongoing and risk-appropriate safety monitoring; and quality improvement and compliance activities. Furthermore, to be effective, HRPPPs should operate within environments that emphasize accountability for the provision of participant protection, assure adequate resources for robust protection activities, provide ethics education programs to those conducting and those overseeing research with humans, and seek open communication and interaction with all stakeholders in the research enterprise.

A series of recommendations focuses on improving ethics review of protocols, reforming the informed consent process, improving access to information by participants and those responsible for review and monitoring of protocols, enhancing safety monitoring, compensating those who are harmed as a result of their participation in research, and developing a standard of quality improvement in HRPPPs.

Recommendations focused at the national level include: extending federal requirements for protection to include every research project involving human participants, regardless of funding source or research setting; collecting, assessing, and disseminating data about the overall system; and establishing an independent, nonpartisan advisory body that includes the perspectives of participants, scientists, ethicists, and research administrators to ensure that the national protection system receives objective and ongoing assessment.

In response to mounting concerns about the well-being of research participants[1] and the capability of current procedures to ensure participant protection, the Department of Health and Human Services (DHHS) commissioned the Institute of Medicine (IOM) to perform a comprehensive assessment of the national system for providing participant protection. Specifically, the IOM was asked to make recommendations regarding mechanisms to improve the structure and function of protection activities, as well as ways to continually evaluate performance of these activities. This in-depth analysis was intended to emphasize the responsibilities and functions of the individual human participant protection program (not restricted to Institutional Review Boards [IRBs]) and was to include the prospect of accreditation as a useful tool to achieve the desired performance improvements. This task was broken into two phases.

---

[1]This committee has elected to use the term "participant" rather than "subject" to reflect its belief that the optimal functioning of research oversight programs necessitates the meaningful integration of research participants and their perspectives (IOM, 2001a).

The first phase of work by the Committee on Assessing the System for Protecting Human Research Participants ("the committee") focused almost exclusively on accreditation. While examining the issues relevant to this subject, the committee introduced the concept of the Human Research Participant Protection Program (HRPPP) as the appropriate functional unit to implement and oversee protection functions. The committee's first report, *Preserving Public Trust: Accreditation and Human Research Participant Protection Programs*, provided a foundation for establishing an HRPPP, but was unable to provide much more than a sketch of the intended program (IOM, 2001a). The current report represents the culmination of the committee's deliberations and provides substantive descriptions of the functions and responsibilities intrinsic to a robust participant protection program.

In phase two, the committee was charged with the following tasks:

1. Review the ethical foundations for protecting human participants in research.
2. Assess and describe the current system for protecting human participants and make recommendations for potential enhancements and improvements to
    (i)   ensure informed consent,
    (ii) monitor ongoing research,
    (iii) accommodate private IRBs, multicenter research, and non-medical research,
    (iv) ensure continuous improvement in the system, and
    (v)   educate researchers, participants, and others involved in research with human participants.
3. Assess the potential impact of recommended changes on resource needs and how to address them.
4. Consider the effects of accreditation on improving human participant protection activities.
5. Determine the need and develop potential mechanisms for on-going independent review of the national system.

Many of the issues and policies pertinent to the committee's task have been in flux, with a number of commissions and organizations, including research institutions, professional associations, and the federal government, all working to find solutions to previously identified problems. In addition to countless news stories highlighting and influencing public discussion,[2]

---

[2]Blumenstyk, 2002; DeYoung and Nelson, 2000a,b; Flaherty et al., 2000; Flaherty and Struck, 2000; LaFraniere et al., 2000; Lemonick and Goldstein, 2002; Nelson, 2000; Shaywitz and Ausiello, 2001; Stephens, 2000; Stolberg, 2001; Wilson and Heath, 2001a,b,c,d,e,f,g.

reports have been issued,[3] accreditation programs have been launched,[4] privacy regulations have been promulgated and revised,[5] Congressional hearings have been held,[6] and legislation has been drafted.[7] This committee has endeavored, however, to formulate recommendations that reflect the current state of policy development, the present regulatory framework, and the efforts undertaken by others.

In contrast to other reports on these issues, this committee focused on the roles and responsibilities of the individual HRPPP, with the majority of recommendations directed toward improving the protection of the individual research participant through HRPPP policy and procedural enhancements.

STATEMENT OF THE PROBLEM

As recently detailed by the National Bioethics Advisory Commission (NBAC), many highly regarded groups have assessed the strengths and weaknesses of the national system for ensuring the ethical protection of volunteer research participants.[8] Proposals for reform have been presented to the public, the Executive Branch of the federal government, and Congress. However, a fact that has repeatedly confounded this committee's deliberations is the lack of data regarding the scope and scale of current protection activities. This absence of information seriously handicaps an objective assessment of protection program performance and needs and the development of useful policy directions. Nonetheless, the evidence is abundant regarding the significant strains and weaknesses of the current system, and this committee has reached the conclusion that major reforms are in order.

---

[3]AAMC, 2001; AAU, 2001; GAO, 2001; NBAC, 2001a,b; NIH COPR, 2001.

[4]Both the National Committee for Quality Assurance (NCQA) and the Association for the Accreditation of Human Research Protection Programs (AAHRPP) launched accreditation programs for human protection programs in 2001.

[5]The Health Insurance Portability and Accountability Act of 1996 regulations were modified in March 2002 and finalized in August 2002 (DHHS, 2002).

[6]The Senate Committee on Health, Education, Labor, and Pensions held a hearing on protecting research participants on April 23, 2002. The House Committee on Veterans Affairs held a hearing on VA research and nonprofit research corporations and educational foundations on May 16, 2002.

[7]Representatives DeGette and Greenwood have proposed legislation in the House of Representatives [A Bill to Amend the Public Health Service Act with Respect to the Protection of Human Subjects in Research. H.R. 4697. 107th Congress, 2nd Sess. (2002)]. Subsequent to the public release of this report, Senator Kennedy introduced the Research Revitalization Act [Research Revitalization Act of 2002. S. 3060. 107th Congress, 2nd Sess. (2002)].

[8]NBAC, the DHHS Office of Inspector General, the General Accounting Office, the Advisory Committee on Human Radiation Experiments, the President's Commission for the Study of Ethical Problems in Medicine and Biomedical and Behavioral Research, and the National Commission for the Protection of Human Subjects of Biomedical and Behavioral Research.

First, significant doubt exists regarding the capacity of the current system to meet its core objectives. Although all stakeholders agree that participant protection must be of paramount concern in every aspect of the research process, a variety of faults and problems in the present system have been noted. The common finding is that dissatisfaction with the current system is widespread.

Second, it has been shown that IRBs are "under strain" and "in need of reform" (AAU, 2001; GAO, 1996; Levine, 2001a; NBAC, 2001b; OIG 1998a, 2000a). The complexity of the issues, the variability in the research settings, the limitations of funding options, the demands of investigators and participants for access to research, and the accountability for institutional compliance have magnified and complicated IRBs' responsibilities. This heavy burden has made it difficult both to recruit knowledgeable IRB members and to allow them sufficient time for the necessary ethical reflection.

Third, the existing regulatory framework (i.e., the Common Rule[9] and the IRB system it created) cannot adequately respond to the complex and ever-changing research environment, with weaknesses related to gaps in authority, structure, and resources. Some of the problems can be addressed through interpretive guidance and clarification issued by the pertinent federal agencies and offices and through collaborations between federal authorities and private entities. However, in instances relating to deficiencies in authority, Congressional action is needed.

MAJOR RECOMMENDATIONS

The major recommendations of this report aim to ensure the protection of every research participant. The committee envisions a three-part strategy to achieve this goal, including refocusing the mission of the IRB on the thorough ethical review and oversight of research protocols; recognizing research participants' contributions and integrating them into the system; and maintaining high standards for and continuing review of HRPPP performance. Specific recommendations are organized around these themes in the following summary. By contrast, the report itself has been sequenced according to the natural progression of the research process. Additionally, two tables at the conclusion of this summary categorize the committee recommendations into those that will require direct government action and those that will not (Tables ES.1 and ES.2). The tables also indicate which agencies, organizations, offices, or individuals have the primary responsibility for the implementation of each recommendation.

---

[9]45 CFR 46, Subpart A.

6

RESPONSIBLE RESEARCH

Protect Every Research Participant

The protection of research participants is fundamental and should remain paramount to any research endeavor. In today's complex research environment, appropriate protection can most effectively be provided through a program of systematic and complementary protection functions within which roles and accountability are clearly articulated. HRPPPs, henceforth referred to as "protection programs" or simply "programs," should be viewed as a system of interdependent elements that involve the research organization, the IRB, the investigators, the sponsors, and most importantly, the volunteer participants. Redundancies in the system that do not add value should be eliminated. To this end, each research entity should develop clear, efficient, and effective processes and procedures. In addition, open and defined communication among those involved in participant protection should be established and maintained.

The diligent application of HRPPP policies and practices will ensure that participants in any research project are protected against undue risk, that informed consent to participate in the research is provided, and that all efforts are made to ensure that participants' rights, privileges, and privacy are protected throughout the entire research process. Therefore, protection requirements should be extended to include every research project that involves human participants, regardless of funding source or research setting.

The specific structure of a protection program is secondary to its performance of several essential functions. These functions include:

1) comprehensive review of protocols (including scientific, financial conflict of interest, and ethical reviews),
2) ethically sound participant-investigator interactions,
3) ongoing (and risk-appropriate) safety monitoring throughout the conduct of the study, and
4) quality improvement (QI) and compliance activities.

Recommendation: Adequate protection of participants requires that all human research be subject to a responsible Human Research Participant Protection Program (HRPPP) under federal oversight. Federal law should require every organization sponsoring or conducting research with humans to assure that all of the necessary functions of an HRPPP are carried out and should also require every individual conducting research with humans to be acting under the authority of an established HRPPP. (Recommendation 2.1)

Establish Accountability Within an Ethical Research Culture

Ultimate responsibility for the adequacy of an HRPPP resides at the highest level of an organization. An effective protection program requires the unequivocal support of the leaders of the relevant research organizations and the research sponsors. These leaders should engender an institutional culture that facilitates and improves the ethical and scientific quality of research within their purview. Four specific conditions should undergird the establishment of such a culture:

1) accountability—to assure the quality and performance of the protection program,
2) adequate resources—to assure that sufficiently robust protection activities are in place,
3) ethics education programs—to provide research personnel and oversight committees with the knowledge necessary to carry out their obligation to conduct or oversee ethically sound research, and
4) transparency—to ensure open communication and interaction with the local community, research participants, investigators, and other stakeholders in the research enterprise.

Each organization should tailor these pre-requisite conditions to its mission, the breadth and substance of its program, and the context of its community. When multiple organizations are involved in a research project, at least one of them should assume responsibility for obtaining appropriate and documented assurances from the other participating organizations that a robust protection program is in place at each site.

Recommendation: The authority and responsibility for research participant protections should reside within the highest level of the research organization. Leaders of public and private research organizations should establish a culture of research excellence that is pervasive and that includes clear lines of authority and responsibility for participant protection. *(Recommendation 2.2)*

Establishing the appropriate research culture will require ongoing efforts to educate researchers, research administrators, IRB members, and participants about research ethics and participant protection issues, as well as continuous QI activities. The Office for Human Research Protections (OHRP), with input from a variety of scholars in science and ethics, should coordinate the development and dissemination of core education elements and practices for human research ethics for those conducting and those overseeing such research. The individual research organization is responsible for ensuring that its personnel are educated about their responsibilities and expected conduct (see Recommendation 2.4). The sponsor also shares some responsibility for ensuring that the research organization it engages employs only qualified personnel and has the resources to conduct the study. The stimulation of a high-quality research culture is one area in which the committee believes that developing accreditation programs may offer a significant contribution by focusing an organization's attention on QI and specific resource needs.[10] The committee suggests in Chapter 6 that adding a standard within accreditation programs directed at establishing and identifying accountability for specific protection functions would facilitate performance improvement within accredited protection programs (see Recommendation 6.3).

Provide Sufficient Resources

Protection programs should have the dedicated financial and nonfinancial resources needed to implement and sustain a sufficiently robust system of protection, including adequate space, equipment, and personnel, in addition to an appropriate annual budget. Research organizations, sponsors, and investigators agree that funds should be allocated for investigators and staff and to cover the out-of-pocket costs of research, but no satisfactory agreement has been reached regarding how to fund specific protection activities.

Unfortunately, few published data quantify the costs of ethics review and other protection activities (such as safety monitoring); thus, it is difficult to determine reasonable funding levels for offices or the individuals involved in the process.

Adequate resources are essential for the protection of research participants and are a real part of the cost of doing research. Therefore, to assure successful protection programs, public and private research sponsors and research organizations should partner to develop benchmark guidelines for critical functions and to provide the necessary funding sources (see Recommendation 2.3).

Refocus Institutional Review Board Mission on Ethical Review of Protocols

As the demands on the research oversight system have grown, so has the reliance upon IRBs to accomplish all protection tasks. This is a disser-

---

[10]Accreditation efforts have been undertaken by AAHRPP and NCQA. The progress and potential contributions of accreditation programs are discussed in Chapter 6.

vice to research participants, because IRBs, which are intended to focus on the ethical review and oversight of proposals, find it exceedingly difficult to both manage the increasing volume of protocol actions and ensure the safety of research volunteers, particularly when these boards are often under-resourced.

In this committee's refocused paradigm, the responsibilities for managing institutional risk, ensuring institutional compliance with all relevant research rules and regulations, and assessing potential conflicts of interest related to proposed research should be assigned to other units within the research program or organization and not the IRB (see Chapter 6). Often, such units already exist and may be retooled to add the relevant participant protection focus to their responsibilities.

To reflect this refocused role, the committee recommends moving away from the term "Institutional Review Board," which conflates institutional interests with those of participants, and suggests adopting a more functionally appropriate term.

> **Recommendation: The Institutional Review Board (IRB), as the principal representative of the interests of potential research participants, should focus its full committee deliberations and oversight primarily on the ethical aspects of protection issues. To reflect this role, IRBs should be appropriately renamed within research organizations' internal documents that define institutional structure and policies. The committee suggests the name "Research Ethics Review Board" (Research ERB).** *(Recommendation 3.1)*

From this point forward in this report, the term "Research ERB" will be used in the context of the committee's envisioned HRPPP, and the term "IRB" will be reserved for comments regarding the existing protection framework.

All members of the Research ERB should have a core body of knowledge, and a critical mass of the membership,[11] either scientist or nonscientist, should possess a specialized knowledge of human research ethics. The research organization's goal should be to create or associate with a Research ERB in which unaffiliated members, nonscientists, and those who represent the local community and/or the participant perspective comprise at least 25 percent of the membership (see Recommendation 3.5). Although the committee recognizes that identifying this increased proportion of willing and able unaffiliated and nonscientist individuals will be difficult and that they will require additional training, the proportional shift is important to the integration of the participant or community and could help

---

[11]That is, a sufficient number of members to influence the tenor of the discussion.

insulate Research ERBs from potential conflicts of interest at the organizational level.

Further, as modern IRBs have tended to become larger and to reflect a broader range of scientific expertise, some IRB deliberations have tended to be dominated by the scientific perspective, increasing the potential to marginalize the perspectives of nonscientist members and those who focus on ethics-based concerns (Cho and Billings, 1997; Peckman, 2001). Therefore, the refocused Research ERB's deliberative objective should aim for consensus rather than majority control (see Recommendation 3.6). No protocol should be approved without three-quarters of the voting members concurring. Just as a vote of unanimity would effectively give a veto to a single dissenting committee member, allowing a simple majority to approve a protocol in the face of substantial minority opinion can too easily suppress responsible ethical opinions.

Distinguish Scientific, Conflict of Interest, and Ethics Review Mechanisms

The scientific and ethical review of protocols should be equally rigorous. Therefore, each review requires distinct, although overlapping, expertise. Research ERBs that are constituted to emphasize the ethical dimensions of protocol review should not be expected to have a primary membership with the range of knowledge and skills needed to adequately assess the scientific and technical merits of every protocol under their purview. Although the in-depth scientific evaluation of proposals is fundamental to the comprehensive ethics review of any protocol, the Research ERB need not conduct the initial scientific review. Instead, summaries of the scientific review should be submitted to the Research ERB as a component of its ethics-focused deliberations.

Furthermore, there is a need to ensure that no financial or other interests on the part of the investigator, research organization, or the Research ERB (as a body or as individual members) will distort the conduct of research with human participants.[12] While there are nonfinancial self-interests intrinsic to the pursuit of research questions, the frequency and complexity of potential financial conflicts of interest in research are expanding, and the federal government and relevant professional and industry groups should continue to consider their potential ramifications and pursue rigorous policies for handling them (see Chapter 6). A process for scrutinizing potential financial conflicts of interest in any protocol is vital to the subse-

---

[12]Potential conflicts of interest should also be considered when constituting Data and Safety Monitoring Boards or Data Monitoring Committees.

quent evaluation of participant risks and benefits by the Research ERB (see Chapter 3).

Despite the need for review from three distinct perspectives (scientific, ethical, and financial conflict of interest), the interrelated nature of these perspectives requires that a *single* body be vested with the authority to make final protocol determinations and be accountable for those determinations. This body is and should remain the Research ERB. The focused reviews of scientific merit and potential financial conflicts of interest should inform the ethics review process for each protocol (see Figure ES.1).

> Recommendation: Research organizations and research sponsors should ensure that Human Research Participant Protection Programs utilize distinct mechanisms for the initial, focused reviews of scientific and financial conflicts of interest. These reviews should precede and inform the comprehensive ethical review of research studies by the Research Ethics Review Board (Research ERB) through summaries of the relevant findings submitted to the Research ERB for full board consideration. *(Recommendation 3.2)*

Emphasize Risk-Appropriate Protection

The degree of scrutiny, the extent of continuing oversight, and the safety monitoring procedures for research proposals should be calibrated to a study's degree of risk. Minimal risk studies should be handled diligently, but expeditiously, while studies involving high risk should receive the extra time and attention they require. Although federal regulations provide several mechanisms for expeditiously reviewing certain kinds of research involving no more than minimal risk,[13] classifications of studies by risk level currently lack refinement and consistency. The development of such a stratification schema would be extremely useful to the research oversight community in their efforts to provide uniform and appropriate protection to research participants. This committee, as well as the panel constituted by the Committee on National Statistics and the Board on Behavioral, Cognitive, and Sensory Sciences and Education to examine issues pertinent to social and behavioral science,[14] believes that federal intervention and guidance nuanced to match the different risk strata are warranted (see Recommendations 3.3 and 5.1, and Appendix B).

---

[13]45 CFR 46.100, 21 CFR 56.104.

[14]The Panel on IRBs, Surveys, and Social Science Research is focusing on issues of human research participant protections in social, behavioral, and economic research. Its initial conclusions and recommendations are in Appendix B; its final report will be released in early 2003.

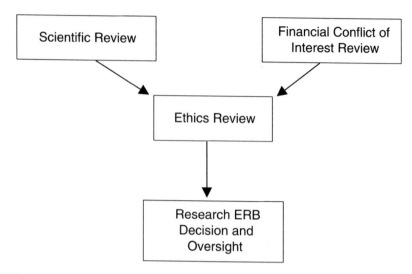

FIGURE ES.1   The Confluence of the Research Review Process

Increase Program Productivity

The effective oversight and management of the rapidly expanding number of multisite studies, particularly in the high-risk clinical domain, is an area of substantial concern (NBAC, 2001b; OIG, 1998a); full-scale IRB review of protocols by all participating organizations does not necessarily increase participant protection. Therefore, the committee encourages the streamlining of multisite trial review, recommending one primary scientific review committee and one primary Research ERB assume the lead review functions, subject to acceptance by the local committees and boards at participating sites (Recommendation 3.7).

The extreme variability in the approval decisions and regulatory interpretations among IRBs is one of the weaknesses in the current protection system. To better clarify regulatory intent and appropriate ethical practices, OHRP and the National Human Research Protections Advisory Committee (NHRPAC)[15] should convene conferences and establish working groups to develop and disseminate best practices, case presentations, and conference proceedings for local HRPPPs, their Research ERBs, and research investigators (Recommendation 3.8).

---

[15]As this report went to press, it was reported that DHHS had disbanded NHRPAC (Otto, 2002c; Weiss, 2002). Committee discussion and recommendations directed to NHRPAC should now be directed to any future advisory body constituted to address participant protection issues.

Recognize and Integrate Participant Contributions

As stated in this committee's first report, participants and their representatives should be meaningfully included in the review and oversight of research to ensure that pertinent concerns are heard and that researchers conduct studies that meet participant needs (IOM, 2001a). The public should also be educated generally about the nature of the research process and the need for well-designed research studies.

Revitalize Informed Consent

Informed consent should be an ongoing process that focuses not on a written form or a static disclosure event, but rather on a series of dynamic conversations between the participant and the research staff that should begin before enrollment and be reinforced during each encounter or intervention (see Box 4.3). Multidisciplinary approaches should be tailored to individual differences in participant education and learning capabilities.

> **Recommendation: The informed consent process should be an ongoing, interactive dialogue between research staff and research participants involving the disclosure and exchange of relevant information, discussion of that information, and assessment of the individual's understanding of the discussion.** *(Recommendation 4.1)*

The informed consent conversation(s), as well as the written consent document, should not be obscured by language designed mainly to insulate the institution from liability.[16] Rather, the process should ensure that participants clearly understand the nature of the proposed research and its potential risks and benefits to them and society.

> **Recommendation: Forms signed by individuals to provide their legally valid consent to participate in research should be called "consent forms" rather than "informed consent forms." Research Ethics Review Boards should ensure that the focus of the informed consent process and the consent form is on informing and protecting participants, NOT on protecting institutions.** *(Recommendation 3.4)*

Increase System Accessibility

The system of protections established by any protection program should be transparent and open to the public if research institutions, federal agen-

---

[16]We refer, for example, to the unnecessarily abundant discussion of remote risks for the purposes of institutional protection, rather than for use by the prospective participant in considering the truly pertinent risks inherent to a particular protocol.

cies, and private companies are to maintain the community's trust and ask individuals to participate in research. Transparency is best achieved by providing graded levels of information and guidance to interested parties (see Recommendation 2.5).

Open communication should also occur among all relevant stakeholders to achieve this transparency and to ensure that individuals can question how research protocols were developed, reviewed, and implemented. Furthermore, those who stand to benefit or be harmed by the research should have an opportunity to comment on the research design and operation, to participate in the research, and to have access to study findings. They should also expect the research will not involve unnecessary duplication of previous studies.

In 2000, the National Library of Medicine established a clinical trials registry,[17] which has expanded to serve as the Food and Drug Administration (FDA)-required site for submissions about clinical trials subject to the FDA databank requirement[18] and to include information from several other trial registries (see Chapter 7). Although the development of such registries is an important first step toward providing high-quality clinical trial information to the public, currently no centralized system exists for disseminating information about clinical trials of drugs or other interventions, making it difficult for consumers and their health care providers to identify ongoing studies.

To ensure that information about all clinical trials is available, the committee proposes the creation of a comprehensive and soundly struc-tured clinical trials registry for use by the public. Material submitted to Research ERBs could serve as the backbone of this registry.[19] The commit-tee believes that although the challenges and resource requirements involved in such an undertaking are significant, clinical trials are of such public con-cern that the effort should be pursued (see Recommendation 7.2).

Compensate Participants for Research-Related Injury

Despite decades of discussion on the ethical obligation to compensate participants for research-related injury, little information is available re-garding the number of such injuries and the cost of providing compensation for them (ACHRE, 1995; DHEW, 1977; NBAC, 2001a,b; President's Com-mission, 1982a). In the face of real potential for diminished public trust in

---

[17]See www.clinicaltrials.gov.

[18]FDA Modernization Act of 1997. P.L. 105-115, 1997. Section 113.

[19]Basic material submitted for approved protocols might include disease target, a general description of the intervention, trial site locations, and contact information to learn more about the study. One option would be to adopt at a minimum the same inputs required for compliance with Section 113 of the FDA Modernization Act (P.L. 105-115, 1997). It should be noted that the basic information submitted to the registry would not need to include trial results.

the research community,[20] providing reasonable compensation for legitimate instances of research harm is critical to restoring credibility.

Although some activities in this area are ongoing, and international experience is available for guidance, determining the portion of participant illness and injury that is attributable to the research itself is a key area that will require de novo research. To guide public policy and accreditation standard development in this area and to help establish the potential magnitude of such claims, DHHS should assemble data on the incidence of research injuries and conduct economic analyses of their costs (see Recommendation 6.7).

It is the committee's impression that many research organizations conducting clinical trials agree to provide at least short-term medical care for those who suffer research-related injuries (DoD, 2002; IOM, 1994a; NIH CC, 2000; 38 CFR 17.85), but that few research organizations cover other relevant costs. These observations refer only to harm resulting from research properly conducted in accordance with the protocol; harm due to negligence or malfeasance in science can and does end up in the tort system. However, a no-fault system could allow injured parties speedier claims resolution while permitting (as now) the pursuit of tort remedies for product defects or for negligent design or execution of studies.

The responsibility for no-fault compensation programs should fall initially on the institution or organization accountable for conducting the research, and its terms should be specified in the documentation accompanying the participant's agreement to participate. The committee supports the findings of the many reports addressing this topic—that a comprehensive research participant protection system should include a compensation mechanism for medical and rehabilitative costs (ACHRE, 1995; DHEW, 1977; NBAC, 2001a,b; President's Commission, 1982a). The committee further believes that the next step in this process should be to pilot test mechanisms to provide remuneration for lost work time.

> **Recommendation: Organizations conducting research should compensate any research participant who is injured as a direct result of participating in research, without regard to fault. Compensation should include at least the costs of medical care and rehabilitation, and accrediting bodies should include such compensation as a requirement of accreditation.** *(Recommendation 6.8)*

---

[20]This assertion is based upon increased media attention to research issues including recent adverse events and financial conflicts of interest, increased attention given by regulatory agencies to institutional noncompliance, and the growing pressures on the research system.

Maintain Vigilance

Collect National Level Data About the System

The absence of sufficient data regarding human research activities significantly impedes the thorough examination of system performance. The value of data to support both problem definition at the national level and QI at the program level cannot be overemphasized (see Chapter 6). Collecting such data would be a considerable and lengthy undertaking, and the committee recognizes that some information needs may be better met through targeted studies. Scientific surveys involving representative samples rather than a full census would serve policy-setting priorities cost effectively (Recommendation 6.1).

Enhance Safety Monitoring

The safety of research volunteers must be guaranteed from the inception of a protocol, through its execution, to final completion and reporting of results. Continual review and monitoring of risk-prone studies is needed to ensure that emerging information has not altered the original risk-benefit analysis. Therefore, risk-appropriate mechanisms are needed to track protocols and study personnel; provide assurances that data are valid and collected according to applicable practices (e.g., Good Clinical Practice); and ensure that participants' safety, privacy, and confidentiality are protected throughout a study. Protection measures should be monitored by various means at all levels to ensure that consent has been properly given and that all adverse events have been identified and appropriately reported by the investigator to the relevant institutional body, sponsor, and federal agency(ies).

> **Recommendation: Research organizations and Research Ethics Review Boards should have written policies and procedures in place that detail internal oversight and auditing processes. Plans and resources for data and safety monitoring within an individual study should be commensurate with the level of risk anticipated for that particular research protocol.** *(Recommendation 5.1)*

An area of intense concern regarding the ongoing safety monitoring of research protocols, particularly high-risk clinical trials, is the ability of protection programs and their Research ERBs to appropriately collect, interpret, and report adverse event information (see Chapter 5). Federal oversight agencies, therefore, should harmonize safety monitoring guidance, develop standardized practices for defining and reporting adverse events, and monitor all federally regulated studies that pose substantial risks to participants with equal rigor and scrutiny (see Recommendations 5.3 and 5.5).

Continuously Improve Quality

To maximize the strength and efficiency of participant protection functions, the effectiveness and value of program policies and practices should be continuously assessed and improved. Protection programs can use systematic QI analysis tools to determine the underlying causes of shortfalls and develop procedures to eliminate them and improve work processes. The committee, in its first phase of deliberations regarding accreditation, emphasized the need to incorporate QI mechanisms into program performance assessment (IOM, 2001a).

The lack of empiric data on the performance of protection programs, the absence of defined measurable outcomes or other criteria for their ongoing evaluation, and the scant knowledge of approaches and methods by which programs have been improved have hindered efforts to initiate QI measures. Research sponsors should initiate programs and locate funding to develop criteria for evaluating program performance and enhancing QI practices. In doing so, specialists from many disciplines could contribute to a new empiric knowledge base that would inform both the leadership of individual HRPPPs and policy makers.

> **Recommendation: Research sponsors should initiate research programs and funding support for innovative research that would develop criteria for evaluating program performance and enhancing the practice of quality improvement.** *(Recommendation 6.2)*

As observed in this committee's first report, accreditation programs represent one promising approach to assessing the protection functions of research organizations in a uniform and independent manner, and may serve as a useful stimulus for QI programs (IOM, 2001a). The committee reiterates its support for pilot testing voluntary accreditation as an approach to strengthening participant protections, but repeats its recommendation that DHHS should arrange for a substantive, independent review and evaluation of HRPPP accreditation before determining its ultimate role in the participant protection system (see Recommendation 6.4).

Manage Potential Conflicts of Interest

Confidence about the current system of participant protection is undermined by the perception that harm to research participants may result from conflicts of interest involving the researcher, the research organization, and/or the research sponsor. This concern is particularly acute regarding financial conflicts of interest, as the relationships between the academic and private research enterprises continue to evolve. Therefore, mechanisms for identifying, disclosing, and resolving conflicts of interest should be strengthened, especially those involving financial relationships (see Chapter 6).

Strong organizational leadership and the promotion of an ethically based research culture (possibly complemented through appropriate accreditation standards) may help avoid the need for management policies regarding potential self-interests; however, a dedicated conflict of interest review process will remain essential. Guidelines for acceptable levels of conflict and policies for managing conflict should continue to be developed so that common professional standards can be implemented and refined.

In the committee's view, because the Research ERB lacks the necessary resources or authority to ensure the appropriate management of potential conflicts of interest, the responsibility for assessing and managing financial conflicts of individuals (investigators, research staff, and Research ERB members) should lie with the research organization (see Recommendation 6.5). Likewise, organizations should ensure that an independent, external mechanism is in place for the evaluation of potential institutional conflicts (see Recommendation 6.6). In both instances, conflict of interest information should be communicated in a timely and effective manner to the Research ERB, which should make the final assessment with regard to ensuring participant protections.

The impact of institutional conflicts of interest as well as nonfinancial conflicts of interest at all levels of the research enterprise have not been explored sufficiently and are issues that, like the development of professional norms for individual conflicts of interest, should be rigorously pursued by federal agencies and appropriate interest groups.

Periodically Assess the National System

Complexity, opacity, and contradiction abound in interpretations of the rules and regulations that apply to human research, often confounding clear communication between agencies and institutions. Although the language of the Common Rule deserves a careful and comprehensive reassessment for clarity and relevancy after more than 20 years of use, its revision would be time-consuming and difficult, as each signatory agency must agree to the changes. Eventually, Congress will need to take the necessary steps to broaden and strengthen the federal oversight system and to make appropriate Common Rule modifications as needed.

One mechanism through which continuing and periodic review of the national participant protection system could be provided is NHRPAC.[21] This committee was created by the Secretary of DHHS in concert with the creation of OHRP in June 2000 to provide expert advice and recommenda-

---

[21]The recent dissolution of NHRPAC underscores the need for Congressional direction in the establishment of a nonpartisan, independent advisory committee focused on the policy issues relevant to ensuring the protection of research participants, as discussed in Chapter 7.

tions to the DHHS Secretary, the Director of OHRP, and other departmental officials on a broad range of topics pertaining to or associated with the protection of human research participants.

If NHRPAC, or any advisory committee, is to successfully guide federal policy and preserve the public trust, there must be no appearance or existence of conflict in its membership or organization, and the committee should be perceived as an independent entity. However, creating the necessary balance in a federal advisory committee presents a significant challenge, considering the breadth of federal agencies with oversight responsibility and the profound stake the public has in human research activities.

The committee therefore proposes the establishment of a nonpartisan, independent body of experts to ensure that the national protection system receives objective public advice (Recommendation 7.1). Inherent within the multidisciplinary concept for this advisory committee's membership is balanced representation of the perspectives of participants, a range of scientific disciplines, bioethics, and IRB experts.

Such a committee could provide ongoing advice and guidance on the scientific, technological, and ethical issues related to participant protection in clinical and social/behavioral research and could provide the capacity and mechanism for examining national system performance changes over time to provide policy makers and the research community with options for ensuring continuous improvement.

CONCLUDING REMARKS

Policy makers and the scientific community should ensure that the interests and dignity of every research participant are diligently protected throughout the research process. The complexity and multifaceted nature of research requires that many offices and individuals interact and coordinate activities to form a systemic HRPPP. Tables ES.1 and ES.2 organize the committee recommendations according to their need for government action, and also serve to highlight those parties within protection programs and the federal government that possess primary responsibility for the implementation of each recommendation. The recommendations offered within this report are intended to guide HRPPPs and policy makers as they work to guarantee that research participants' safety and rights are protected throughout their involvement in any research study and that the national research enterprise is worthy of the public's trust and continued support.

TABLE ES.1 Recommendations That Require Direct Government Action

Recommendation	Congress	The Department of Health and Human Services					Relevant Regulations[a]
		Office of the Secretary	NHRPAC	OHRP	FDA	NIH	
2.1 Require federal protections to be in place for all research with human participants, regardless of the source of research funding.[b]	X	X					45 CFR 46.101
2.4 Coordinate the development and dissemination of ethics education practices.				X			45 CFR 46.107(a) and 46.111(a)(1)
3.3 Coordinate the development of guidance for risk classification.				X			45 CFR 46.111(a)(b) 21 CFR 56.111(a)(b)
3.8 Convene conferences and/or establish working groups to develop and disseminate best practices, case presentations, and conference proceedings for use by local protection programs.			X	X			
5.2 Ensure that research organizations are notified of deficiency warnings and all related communications issued by regulatory agencies.				X	X		
5.3 Harmonize safety monitoring guidance for research organizations, including standard practices for defining and reporting adverse events.[c]				X	X	X	45 CFR 46.103(b)(5) 21 CFR

Recommendation				CFR
5.4 Issue a yearly report summarizing the results of research monitoring activities in the United States, including OHRP and FDA findings from inspections conducted the previous year.	X	X	X	56.108(b) 21 CFR 312.32
5.5 When potential risks to participants warrant high levels of scrutiny, NIH-funded studies should be monitored with the same rigor and scrutiny as trials carried out under an IND.			X	21 CFR 312.23 21 CFR 312.53
6.1 Commission studies to gather baseline data on the current national system of protections for research participants.	X			
6.4 Pilot test and evaluate voluntary accreditation as an approach to strengthening human research participant protections.[d]	X			
6.7 Assemble data on the incidence of research injuries and conduct economic analyses of their costs to establish the potential magnitude of claims that would arise under a no-fault compensation system for such injuries.	X			
7.1 Authorize and appropriate support for a standing independent, multidisciplinary, nonpartisan committee on human research participant protections.	X			

(continued)

TABLE ES.1 Continued

| Recommendation | Congress | The Department of Health and Human Services | | | | | Relevant Regulations[a] |
		Office of the Secretary	NHRPAC	OHRP	FDA	NIH	
7.2 Facilitate the establishment of a comprehensive clinical trials registry.		X		X	X	X	
7.3 Groups addressing bioterrorism response mechanisms and research should pay special attention to the protection of research participants.		X		X	X	X	

NOTE: Within the table, entities with primary responsibility for the implementation of committee recommendations are indicated by an X. In many instances, additional agencies may be involved in the implementation of recommendations (e.g., FDA should participate in the development of guidance for risk classification [Recommendation 3.3]); however, only the lead responsibilities are indicated within the table.

[a]The relevant regulations are provided for reference. Unless otherwise noted, the committee recommendations can be implemented without further promulgation or revision of regulations. In several instances, the development of guidance documents directed at specific issues may be useful to facilitate the recommended action.

[b]Implementation would necessitate modification to current regulatory language.

[c]In addition to the agencies within the Department of Health and Human Services (DHHS), all federal agencies sponsoring or overseeing human research should be consulted to ensure that reporting requirements for adverse events involving nonphysical harms are similarly harmonized.

[d]DHHS is responsible only for ensuring that an independent *evaluation* of accreditation is undertaken.

TABLE ES.2 Recommendations That Can Be Implemented in the Absence of Direct Government Action

Recommendation	Research Organization	Sponsors	Research ERBs[a]	Investigators	Research Participants	Accreditation Programs	Relevant Regulations[b]
2.2 Establish a pervasive culture of research excellence that includes clear lines of authority and responsibility for participant protection.	X	X					45 CFR 46.103(a)(b)
2.3 Provide the necessary financial support to meet the obligation to ensure HRPPPs have adequate resources.	X	X					
2.4 Ensure that investigators, IRB members, and other individuals substantively involved in human participant research are adequately educated to perform their respective duties.	X	X				X	45 CFR 46.107(a) and 46.111(a)(1)
2.5 Foster communication with the general public and research participants to assure that the protection process is open and accessible to all interested parties.	X	X					

(continued)

TABLE ES.2 Continued

Recommendation	Research Organization	Sponsors	Research ERBs[a]	Investigators	Research Participants	Accreditation Programs	Relevant Regulations[b]
3.1 Rename the Institutional Review Board to reflect its role as the principal representative of the interest of potential research participants.	X						45 CFR 46.102(g) 21 CFR 56.102(g) 21 CFR 50.3(i)
3.2 Ensure that focused scientific and financial conflicts of interest reviews precede and inform the comprehensive ethical review of research studies by the Research ERB.	X	X					45 CFR 46.107(e)(f), 46.115(a)(1), and 46.116
3.4 Ensure that the focus of the informed consent process and consent forms is on informing participants, NOT protecting institutions.	X	X	X	X			45 CFR 46.116 21 CFR 50
3.5 Reserve 25 percent of Research ERB membership for individuals with unaffiliated and non-scientific perspectives.	X		X				45 CFR 46.107 21 CFR 56.107

25

Recommendation	CFR Citation			
3.6 Conduct Research ERB deliberations by consensus and, in the absence of consensus, require 3/4 majority for approval.	45 CFR 46.108(b) 21 CFR 56.108(c)			X
3.7 Streamline the reviews of multisite trials by assigning lead review committees	45 CFR 46.114 21 CFR 56.114		X	X
4.1 Conduct the informed consent process as an on-going, interactive exchange between research staff and research participants.	45 CFR 46.116 21 CFR 50	X	X	X
4.2 Research participants should understand their potential role in the study, the rationale of the study, and what is required of them to prevent unanticipated harm to themselves and to maintain the scientific integrity of the study.	45 CFR 46.116 and 21 CFR 50	X	X	
5.1 Create written policies and procedures that detail internal monitoring and auditing processes.	45 CFR 46.103(b) 21 CFR 56.108(a)	X	X	X

(continued)

TABLE ES.2 Continued

Recommendation	Research Organization	Sponsors	Research ERBs[a]	Investigators	Research Participants	Accreditation Programs	Relevant Regulations[b]
5.2 Ensure that Research ERBs are notified of deficiency warnings and all related communications issued by regulatory agencies and of any serious violations identified through sponsor-requested monitoring reports.	X	X					21 CFR 312.23 21 CFR 312.53
5.5 When potential risks to participants warrant high levels of scrutiny, NIH-funded studies should be monitored with the same rigor and scrutiny as trials carried out under an IND.	X	X					
5.6 Ensure an independent Data and Safety Monitoring Board/ Data Monitoring Committee is assigned to high-risk studies or those involving participants with life-threatening illnesses.	X	X	X				45 CFR 46.111(a)(6) 21 CFR 56.11(a)(6)

Recommendation			Regulatory citation
6.2 Initiate research programs and funding support for innovative research that would develop criteria for evaluating program performance and enhance the practice of quality improvement.		X	
6.3 Include an accreditation standard directed at establishing and identifying accountability for specific protection functions.	X		
6.4 Pilot test and evaluate voluntary accreditation as an approach to strengthening human research participant protections.	X		
6.5 Ensure prospective, in-depth review of potential individual financial conflicts of interest.		X	42 CFR 50 21 CFR 54 45 CFR 46.116
6.6 Establish an external mechanism to review potential institutional conflicts of interest.		X	
6.8 Compensate any research participant who is injured as a direct result of participating in research, without regard to fault. Include compensation for research-related injury as a requirement of accreditation.c	X	X	45 CFR 46.116(a)(6)

(continued)

TABLE ES.2 Continued

Recommendation	Research Organization	Sponsors	Research ERBs[a]	Investigators	Research Participants	Accreditation Programs	Relevant Regulations[b]
7.3 Groups addressing bioterrorism response mechanisms and research should pay special attention to the protection of research participants.	X	X	X	X			

NOTE: Within the table, entities with a primary responsibility for the implementation of committee recommendations are indicated by an X. In several instances, other elements within an HRPPP may possess a secondary role in the systemic implementation of the recommendation (e.g., the Research ERB); however, to preserve the clarity of the table, only primary relationships are indicated. Likewise, while the pursuit of a recommended action may be facilitated by a government organization, this indirect role is not represented within the table. Some recommendations are contained within both tables due to their multistep nature or substantial overlapping responsibility.

aIn accordance with Recommendation 3.1, Research Ethics Review Board (Research ERB) is used to designate the traditional IRB panel.

bThe relevant regulations are provided for reference. Unless otherwise noted, the committee recommendations can be implemented without further promulgation or revision of regulations. In some instances, the development of guidance documents directed at specific issues may be useful to facilitate the recommended action.

cIf it is determined through the evaluation of the suggested demonstration programs covering lost income due to temporary or permanent disability resulting from research harm that a federal insurance program is the appropriate solution to broad implementation of this responsibility, Congressional intervention could be required (see Chapter 6).

1

Introduction

S ince the beginning of modern history, we have sought cures for disease and injury and searched for ways to improve the well-being of societies through the understanding of cultures and civilizations. Scientific progress has been central to these efforts, leading to vast improvements in the way we live. Often, this progress has occurred by studying humans and the human condition. Thus, those who participate as the subjects of research studies should share in the accolades usually accorded great scientists. In some studies, research participants[1] assume great risks, even though the prospect for personal benefit is slim or nonexistent. By volunteering to participate, they provide researchers with a capability that they would otherwise lack. In return, research participants deserve to be fully informed, treated with respect, listened to, and protected from foreseeable harms. At the very least, they deserve respect and the highest level of consideration for their safety and well-being. Concern for their rights and welfare should permeate every aspect of the research process, from protocol design to dissemination of results.

A series of events in the late 1990s involving mishaps and errors—some tragic—in the conduct of human research focused renewed attention on the ethical requirement to protect the rights and welfare of those who volunteer

---

[1]This committee has elected to use the term "participant" rather than "subject" to reflect its belief that optimal functioning of research oversight programs necessitates the meaningful integration of research participants and their perspectives (IOM, 2001a).

to participate in research. The rapid growth in the size and breadth of the research enterprise in the United States makes it imperative to determine how improvements can be made in the system of protections to ensure that, given the volume and sometimes complex nature of research, institutions and investigators fulfill their ethical responsibilities to research participants.

CONTEXT FOR THIS REPORT

In October 2000, the Department of Health and Human Services (DHHS) asked the Institute of Medicine (IOM) to conduct a two-phase study to address concerns about protecting the rights and interests of research participants. The first-phase report, *Preserving Public Trust: Accreditation and Human Research Participant Protection Programs*, was released in April 2001 (IOM, 2001a). In that report, the Committee on Assessing the System for Protecting Human Research Participants ("the committee") developed terminology to describe a set of activities and functions critical to protecting research participants. The term "Human Research Participant Protection Program" (HRPPP), although perhaps unwieldy, reflects the committee's vision of a system of components, functions, and accountability that should exist, at a minimum, when human research is conducted.

In its first report, the committee addressed the potential for accreditation of HRPPPs to enhance the function of the current protection system. The committee also outlined the basic elements of an HRPPP, envisioning a *system* with appropriate functions within which roles and accountability would be articulated. The committee suggested that HRPPPs are the appropriate units for accreditation, that human research participant protection should be integral to every aspect of the research effort, and that it can most effectively be provided through an HRPPP. However, it will be critical to evaluate the effects of accreditation to determine whether it actually improves protections.

In this second-phase report, the committee broadens its focus, refining the concept of an HRPPP and examining the overall system of protections within which accreditation is merely one factor. The two primary questions addressed in this phase are, "What should be the functioning units of the protection system?" and "How can performance be assessed to ensure the public safety and effectively maintain public trust?"

It should be noted that the current system is a moving target, and the committee acknowledges that a number of individuals and groups are working within this framework to improve protections for human research participants. It could be said that many institutions already have an HRPPP in place, some more fully developed than others and perhaps applying different names and functions while seeking to achieve the same goals.

In this report the committee was specifically charged with the following tasks:

1. Review the ethical foundations for protecting human participants in research.
2. Assess and describe the current system for protecting human participants and make recommendations for potential enhancements and improvements to
    (i)   ensure informed consent,
    (ii)   monitor ongoing research,
    (iii)   accommodate private Institutional Review Board (IRBs), multicenter research, and nonmedical research,
    (iv)   ensure continuous improvement in the system, and
    (v)   educate researchers, participants, and others involved in research with human participants.
3. Assess the potential impact of recommended changes on resource needs and determine how to address them.
4. Consider the effects of accreditation on improving human participant protection activities.
5. Determine the need and develop potential mechanisms for continual independent review of the national system.

BASIC TENETS OF ETHICAL HUMAN RESEARCH

It is widely recognized that research involving humans must follow general ethical principles. The National Commission for the Protection of Human Subjects of Biomedical and Behavioral Research (1974-1978) (National Commission) was charged by the U.S. Congress to investigate the ethics of research and to study how research was conducted and reviewed in U.S. institutions; it was also charged with determining the basic ethical principles that should govern research with humans. In response, the National Commission developed a schema of basic ethical principles and related it to the subject areas of research ethics to which the principles apply. The *principle of respect for persons* states that informed consent should be received from subjects before their involvement in research. The purpose of consent provisions is the protection of autonomy and personal dignity, including the dignity of incompetent persons who are incapable of acting autonomously. The *principle of beneficence* requires that an appropriate risk-benefit assessment be conducted in order to protect subjects from harm, and the *principle of justice* requires that there be an appropriate selection of subjects so that certain populations of participants are not over- or underused (National Commission, 1979). These three principles have come to form the ethical foundation upon which participant protection mechanisms are built. As described within this report, the core functions necessary to provide adequate protection are comprehensive protocol review, ethically sound investigator-participant interactions—including an appropriate informed consent process—ongoing safety monitoring, and quality improvement and compliance.

The principles discussed above are necessary conditions of justified research involving humans, but they do not speak directly to the justification of research as a collective social enterprise. The ultimate justification for placing persons at (some level of) risk as research participants is the creation of new and beneficial knowledge. This is the only tenet that allows research investigators or institutions to balance the assumption of risk by the research participant against the individual and social benefits reasonably expected from the research itself. Inherent in this tenet is the responsible use of resources (time, money, people). In addition, although it is not possible to completely eliminate the possibility of harm to participants when conducting research, every effort should be made to minimize risks to the extent possible.

The requirement of a reasonable expectation that the research will benefit society may be more direct when the research is federally funded. However, this requirement still applies to privately funded research, because it also involves the assumption of risk by the participant.

The moral imperative that answering the research question should be of justifiable value to society is articulated in every professional code of research ethics, including the Nuremberg Code and the Declaration of Helsinki, and in federal regulations governing human research (Nuremberg Code, 1949; World Medical Association, 2000; 45 CFR 46; 21 CFR 50 and 56) (see Box 1.1).

THE RANGE OF HUMAN RESEARCH

The term "human research" often evokes the image of experimental studies in biomedicine, such as clinical trials. Although these studies may well represent those for which the most frequent ethical concerns arise, this report considers other types of studies as well.

Biomedical Research

Biomedical research studies can be classified in two ways—experimental or observational. In experimental studies, the investigator manipulates the participants in some way, either to learn more about biological mechanisms or to observe a clinical effect. Examples of studies of biological mechanisms might be the administration of a substance to examine its bioavailability or the administration of a substance to allow the study of the

Box 1.1
The Imperative Within Professional Ethics Codes Regarding the Importance of Scientific Questions

Thomas Percival's Code of Medical Ethics (1803)

"Whenever cases occur, attended with circumstances not heretofore observed, or in which the ordinary modes of practice have been attempted without success, it is for the public good, and in especial degree advantageous to the poor (who, being the most numerous class of this society, are the greatest beneficiaries of the healing art) that new remedies and new methods of chirurgical treatment should be devised but, in the accomplishment of the salutary purpose, the gentlemen of the faculty should be scrupulously and conscientiously governed by sound reason, just analogy, or well-authenticated facts. And no such trials should be instituted without a previous consultation of the physicians or surgeons according to the nature of the case" (Annas and Grodin, 1992, p. 124; CIOMS, 1982, p.1435).

William Beaumont's Code of Ethics (1833)

"There must be recognition of an area where experimentation in man is needed...

Some experimental studies in man are justifiable when the information cannot otherwise be obtained;

The investigator must be conscientious and responsible...for a well-considered, methodological approach is required so that as much information as possible will be obtained whenever a human subject is used. No random studies are to be made" (Annas and Grodin, 1992, p.125; CIOMS, 1982, p.66).

The Nuremberg Code (1949)

"The experiment should be such as to yield fruitful results for the good of society, unprocurable by other methods or means of study, and not random and unnecessary in nature;

The experiment should be so designed and based on the results of animal experimentation and a knowledge of the natural history of the disease or other problem that the anticipated results will justify the performance of the experiment...

The degree of risk to be taken should never exceed that determined by the humanitarian importance of the problem to be solved by the experiment...

The experiment should be conducted only by scientifically qualified persons. The highest degree of skill and care should be required through all stages of the experiment of those who conduct or engage in the experiment" (Nuremberg Code, 1949, Principles 2,3,6,8).

The Declaration of Helsinki (1964, revised 2000)

"Medical research involving human subjects must conform to generally accepted scientific principles, be based on a thorough knowledge of the scientific literature, other relevant sources of information...

Medical research involving human subjects should be conducted only by scientifically qualified persons and under the supervision of a clinically competent medical person. The responsibility for the human subject must always rest with a medically qualified person and never rest on the subject of the research, even though the subject has given his or her consent...

(continued)

Box 1.1 Continued

Medical research involving human subjects should only be conducted if the objective outweighs the inherent risks and burdens to the subject..." (World Medical Association, 2000, Principles 11,15,18).

Council for International Organizations of Medical Sciences Guidelines (1993)

The objectives of the research are directed to a justifiable advancement in biomedical knowledge that is consonant with prevailing community interests and priorities;

The interventions are justifiable in terms of these objectives: the required information cannot be obtained from animal models; and the study has been designed with a view to obtaining this information from as few subjects as possible who will be exposed to a minimum of risk and inconvenience;

The responsible investigator is appropriately qualified and experienced, and commands facilities to ensure that all aspects of the work will be undertaken with due discretion and precaution to protect the safety of the subjects (CIOMS, 1993).

Code of Federal Regulations

"Risks to subjects are reasonable in relation to the anticipated benefits, if any, to subjects, and the importance of the knowledge that may reasonably be expected to result" [45 CFR 46.111(a)(2); 21 CFR 56.111(a)(2)].

biochemical events associated with the symptoms provoked. These types of experimental studies are basic science involving humans that may involve either minor or serious risks.

Another type of experimental study is the clinical trial, which typically involves the administration of an intervention for diagnosis, treatment, or prevention. The intervention could be a drug or biologic; a device; a behavioral intervention, such as counseling or education; a procedure, such as surgery, laser treatment, or a diagnostic test; or a specific service, such as home or hospice care. A clinical trial can be designed and supported for commercial reasons, such as approval of a new drug, or in response to interest by an individual investigator or research group.

Drug companies are required to submit data from clinical trials in order to receive new drug approval. New drug trials have four generally recognized sequential phases. Phase 1 trials test dosage and safety and typically involve a small number of people who are either healthy, paid volunteers or patients with the condition for which the treatment is being developed—cancer patients in the final stages of their illness, for example. Phase 1 studies can involve serious risks and, perhaps most importantly, are not designed to benefit the participant volunteer's health. Phase 2 trials continue testing of the dosage and safety of the new drug and also look for evidence of the intervention's efficacy. Phase 2 studies involve more patients than Phase 1 studies, may involve a comparison group, and may be randomized. Phase 3 trials are randomized and are designed to test the drug's efficacy. Phase 4 trials occur after approval and examine the long-term benefits and risks of the new drug.

In observational studies, the investigator does not perform any intervention on the study participant, but instead observes or studies the experiences of the participant. Observational studies can include focus groups; surveys or cross-sectional studies; studies involving analysis of large patient datasets, such as those collected by Medicare; studies that follow a cohort of individuals, examining or surveying them at regular intervals (e.g., the Framingham Heart Study); studies in which medical records are reviewed (e.g., to learn the outcome for women treated for osteoporosis); or studies in which cases and unaffected controls are compared to examine a possible association with a past exposure or characteristic (e.g., comparison of young women with and without vaginal cancer who had in utero exposure to diethylstilbestrol). The primary potential harms in observational studies are those related to confidentiality of medical records and information collected as part of the study, the effect of the interactions related to the study itself (e.g., the interview process), and the time and resources (e.g., extra doctor visits or telephone calls) that could be required of participants.

Clinical trials constitute only a subset of research, but because of the heightened concerns that surround them, they are an important subset and are the focus of much of the discussion in this report. Clinical trials comprise a sizeable fraction of the studies that entail medical risks to participants and are a large and growing segment of medical research. Also, on the basis of the growth of organizations dedicated to managing clinical trials and other evidence, it appears that the number of privately financed clinical trials has grown dramatically over the past decade (Rettig, 2000). Furthermore, many trials are multicenter trials involving participants drawn from academic medical centers, private physicians' practices, community hospitals, clinics, and other institutions and are therefore not subject to a single formal oversight structure.

Genetic research is one form of biological or medical research, and like other types of medical information, it can reveal sensitive information about an individual, his or her family, or even entire groups of people. Moreover, because DNA can be stored, samples studied at later dates can provide new information about individuals or groups in unanticipated ways. Some believe that the major distinguishing characteristics of genetic research and the uncovering of genetic information are its predictive capabilities and its implications for family members and future generations (IOM, 1994a). Thus, any harms that might occur from participating in research could include emotional, psychological, social, and even economic harms (if such information resulted in discrimination in employment or insurance). Others argue that genetic information is not inherently different from other types of medical information and that caution should be exercised to protect research participants from psychosocial harm in all forms of research (Murray, 1997).

Non-biomedical Research

The social sciences, which include sociology, psychology, and anthropology, also employ both experimental and observational methods. Observational studies and survey work tend to predominate in these disciplines. Traditional research methods include qualitative as well as quantitative approaches, with qualitative methods more prevalent than they are in biomedical research. In terms of subject matter, the boundaries between biomedicine (especially public health) and the social sciences are not always clear. For example, issues such as violence, the health effects of poverty or racism, depression, and child development are encompassed by both fields.

Finally, some research in the humanities may also involve human participants. For example, research in the fields of history, English, and other disciplines might involve interviews with individuals and groups about their past or current experiences.

The United States requires review of federally funded research in disciplines both inside and outside of medicine, but many other countries review only medical research. Although the principles of informed consent and the importance of oversight apply to all research, the principles may be applied in different ways when the risks are social rather than medical and when the goals of research may not be the prevention, detection, or treatment of disease. Therefore, the risks and benefits of such projects might be analyzed differently from those of clinical trials, and such projects might require the application of different kinds of expertise and sensitivies to different categories of research participants. (See Appendix B for a more in-depth discussion of issues related to the social and behavioral sciences.)

RECENT EVENTS

Much of the recent debate and analysis about the protection of research participants has focused on the federal and local institutions and agencies charged with this task, including the federal regulatory agencies, academic and industrial laboratories, IRBs, and funding organizations. To a great extent, examinations have focused on IRBs—the bodies responsible for reviewing the ethical acceptability of proposed human research. In June 1998, the Office of the Inspector General (OIG) of DHHS issued a report,

Institutional Review Boards: A Time for Reform (1998a). Its foremost finding was that "the effectiveness of IRBs is in jeopardy," and it found that IRBs are facing overwhelming demands (1998a, p. ii). OIG concluded that the system originally devised as a volunteer effort to oversee a much smaller research effort in the 1970s was having difficulty contending with its growing and broadening workload with scant resources.

But the focus of national attention has not been exclusively on IRBs; the institutions in which research is conducted have also been in the spotlight. In May 1999, the federal office charged with overseeing federally funded research, the Office for Protection from Research Risks (OPRR), halted human research studies at Duke University Medical Center. This was shocking to the research community and the public, for if a highly respected institution such as Duke could be noncompliant, then problems were likely to be more widespread than previously imagined. From October 1998 through December 2001, OPRR and its successor, the DHHS Office for Human Research Protections (OHRP), restricted or suspended a number of multiple project assurances and cited 113 research organizations for noncompliance (OHRP, 2001); the Food and Drug Administration (FDA) has also suspended clinical research at other organizations. In addition, issues concerning conflicts of interest at the investigator and institutional levels have forced professional groups and academic institutions to revisit or create policies to ensure that research participants are not placed in harm's way because the financial interests of those funding or conducting the research conflict with the need to assure participant protection.

Attention was already focused on the protection of human research participants in 1999 when 18-year-old Jesse Gelsinger died in a Phase 1 gene transfer study at the University of Pennsylvania. He was a relatively healthy (i.e., medically stable) young adult with a genetic condition—ornithine transcarbamylase deficiency—who had suffered intermittent health crises throughout his life but was responding relatively well to medications when he entered the gene transfer trial (Gelsinger, 2000; Lehrman, 2000a,b). The details of the case are complex and to some extent contested. Although Gelsinger was aware that he was participating in a gene transfer study, FDA found that the consent form had been altered from the original approved document and that data relevant to safety had not been reported. Questions were raised about whether some participants in the trial, including Gelsinger, fit the revised inclusion criteria and whether the IRB and relevant federal agencies were notified of adverse events that had occurred in studies with animals and in previous participants (Weiss and Nelson, 1999).

The Gelsinger case was heavily reported in the national media and drew the attention of clinical investigators and research administrators throughout the world. It also became the focus of a Senate hearing and commanded direct attention from the Secretary of DHHS, who subsequently requested the IOM study presented in this report (Shalala, 2000; U.S. Congress, Senate, Subcommittee on Public Health, Committee Health, Education, Labor, and Pensions, 2000). Gelsinger's death brought a sharp escalation in attention to problems with the system of research participant protections because it resulted more from the experimental intervention and failures in the system of protections than from his underlying condition. The failure to protect this young man in many ways was paradigmatic of failures in the system of protections itself—lack of accountability, conflicts of interest of the investigators and the institutions, insufficient monitoring upon trial commencement, a questionable scientific review procedure, and inadequate resources for comprehensive and stringent review and oversight.

At the institutional level, OPRR/OHRP sanctions have been imposed when systematic deficiencies and concerns regarding systemic protections for human research participants have been found. The deficiencies could be in such areas as IRB membership, education of IRB members and investigators, institutional commitment, initial and continuing review of protocols by IRBs, review of protocols involving vulnerable persons, or procedures for obtaining voluntary informed consent. Although the federal government has been finding fault at the institutional level, some have turned attention to the federal system itself, suggesting that it is in need of consolidation, harmonization, clarity, and a change in organizational culture.

In 2001, the National Bioethics Advisory Commission issued a comprehensive report on ethical and policy issues in human research. The report recommended that federal oversight be centralized and that various components of the oversight system be revised to clarify regulatory responsibilities and to provide more guidance to assist institutions in formulating and implementing policies (2001b).

Calls for such reform are not new. Since the 1974 formation of the National Commission and the activities of the President's Commission for the Study of Ethical Problems in Medicine and Biomedical and Behavioral Research (1980-1983), an evolving system of protections has consistently, albeit not always successfully, tried to enhance protections for human research participants.

In response to recent concerns, many groups have taken steps to improve protections for research participants. For example, Public Responsibility in Medicine and Research, the Applied Research Ethics National Association, the Association of American Medical Colleges, and the Association of American Universities have issued policy statements, instituted workshops and training, or encouraged their member organizations to strengthen their protection procedures.

Federal agencies also have moved to strengthen and streamline the oversight system. The DHHS elevated its oversight office from NIH to the

Office of the Secretary and formed the National Human Research Protections Advisory Committee to make policy recommendations regarding human participant protection issues to OHRP and DHHS. FDA has centralized and elevated its coordination of participant protection activities into a new office, the Office for Good Clinical Practice. In addition, several federal initiatives provide education and training of investigators or support for institution-based programs.

A System Under Pressure

The federal policies for protecting research participants, as codified in 45 CFR 46 (DHHS regulations) and 21 CFR 50 and 56 (FDA regulations) provide a regulatory framework through which to implement the ethical principles incumbent to human research. Based on this ethical and regulatory guidance, national and international policies have evolved to create a system of protections requiring the involvement of investigators, research sponsors, research institutions, health care providers, federal agencies, and patient and consumer groups. However, the system's sheer size and complexity and the changing nature of research and relationships within the research enterprise have challenged its ability to fully protect research participants. There is no single cause of failure in the system. Rather, it results from a confluence of factors—a combination of stresses, weaknesses, vagaries, and lack of accountability—that has pushed the system to the point where change should occur or the public trust in the research enterprise will be further eroded.

Investigators and research institutions complain that there is a lack of national guidance on the administrative and ethical requirements of providing adequate protections and that the current federal posture is reactive and punitive rather than proactive and positive. Institutions complain about an overemphasis on documentation, which can lead to unproductive use of time that would be better spent seeking substantive protections. IRBs complain that the regulatory language is not easily understandable and is subject to wide interpretation—sometimes by federal regulators and research sponsors in ways that differ from local views. What sometimes appears to be a senseless bureaucracy has led to cynicism on the part of investigators, which could detract from a genuine commitment to ensuring protections. IRBs themselves are overburdened and at times focus on avoiding risk in the face of rising regulatory pressures. IRB members, who must also fulfill other professional duties and who are often ill rewarded for their IRB service, are reviewing growing numbers of increasingly complex studies that may be conducted at multiple sites and reviewed by multiple IRBs. In addition, IRBs are asked to address conflicts of interest, the science underlying protocols, and a number of other issues in addition to fulfilling their primary obligations of ensuring appropriate informed consent and properly weighing the risks and benefits of the research.

Most importantly, research participants too often report that they do not understand the nature or risks of research, that they find the informed consent process confusing, and that they are frequently divorced from the decision-making processes involved in the conduct of research. Numerous articles have demonstrated that the current informed consent process is not achieving its purpose (Amdur, 2000; Bohaychuck et al., 1998; Ganter, 2002; Kass and Sugarman, 1996; Moreno et al., 1998). In our litigious society, informed consent documents have become increasingly complex and legalistic and too often are used inappropriately to protect the institution rather than the participant (Annas, 1991). As a practical matter, those participating in research are in the best position to appreciate their own wants and needs, and the principle of autonomy suggests that their wishes should be respected (Faden and Beauchamp, 1986). Although participants might not always be in a position to judge the scientific validity of a protocol, their perspectives can improve the study design, the review of protocols, and the oversight of ongoing research.

In addition, new notions of justice are emerging within the research environment. In some cases, participants now want access to research and are actively seeking protocols that are relevant to their disease or condition (Gifford et al., 2002; Kahn, et al., 1998; Levine, 1986; Mastroianni and Kahn, 2001). Although this development enhances the autonomy of research participants, it should be monitored, as it is often difficult to distinguish research from treatment when routine health care is nonexistent, inadequate, or inaccessible (NBAC, 2001b). Individuals, particularly those who are ill, should not be forced to pursue participation in research as the only means to secure treatment for their condition.

THEMES AND ORGANIZATION OF THIS REPORT

As Figure 1.1 demonstrates, the well-being and interests of participants should be considered at all phases of the research process, from conception of the research question (i.e., will answering this question serve a purpose worthy of exposing human participants to even minimal risks or unnecessary inconvenience?) to dissemination of study results (i.e., ensuring that participants' personal information is protected and that the study information is accurately reported in order to contribute to the advancement of knowledge). The informed consent process is an ongoing expression of participant protection and should begin from the time a participant first becomes involved in the research and continue throughout his or her participation. Likewise, safety monitoring activities are essential to ensure that participants are protected throughout the entire research process. This re-

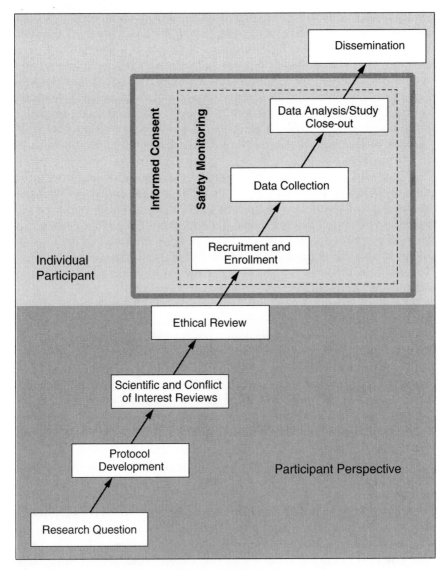

FIGURE 1.1 The Phases of Human Research

Research studies involving human participants are conceived, developed, and implemented through a serial progression of discrete phases. Consideration of the rights, interests, and safety of participants is fundamental to the ethical conduct of each of these phases. Therefore, prior to the recruitment and enrollment of participants, consideration and integration of the perspectives of potential participants is central to ensuring comprehensive protection. With the entrance of an individual participant into a study, informed consent and safety monitoring provide the most direct protection mechanisms to safeguard volunteers and facilitate responsible research.

port is organized to follow a research protocol from initial review through implementation and safety monitoring to completion. In doing so, the committee targeted the HRPPP elements and functions that should be in place at each step in the process to provide and enhance participant protections. In addition, because the greatest concerns exist for studies that pose the highest risk, much of the orientation of this report is focused on creating a system of protections commensurate with the risks involved. Minimum protection requirements exist for all studies with human participants, regardless of the level of risk. However, as risks increase, so should those requirements.

Chapter 2 presents the HRPPP and its functions as a set of organizational policies and practices that ensure adequate protection of participants in any type of research. The diligent application of HRPPP policies and practices will ensure that individual participants in any research project are protected against undue risk, that they provide informed consent to the research, and that their safety, rights, privileges, and privacy are protected. The precise composition of an HRPPP within a given organizational setting depends on the applicable circumstances and context.

Chapter 3 describes the need for independent scientific, ethical, and financial conflict of interest reviews to ensure that the proposed research is meritorious, that it does not expose participants to unnecessary risk, and that the interests of the investigator, institution, or IRB are not in conflict with those of the participants. Chapter 4 focuses on the qualifications of the investigator in designing and conducting a study, the roles of the research participant, and the primary focus of their interactions—the informed consent process. Chapter 5 addresses the need for ongoing oversight and monitoring at the federal, institutional, and local levels to increase safety during the conduct of studies.

Chapter 6 focuses on organizational responsibilities to ensure the optimum performance of HRPPPs, discussing accreditation, quality assurance and improvement, and the need for role clarification within research organizations. Also included in Chapter 6 are recommendations regarding compensation for research-related injury, a topic that has been discussed for decades but never adequately addressed. Chapter 7 addresses broader issues affecting HRPPPs that should be addressed at the national level and mechanisms to provide continuing assessment of the national protection system.

This report is not intended to be comprehensive. Many important issues in human research have received extensive analysis and review by other groups or remain unresolved and deserve further discussion. Although these issues periodically emerged during committee discussions, they were beyond the scope of the committee's mandate or were too important to be treated in a cursory fashion. For example, although the ethical obligations of researchers in conducting studies in international settings have been explored in depth by others, the continuing issues involved merit explicit and ongoing discussion (NBAC, 2001a; World Medical Association, 2000). In addition, the complexities of ethically involving minors or individuals with impaired decisional capacity in research continue to be reviewed by several other groups, and ethical issues in research utilizing large databases and human biological materials will continue to evolve as the volume of such research expands (NBAC, 1999).

Furthermore, a recent report by IOM demonstrated that race is important in understanding how people of color are treated by the health care system (IOM, 2002). And, given the lack of health insurance coverage for many persons in this country, research studies increasingly are seen as a way to receive access to otherwise unavailable health care services—a pattern that has been most evident in HIV/AIDS studies, but that can be seen in many other types of investigations. Although the committee recognizes the critical importance of these issues, as well as the issue of social class, to matters of participant choice in enrolling or refusing to participate in a particular study or protocol, they cannot be sufficiently considered within the scope of this report.

Finally, ongoing debates about ethical issues in social science research, as distinct from biomedical research, call for focused attention. In the process of its work, the committee heard concern that draft accreditation standards would require the elaboration of formal policies and documentation that would be irrelevant for IRBs that primarily review social science, behavioral research, anthropology, sociology, oral history, epidemiology, and population studies (Levine, 2001b; Overbey, 2001; Shopes, 2001). However, pleas to exempt nonbiomedical research from oversight were not heard; rather, the committee received suggestions to reduce paperwork, to develop criteria sensitive to social and behavioral research, and to expand the categories of research exempt from review when the risks of nonmedical research are inherently minimal and informed consent can be "presumed" (e.g., by returning a survey form or answering interview questions) (Erickson, 2001; Rubin, 2001; Rudder, 2001).

The American Association of University Professors has addressed this topic (AAUP, 2001), and at The National Academies, the Committee on National Statistics, in collaboration with the Board on Behavioral, Cognitive, and Sensory Sciences and Education (CNSTAT/BBCSS), is conducting a study of research oversight for the social and behavioral sciences that is intended to complement and inform the work of this committee. The initial conclusions and recommendations of that group can be found in Appendix B and are referenced as they apply throughout this report. The CNSTAT/BBCSS Panel on IRBs, Surveys, and Social Science Research is expected to issue its final report in early 2003.

SUMMARY

Conducting research with human participants is a privilege granted by willing volunteers. Such research is central to the translation of scientific knowledge into societal goods and should be encouraged. However, in doing so, it should be realized that we have a solemn responsibility to protect research participants and to ensure that this protection is integral to every aspect of the research process.

Our current system of protection, however, is not functioning as intended, a message that this committee as well as a long line of analysts and observers have delivered. The committee believes that the system should be adapted to overcome its current constraints in order to ensure that the oversight of comprehensive participant safety occurs in a manner that does not curb the quality of research. Previous groups have made recommendations to the federal government, to IRBs, and to investigators. This committee also offers recommendations to those entities, but in addition it seeks to emphasize a systems approach (i.e., the HRPPP) for protecting research participants.

The envisioned HRPPP should strive to prevent research harms through systematic and interlocking protection functions within which discrete roles and accountability are clearly articulated; the program should be buttressed by an infrastructure that is adequately funded and embraced by its leadership; and the level of protection it provides should be commensurate with the anticipated risks of the research. To achieve these goals, each research entity should develop processes and procedures that are clear, efficient, and effective. Finally, clear and open communication among those who are involved in protecting research participants should be established and maintained.

2

A Systemic Approach to Human Research Participant Protection Programs

The current system for protecting research participants is based on established ethical principles and federal regulations that grew out of a research context consisting largely of single investigators at single institutions developing, conducting, and publishing the results of original research. Today's research environment is far more complex and requires a more multifaceted and interconnected system of protections. To sustain the current level of research, the protections that are thought to be essential should be reviewed and a more responsive and flexible organizational structure that will better assure that the necessary protections are in place should be created.

This chapter describes what the committee has termed a "Human Research Participant Protection Program" (HRPPP), also called throughout this report a "program" or a "protection program," and introduces the protection functions intrinsic to its overarching framework. Subsequent chapters elaborate the specific mechanisms and accountability provisions needed to carry out program functions.

THE NEED FOR A SYSTEMIC APPROACH

In envisioning such a protection program, the committee attempted to examine the perspective of the individual who volunteers to participate in a research study. This individual might be a healthy volunteer, might have a specific disease or condition, or might be a participant in a sample survey. The focus the committee adopted in devising the program is best represented by the following question—"*What protections would a potential participant want in place before and after he or she has consented to be a part of a study?*" Based on testimony from research participants and their families (Cohen, 2001; Gonsalvez, 2001; Pedrazzani, 2001; Terry, 2001; Wayne, 2001) and the committee members' own experiences as research participants, investigators, and research administrators, the committee believes that the goals of an effective program are to ensure that

• Participant welfare is of central concern to the investigator(s) and staff and that researchers take steps to minimize the level of harm to which participants may be exposed and treat participants with respect and dignity throughout the study.

• The investigator(s) who designed the study, those who will collect the data, and others who interact with participants are appropriately trained and well qualified to conduct research with humans and to perform all study procedures.

• The investigator(s) who designed the study, those who will collect the data, and those who oversee the research have no financial or other conflicts of interest that could bias the study or negatively affect participant care, and unavoidable potential for conflict has been disclosed to participants before enrollment and adequately managed throughout the study.

• The proposed study has been reviewed by neutral scientific experts to ensure that the question(s) asked are important; that the protocol is feasible, well designed, and likely to result in an answer(s) to the research question(s); that the risks have been minimized and do not outweigh the benefits (even if the participants will not directly benefit); and that participants are given all the information necessary to make an informed decision[1] about participation in language they can understand.

• An advocate or friend can help explain the details of the study to participants if necessary or desired.

• Participants understand that they are free to refuse to participate or to withdraw from the study without fear of retribution or loss of benefits to which they are otherwise entitled.

• The investigator(s) or a central coordinator will monitor the progress of longitudinal studies, and if new information pertinent to the protocol becomes available during the study that might be important to participants, the research team will share it with participants and adjust their individual involvement as appropriate (similarly, if the risks are greater than first believed or if the intervention is found to be successful earlier than predicted, the study might be stopped by the central coordinator).

---

[1]Such information should include mention of any major controversy within the research community involving the protocol's methods.

- Provisions are in place to cover the cost of participants' medical and rehabilitation services should they experience an adverse event related to the research.
- The data analysis is of high quality and free from bias, and study findings are reported to the scientific community and study participants, regardless of the outcome.

Recommendation 2.1: Adequate protection of participants requires that all human research be subject to a responsible Human Research Participant Protection Program (HRPPP) under federal oversight. Federal law should require every organization sponsoring or conducting research with humans to assure that all of the necessary functions of an HRPPP are carried out and should also require every individual conducting research with humans to be acting under the authority of an established HRPPP.

In its 2001 report, *Ethical and Policy Issues in Research Involving Human Participants*, the National Bioethics Advisory Commission (NBAC) states that "Federal policy should cover research involving human participants that entails systematic collection or analysis of data with the intent to generate new knowledge" (2001b, p.40). The committee agrees with NBAC that research protections should extend to the entire private sector, as a responsible system of protections should be afforded to all who volunteer to participate in research, regardless of sponsor or location. Therefore, a first and essential step in improving the current system of protections is to require that it be in place universally.[2]

Congress should extend federal regulatory jurisdiction to all research, whoever sponsors or conducts it. Although a number of mechanisms might be used to bring privately sponsored and conducted research within the constitutional reach of the federal government, one approach could be to extend jurisdiction to all providers or entities that receive federal funds for health care, education, or any other relevant activity. In the meantime, until federal authority is extended, state legislatures have the authority to regu-

---

[2]A bill proposed by Representatives DeGette and Greenwood would require that all human research in the United States be conducted in accordance with the Common Rule (45 CFR 46, subpart A) [A Bill to Amend the Public Health Service Act with Respect to the Protection of Human Subjects in Research. H.R. 4697. 107th Congress, 2nd Sess. (2002)]. Senator Kennedy's Research Revitalization Act, introduced subseqeunt to the public release of this report, also calls for universal protections [Research Revitalization Act of 2002. S. 3060. 107th Congress, 2nd Sess. (2002)]. Past proposed legislation has also included this provision [Human Research Subject Protections Act of 2000. H.R. 4605. 106th Congress. 2nd Sess. (2000); Human Research Subjects Protection Act of 1997. S. 193. 105th Congress, 1st Sess. (1997)].

late research conducted within their borders that has not been regulated by the federal government. To avoid confusion, the committee encourages the states to do so in a manner that is consistent with the existing federal regulations and with the recommendations and approach offered in this report. The Maryland statute adopted in 2002 provides one such model for this approach (An Act Concerning Human Subject Research—Institutional Review Boards. House Bill 917. General Assembly of Maryland. 2002).[3]

DEFINING PROTECTION PROGRAMS

Appropriate protection that incorporates the necessary safeguards can most effectively be provided through a program of systematic and complementary functions within which discrete roles and respective accountability are clearly articulated. By definition, "a system is a set of interdependent elements interacting to achieve a common aim..." (Reason, 1990). The critical factor in the effectiveness of any given system lies in how the discrete elements are brought together to achieve their common aim (IOM, 2001b)—in this context, the protection of research participants. Therefore, the form the program assumes is less important than the functions it performs. However, each entity that conducts human research should have a defined set of processes and procedures that are appropriate to its research portfolio. In some cases, this may involve the utilization of an independent IRB or Contract Research Organization, while in other cases, all oversight activities would be performed by "in-house" entities. Regardless of the specific program configurations, the system should be developed to maximize participant protection and minimize unproductive administrative activities and excessive costs.

In its first report, *Preserving Public Trust: Accreditation and Human Research Participant Protection Programs* (IOM, 2001a), the committee adopted the term "HRPPP" to embrace a set of functions somewhat broader than is represented in the customary emphasis on the Institutional Review Board (IRB). In that report, the key components of the program were defined as follows:

1) the participants involved in the research;
2) the investigators carrying out the research;
3) the review boards responsible for reviewing the scientific and ethical integrity of the research;

---

[3]In addition to the Maryland statute, New York, Virginia, and California have extended some level of research participant protection requirements to the private sector at the state level (Schwartz, 2001).

4) the organizational units (which may include the investigator) responsible for designing, overseeing, and conducting the research and analyzing data and reporting study results; and

5) the monitoring bodies, including Data and Safety Monitoring Boards/Data Monitoring Committees (DSMB/DMCs),[4] ombudsman programs, and data collection centers.

The program's most basic function is to develop and implement policies and practices that ensure the adequate protection of research participants. Because the conduct of human research has expanded to diverse settings—including the public and private sectors, academic centers, and community clinics, as well as unisite, multisite, and international sites—the requirements of the system for protection should be universal and should adhere to a basic set of principles that encompass the items outlined above.

Box 2.1 includes several examples of such policies from a range of research contexts. The diligent application of program policies and practices will ensure that participants in any research project are protected against undue risk, that they provide informed consent to participate, and that all efforts are made to ensure that the rights, privileges, and privacy of participants are protected throughout the study, the subsequent analyses of collected data, and the dissemination of study results.

Four basic functions are intrinsic to any program, regardless of research setting or sponsor:

1) comprehensive review of protocols (including scientific, financial conflict of interest, and ethical reviews),

2) ethically sound participant-investigator interactions,

3) ongoing (and risk-appropriate) safety monitoring, and

4) quality improvement (QI) and compliance activities.

The precise structure of a program will vary from organization to organization and from protocol to protocol. In fact, the program may be most appropriately conceptualized as a modular framework assembled to meet the participant protection needs intrinsic to a particular protocol. An illustration of such a framework that might be assembled for a clinical trial is depicted in Figure 2.1. In this case, the collective HRPPP includes modules and activities within several individual HRPPPs. The elements of these

---

[4]Currently, the independent data monitoring committees are referred to by synonymous terms. The most common of these are Data and Safety Monitoring Board (DSMB) and Data Monitoring Committee (DMC). Therefore, the committee will refer to this mechanism as the DSMB/DMC.

Box 2.1
Descriptions of HRPPPs at Various Levels Within the
Research Environment

International or National HRPPP: The set of policies and practices dictated by legislation and regulation (e.g., 45 CFR 46, 21 CFR 50 and 56, Guideline for Good Clinical Practice [GCP]) and enforced by governmental authorities (e.g., Office for Human Research Protections [OHRP], the Food and Drug Administration [FDA], the National Institutes of Health [NIH]) or recommended by international bodies (e.g., International Conference on Harmonisation, for drug trials).

Academic HRPPP: The set of policies and practices existing at a particular research institution, consistent with regulations, guidelines, and other applicable standards but enhanced with local laws and/or research-specific considerations and community-specific input.

Industry HRPPP: The set of policies and practices existing at a particular industrial organization, consistent with GCP or other applicable standards but enhanced with local and/or research-specific considerations.

Collaborative HRPPP: The set of policies and practices existing at particular research institutions and industrial firms engaged in collaborative research (e.g., multicenter trials), consistent with GCP or other applicable standards but enhanced with considerations applicable to the collaborative research. In most cases, the sponsor HRPPP would retain ultimate accountability for the conduct and oversight of the study; however, various functions may be contracted out to other appropriate entities (such as contract research organizations or academic institutions) with the necessary assurances.

individual HRPPPs come together to form the system responsible for carrying out all necessary protection functions for a particular protocol. Despite this flexibility, however, it is essential that *all* basic protection functions be met—although various organizations, depending on their missions and activities, might utilize different individuals, offices, or authorities to exercise each function.

For example, in some research universities a separate office might manage all issues related to financial conflicts of interest, while a smaller research institution might address those issues through the Office of General Counsel (see Chapter 6 for further discussion). In most instances, *who* ensures that certain functions are being addressed matters less than the fact that responsibility and accountability are clearly defined for each function and that each unit of the protection program understands the system and its role within it. Thus, although systems-based protection programs could take many forms, currently, it is likely that a significant portion of them

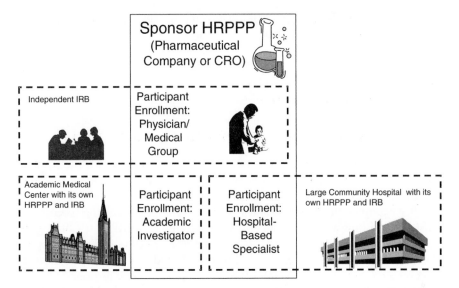

FIGURE 2.1   A Schematic Illustration of Roles and Interactions of HRPPPs in a Typical, Multisite Clinical Trial

Multiple HRPPP modules often collaborate to form the HRPPP for a specific protocol. In this situation, the sponsor's HRPPP is ultimately accountable for the entire trial. For participants enrolled by the community physicians, the sponsor's HRPPP bears direct responsibility for all of the protection functions except the protocol ethics review conducted by the independent IRB under contract with the sponsor. For participants enrolled by the academic investigator and the hospital specialist, it is likely that the sponsor will contract, respectively, with the academic medical center and the community hospital to carry out many (though perhaps not all—data and safety monitoring may be retained, for example) of the protection functions, including science and ethical review (which may be ceded to a lead IRB); education of investigators, board members, participants, etc.; conflict of interest review; and quality improvement for their portions of the study.

employ a set of processes conducted by IRBs and a few other entities within an organization—e.g., regulatory compliance.

The committee acknowledges that the research process itself is a complex and adaptive one and that efforts to integrate an additional complex system within it will be challenging and could create bureaucratic and administrative distractions rather than contribute value and enhance performance. However, the committee has concluded that appropriate participant protection can best be assured through a systemic approach that utilizes diversified and distributed elements with clearly defined and articulated responsibilities. A similar systems-based approach to ensuring patient safety has been recommended by panels that have examined the quality of health care (IOM, 2000b, 2001b). Minimizing duplication, role confusion, and red tape among the varied program components will be critical to the success of the committee's proposed reconfiguration of the existing approach to participant protection. Thus, the coordination of protection functions requires deliberate attention if we are to surmount the current difficulties that confront us as we work to achieve a performance-based system.

ESTABLISHING A BALANCED PROGRAM

Research is a societal enterprise, with the responsibility for the strength and appropriateness of the endeavor transcending the various layers of involvement in the process. As depicted in Figure 2.2, a stream of accountability begins with the individual research participant agreeing to enroll in a study and follow its protocol and runs through the HRPPP (including the investigator, the research organization, the oversight bodies, and the sponsor), to the federal agencies charged by our elected officials with overseeing the research enterprise. It is important that the respective responsibilities at each level are reflected in the composition of any individual HRPPP, and to ensure the optimum performance of protection programs, the perspectives of the various stakeholders should be effectively balanced. Although formal operating and communication procedures are essential to achieving such balance, the establishment by program leadership of an ethically sound research culture throughout the program is critical to ensuring the comprehensive protection of research participants.

Necessary Conditions for a Sound Protection Program

As illustrated in Figure 2.3, the prerequisite conditions of any protection program are

1) accountability—to assure the quality and performance of the protection program,

2) adequate resources—to assure that sufficiently robust protection activities are in place,

3) ethics education programs—to provide research personnel and oversight committees with the knowledge necessary to carry out their obligation to conduct or oversee ethically sound research, and

4) transparency—to ensure open communication and interaction with the local community, research participants, investigators, and other stakeholders in the research enterprise.

Each organization involved in research should ensure that these conditions are met for studies conducted under its purview in a manner that is

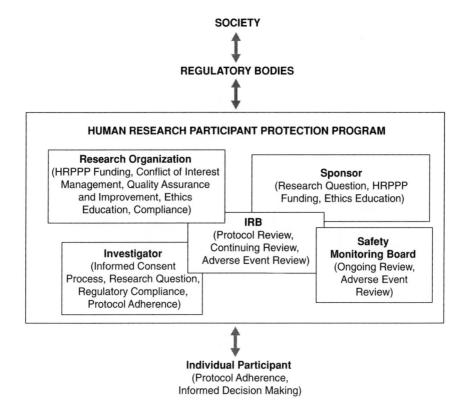

FIGURE 2.2   Accountability for Human Research Activities

Responsibility for the protection of research participants and the quality of the human research enterprise is shared among all those involved. Individuals considering participation in a research study should do so carefully and with regard to the responsibilities entailed. Human Research Participant Protection Programs (HRP-PPs) have a direct responsibility for the safety of those enrolled in studies carried out under their purview. Regulatory bodies should provide HRPPPs with cogent guidance and able leadership, and society should ensure that regulatory bodies have the tools necessary to oversee and guide the national protection system. Owing to the modular nature of HRPPPs, the specific relationships that track participant protection duties within a protection program may vary from project to project. However, this flexibility does not alleviate the absolute obligation of all parties to ensure adequate safeguards are in place for every research participant.

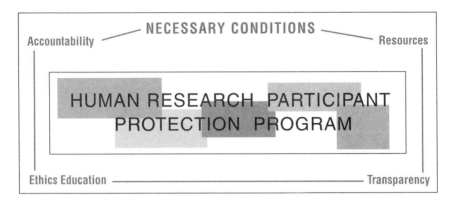

FIGURE 2.3   Effective Human Research Participant Protection Programs Require Four Necessary Conditions

In order to establish and operate a sufficiently robust Human Research Participant Protection Program (HRPPP), four necessary conditions should be pervasive throughout a research culture. These conditions include accountability for all participant protection activities; sufficient resources to carry out those activities (monetary and non-monetary); ethics education programs for those who conduct and those who oversee research with humans; and transparency, in terms of open communication with the public and other stakeholders regarding HRPPP policies and procedures.

tailored to its mission, the breadth and substance of its research program, and the specific context of its community.

Accountability

> Recommendation 2.2: The authority and responsibility for research participant protections should reside within the highest level of the research organization. Leaders of public and private research organizations should establish a culture of research excellence that is pervasive and that includes clear lines of authority and responsibility for participant protection.

Administrative responsibility for the program may reside within a designated office of the organization (perhaps called "Office for the Protection of Research Participants"), but ultimate responsibility for the adequacy of the program resides at the highest level of the research organization. In private organizations, the Chief Executive Officer (CEO) is ultimately responsible for participant protection; in an institutional academic setting, the responsibility lies with the president. Authority for implementing the protection program could be delegated to others within the organization or institution, such as a vice president or a dean, but final accountability for the program's mission, goals, and success (or failure) resides with the CEO or president.

Some elements of the HRPPP may reside within the same research organization or they may be external entities with which the sponsor or the research organization has contracted. Whatever the structure, mechanisms should be in place to assure that appropriate integration of the different elements occurs. For example, financial conflict of interest issues may be subsumed in a more general institutional policy on conflict of interest, but such determinations relevant to research involving humans should be made available to the IRBs reviewing the research in order to be included in the comprehensive ethical review of the study. Lack of coordination and communication within a program leads to duplication of effort that can result in a significant loss of time and resources. Most significantly, lack of communication diminishes a program's capacity to protect research participants.

When multiple organizations are involved in the research, at least one organization should have primary responsibility for obtaining appropriate and documented assurances from the other participating organizations. In the case of a university and a pharmaceutical firm, for example, the firm would be responsible for meeting FDA sponsor regulations (including safety monitoring) and for choosing qualified investigators and site(s) where an institutional protection program was in place. The university would be responsible for ensuring that the investigators conducting the research at their facilities are appropriately trained in GCP or other relevant standards, that the study is scientifically sound, that the study's potential benefit outweighs the potential risks, and that the participants are properly informed about these potential risks. The university would also be responsible for complying with all applicable federal, state, or local regulations. In a multisite project, each site could designate its own IRB as the responsible oversight body, or several sites could designate one of the IRBs as the primary IRB (see Chapter 3).

The organization with primary responsibility for obtaining the assurances should also be responsible for acting decisively should violations occur. Such actions could include termination of the study or the site and/or reporting violations and violators to relevant authorities. However, it should not be assumed, for example, that an industry sponsor participating in FDA-regulated trials has sole responsibility for the protection program. Participants are best protected if all organizations and individuals involved share equally in that responsibility, particularly because research organizations and investigators are more directly and closely involved with the research participants than would be a remote sponsor.

One committee suggestion for ensuring that accountability within any approved human research study is clearly articulated is the use of a document that explicitly defines the roles and responsibilities of all relevant parties at various stages of a protocol's development. Such a document could be very useful to the IRB and others in the program as a tool for confirming that the necessary protection elements are in place within an HRPPP for a specific protocol. One template that could be adapted to address the protection needs within individual protocols is presented in Appendix C, along with several case scenarios developed to illustrate how this template might be used to establish protocol-specific accountability plans.

Within an organization such as an academic institution, the roles and responsibilities would likely remain the same for most single-site investigator-initiated trials, with the specific protection-related tasks determined by the degree of risk posed and protocol methodology. In contrast, the roles and responsibilities in large multicenter trials involving both private industry and academic institutions may vary widely from study to study. Again, the composition of the program for any protocol may be distributed among different elements or organizations as long as all parties clearly understand and meet their respective protection obligations.

A key to assuring accountability throughout the conduct of human research is efficient and frequent communication among all components of the protection program. This process is particularly critical when program components are geographically dispersed (i.e., multisite studies). HRPPPs will benefit from improved electronic linkages that will expedite communication and facilitate a "seamless" system of protections. For example, an electronic version of the template presented in Appendix C could be used to track the completion of tasks by each component of the HRPPP for a particular research study.

Two fundamental assumptions should underlie the interactions among program elements: 1) sound research is necessary for improvement of the human condition and 2) all research must be conducted in an ethical manner. Communication between the organizations sponsoring, reviewing, and conducting human research and the overseeing regulatory agencies provides the primary framework within which protections are provided.[5] Thus, programs should establish mechanisms for ensuring that effective communication occurs between all entities. Just as individual program components are accountable to the senior leadership of research organizations, the overall program is accountable to the appropriate federal oversight office(s). Based upon their research portfolios, educational institutions may be ac-

---

[5]As HRPPP accreditation programs evolve, the web of communication paths in place may become more complex.

countable to several federal agencies, while commercial enterprises may be primarily accountable to FDA. Accreditation by one of the independent accrediting agencies, presuming that accreditation is found to be effective, may provide assurance that the organization is achieving a particular level of protection. However, the goal of any organization should be an ongoing commitment to improve participant protections, not simply to comply with regulations. As stated in the committee's first report, regulatory compliance should be the floor below which organizations do not fall; in no way should it represent the ceiling (IOM, 2001a).

Resources

Recommendation 2.3: Research sponsors and research organizations— public and private—should provide the necessary financial support to meet their joint obligation to ensure that Human Research Participant Protection Programs have adequate resources to provide robust protection to research participants.

No research study involving human participants should be allowed to proceed without ensuring adequate financial support for the proper functioning of the relevant HRPPPs. Providing the resources needed to establish and maintain the infrastructure for a robust protection program is the joint responsibility of the institution (or other organization) conducting the research and the research sponsor. Necessary resources for the HRPPP would include adequate space, equipment, and personnel, as well as a sufficient annual budget.

Assumption of the responsibility to pay for participant protection has been an issue of dispute within the funder/researcher alliance for some time. Although both sponsors and investigators agree that funds must be allocated to pay investigators and staff and to cover the out-of-pocket costs of research,[6] no satisfactory agreement has been reached regarding how the increasing costs of protecting participants should be distributed. Not surprisingly, and as the recent tragedies and citations for administrative infractions at various academic medical centers demonstrate, the responsibility for protecting research participants ostensibly was not sufficiently funded at otherwise prestigious institutions (OHRP, 2000, 2001; Zieve, 2002). Agreements with OHRP that permitted the centers in question to continue federally funded research required significant increases in institutional support, in terms of both finances and personnel (McNeilly and Carome, 2001; NBAC, 2001b).

---

[6]45 CFR 46.103(b)(2) requires that the IRBs must have sufficient meeting space and staff.

For example, one seriously overlooked cost in providing participant protection is that of providing the highly skilled professionals who are required to staff, manage, and serve on IRBs the time necessary to perform their duties, and monetary compensation for their services. Evaluation of protocols requires a variety of skills and knowledge, ranging from technical scientific design expertise to a strong working knowledge of the ethical literature. Both senior staff and IRB members should be familiar with the potential participant communities that will be enrolled and affected by a particular study. Even assuming that an individual—or a collection of individuals—possesses the needed skills, a rigorous and thoughtful review of protocols will still be time consuming. In most academic settings, unfortunately, the time needed to participate in dedicated IRB service is not provided.

To help address these issues, IRB membership should be viewed as an institutional obligation, and those who serve on IRBs should receive release time from other job responsibilities without financial or academic penalty (similar to that provided for jury duty). Ideally, such coverage might also be extended to community representatives who serve on IRBs. At a minimum, research organizations should provide such allowances to their faculty members so that they have more time to participate in dedicated IRB efforts.

Few data have been published that quantify the costs of ethics review, making it difficult to determine reasonable compensation for offices or individuals involved in the process (NBAC, 2001b; Wagner, unpublished data).[7] The committee once again stresses the need for data collection and applauds the efforts now under way by the Consortium to Examine Clinical Research Ethics at Duke University to systematically begin addressing this task (Duke University, 2002).

One existing model that might be instructive in estimating costs are for-profit and not-for-profit independent fee-for-service IRBs; their fee structure can provide some notion of what the private sector now pays for protocol review. Although the committee acknowledges that academic and nonacademic boards operate under different frameworks, because both must accomplish the same mandated tasks, some comparability exists.

In general, research is funded by NIH, the National Science Foundation, or other federal agencies, private foundations, or industry. The private sector generally pays for its initial and ongoing IRB review explicitly, and other sponsors should do so as well.

The committee anticipates that some government agencies will argue that the funds for obtaining ethical review of individual protocols are pro-

---

[7]RAND has published a report, "Paying for University Research Facilities and Administration," that addresses the "indirect" cost issues of research, but not the costs of research involving human participants explicitly (Goldman, 2000).

vided through the indirect rate attached to the direct costs of research. Due to the infrastructure nature of HRPPP activities, officials claim that they have already paid for this review, as it is a cost that transcends individual projects. However, not all research projects involve humans, and even in the case of human research, the extent of the review and ongoing monitoring will vary widely according to the risks presented by a specific protocol. Consequently, the costs per project are discrete.

In response to this argument regarding indirect cost recovery, academic institutions counter that the limited overhead funds available for facilities and administrative costs must be used to meet a number of competing needs. This is especially challenging for academic medical centers in the current era of managed care, in which payments for patient care have markedly diminished, restricting their ability to subsidize research programs at past levels. However, the committee asserts that because sufficient resources are fundamental to implementing a robust participant protection program, providing the needed funds is a real cost of doing research.

Private foundations, which frequently provide much lower indirect costs than federal grants, should also provide money for HRPPP review within their yearly project budgets. Ethics review of investigator-initiated protocols that receive only internal funding should be paid for by the academic department or the institution supporting the research. If an organization cannot provide the resources for the protections, it should not conduct the research.

Payment schemes can be determined by attempting to calculate the actual cost of the time and effort involved in the review process or by agreeing to a fixed percentage of directly expended research dollars. In either event, a robust quality assurance process should determine whether the amounts committed are sufficient to accomplish the required tasks (see Chapter 6). Institutional funding might come from a variety of sources. IRBs could charge for their services, as many already do (IRB teleconference[8]). Overhead funds allocated through industry grants and federal indirect costs could include a specific percentage designated for such activities.

The committee commends NIH for beginning to address this fundamental need through its Request for Applications to support one-time infrastructure building activities and its ongoing grant mechanisms in research ethics, informed consent, and clinical research education programs (NIH, 2001; NIH, 2002b,c). This most recent initiative is soliciting creative solutions to improve HRPPP infrastructure, such as better methods for ongoing monitoring of adverse events or better software systems for tracking clinical trials within a program, that will benefit protection efforts across the

---

[8]See Appendix A, "Methods," for more information.

country. Unfortunately, this particular mechanism does not provide for ongoing support to stabilize the enhanced operations of most programs. The committee encourages NIH and other research sponsors to continue working with research institutions to bridge the gap between resource needs and the availability of funding mechanisms to meet them.

Ethics Education

Recommendation 2.4: Research organizations should ensure that investigators, Institutional Review Board members, and other individuals substantively involved in research with humans are adequately educated to perform their respective duties. The Office for Human Research Protections, with input from a variety of scholars in science and ethics, should coordinate the development and dissemination of core education elements and practices for human research ethics among those conducting and overseeing research.

Education regarding the research process and the ethical issues intrinsic to research involving human participants is essential at every level of accountability in the program. Investigators, key research personnel, IRB members, and institutional officials should all possess a core body of knowledge relating to the ethical design and conduct of a research protocol.

The research organization is responsible for ensuring that program personnel are educated about their responsibilities and proper conduct. The research sponsor also shares responsibility for ensuring that a research organization has the qualified personnel and resources needed to carry out a study—and the adequate education of personnel is part of this responsibility. If an investigator is not part of an institution, the sponsors themselves must provide sufficient education in order to enlist an investigator in a particular project. For example, CROs enlisting private practice clinicians to carry out a study should ensure that they are appropriately trained in ethical research practice, good clinical practices, and the specific protocol (Wyn Davies, 2001). Therefore, both entities must provide adequate resources for initial and continuing education.

One-time education modules do not ensure that these individuals fully appreciate the complex issues involved in human research. Education and consultative services should be ongoing in order to create a rich culture of ethical research. Continuing education options might include activities at annual professional meetings focused on various aspects of ethical research design and conduct, tuition reimbursement for participation in formal education courses, formal mentoring programs to facilitate the training of new investigators, "brown bag" sessions on particularly complex topics or new information, seminars, Web-based tutorials, or in-house research consultation services. Because of the many competing demands on all parties involved (i.e., those developing the protocols as well as those reviewing them), these educational programs should be efficient as well as effective.

It should be noted, however, that the effectiveness of Continuing Medical Education programs has been in question (Davis, et al., 1995; Davis and Taylor-Vaisey, 1997; Thomson O'Brien, et al, 2002), and that although education is important, other program elements also are essential in ensuring that participants are protected and research is conducted ethically. Ideally, the cumulative effect of a comprehensive education program and the inculcation of an ethically sound research culture will enhance the performance of all parties involved in human research, thereby improving the protection participants receive.

An evolving core body of knowledge and best practices that focuses on ethical considerations, contextual concepts and issues, applicable regulations, and case law should be established. OHRP, in consultation with other federal agencies, should pursue efforts to facilitate the development and dissemination of this knowledge and best practices. The pertinent content for education programs at the various levels of the HRPPP is discussed below.

Organizational Leadership. Consistent with Recommendation 2.2 regarding ultimate accountability for human research protections, those within the administrative structure who have oversight responsibility for program functions should be knowledgeable about the ethical tenets underlying an effective program. Box 2.2 describes the type of information that those who oversee program activities should have and suggests that appropriate professional organizations work together to develop the relevant curriculum.

Investigators. Research investigations that enroll participants require a specialized knowledge base that goes beyond that provided through traditional scientific training. Research investigators and key personnel should be versed in the ethical foundations underlying research participant protection, the regulatory requirements for carrying out such research (including confidentiality issues), the relevant research administration and management skills (Phelps, 2001), and, as applicable, GCP and medical ethics. Failure to understand the complexities of conducting research with humans may lead to serious errors in the implementation of a study that would compromise the safety of the participant(s) and/or the integrity of the data and its subsequent interpretation, possibly exposing participants to unnecessary risks, however minimal the risks may have been.

Until recently, few research investigators have received formal education in the human participant protection issues underlying the theory, de-

Box 2.2
Necessary Education Requirements for
Organizational Leadership

President, Chancellor or CEO: The Association of American Medical Colleges (AAMC) and the Pharmaceutical Research and Manufacturers of America (PhRMA), in concert with Public Responsibility in Medicine and Research (PRIM&R) and the Applied Research Ethics National Association (ARENA) should develop educational materials and programs for executive leadership positions in private industry and academic institutions. These could include knowledge of the federal regulatory structure, especially the assurance process; an overview of the federal regulations governing human research; the definition and function of each component of a program; an overview of the program accreditation process and specific knowledge of the accreditation standards at the level of the institution; continuing education on evolving issues in human participant protections.

Dean for Research or Industry Counterpart: AAMC and PhRMA, in concert with PRIM&R and ARENA should develop educational materials and programs for Deans, Vice Presidents, and Department Chairs. These would include knowledge of the federal regulatory structure, especially the assurance process; an overview of the federal regulations governing human research; the definition and function of each component of a program; an overview of the program accreditation process and specific knowledge of the accreditation standards for the institution; continuing education on evolving issues in participant protections.

Federal Research Assurance Signatory: In-depth knowledge of the federal regulatory structure, especially the assurance process; an overview of the federal regulations governing human research; the definition and function of each component of a program; an overview of the program accreditation process and specific knowledge of accreditation standards at all levels; continuing education on evolving issues in participant protections.

Institutional Compliance Officer: In-depth knowledge of the federal regulatory structure, especially the assurance process; an overview of the federal regulations governing human research; an understanding of the certification process for IRB professionals and investigators; the definition and function of each component of a program; an overview of the program accreditation process and specific knowledge of accreditation standards at all levels; continuing education on evolving issues in participant protections.

Academic or Unit Department Head/Scientific Merit Signatory: Certification as an investigator; overview of the federal regulatory structure and assurance process; overview of federal regulations governing human research; knowledge of professional codes of research ethics and conduct such as the Nuremberg Code and the Declaration of Helsinki; a working knowledge of the IRB process of ethics review; in-depth knowledge of the review process for scientific merit; specific knowledge of program accreditation standards for investigators; review of accreditation standards for other program components; continuing education on evolving issues in participant protections.

NOTE: Inclusion of accreditation elements within the requisite education content is dependent upon its applicability to an organization and contingent upon the determination that accreditation programs effectively contribute to participant protection, as discussed in Chapter 6.

sign, or conduct of biomedical or behavioral studies (NBAC, 2001b). This standard is not acceptable, as researchers should have a strong working knowledge of these topics. The committee believes that as individual researchers increase their understanding of the ethical principles and the regulations (state and federal) that govern research, and their intent, they are more likely to comply with them.

IRB Members and Staff. The specialized education requirements for IRB members are even more substantial than those for investigators, yet as a group, IRB members are similarly undereducated. A 1995 survey of 186 IRBs at major universities found that almost half provided no training or less than an hour of training to IRB members (Hayes et al., 1995). Although research institutions and IRBs increasingly recognize the need for training, and the ARENA certification program has resulted in more trained IRB professionals, the extent to which such training occurs nationwide and the effectiveness of such programs remain unclear (NBAC, 2001b).

IRB members are responsible for the comprehensive review, safety assessment, and continuing monitoring activities of protocols, and uniquely within the research organization, for considering the participant advocacy perspective in protocols. In some cases, individuals serving on the board are providing a nonscientific, community perspective in the protocol review process and are likely to need a general knowledge of the research process to facilitate their IRB activities.[9] To be effective, IRB members should understand the ethics and history of research with humans, the current structure and funding of research projects, and the regulatory structure of research, including local laws (see Chapter 3 for an elaboration of IRB education needs). In addition, IRB members should be able to read scientific literature and protocols at some level, understand scientific methods for various disciplines, assess the impact of the research on the community and vulnerable populations within it, conduct a risk-benefit analysis for the proposed protocols, and appreciate and enforce the principles of informed consent. The committee does not expect that every IRB member will possess all the requisite expertise, but rather that as a group the full complement of knowledge is provided within the IRB and that individuals maintain a basic appreciation for all issues. IRB professional staff should have similar knowledge to facilitate the effective operation of the board and to support members, investigators, and organizations in their respective roles. The organizations of Public Responsibility in Medicine and Research and

---

[9]For example, Project LEAD conducted by the National Breast Cancer Coalition, introduces its participants to scientific concepts and the research oversight process as tools to empower their IRB participation.

ARENA should be encouraged to continue developing their education tools for IRB members and staff.

Research Participants. An even more underserved partner in this process is the research participant. Research participants should have a general understanding of the research process in terms of how ideas are generated and decisions are made. At the very least, participants should know that they are able to ask questions about their potential participation and the types of questions to consider in their decision making process regarding participation (see Chapter 4).

Recently, two guides directed at potential research participants have been published (ECRI, 2002; Getz and Borfitz, 2002). These documents include explanations of the clinical trial process and the phases of research, factors to consider and questions to ask before participating, what a participant should expect from study staff, how to evaluate the consent form and the participant's consent obligations, the potential costs of participating in research, what do to if things go wrong, and how to find and enter clinical trials.

Transparency

> **Recommendation 2.5: Human Research Participant Protection Programs should foster communication with the general public, research participants, and research staff to assure that the protection process is open and accessible to all interested parties.**

The system of protections established by any HRPPP should be transparent and open to the public. Yet, recent press reports have described IRB activities as closed and "insulated from public accountability" (Wilson and Heath, 2001d). If research institutions, federal agencies, and private companies seek to maintain the trust of those in the community and continue to ask individuals to participate in research studies, the mechanisms used to protect participants from undue harm and to respect their rights and welfare must be apparent to everyone involved. This transparency requires communication among all parties to ensure that current or prospective research participants can question the mechanisms used to develop, review, and implement research protocols.

Program transparency can be achieved by providing graded levels of information and guidance to interested parties. At the first level, the general public should have access to information about how the local programs operate. All protection programs (both private and public) should provide basic information regarding the principles of human research protection and the structure and functions of their own programs. In some cases, it may be useful to provide the names of individuals responsible for carrying out particular program functions. This general information should be available upon request as pamphlets or through Web-based media with links to relevant federal Web sites. Beyond general program information, IRBs in particular are increasingly likely to be held publicly accountable for their actions. A recent Maryland law begins to move in this direction by requiring that copies of IRB minutes, redacted to remove confidential information, be made available within 30 days of being requested (An Act Concerning Human Subject Research—Institutional Review Boards. House Bill 917. General Assembly of Maryland. 2002). It may also be helpful to provide general contact information for individuals interested in future research participation. Public education is a key component in the promotion of transparency and the sustenance of public trust in the research process.

At the second level, prospective research participants should be provided access to detailed, project-specific information, which may include more information about the overall protection process and relevant financial conflict of interest information regarding the investigators or institution. For example, prospective participants may want assurances that indemnification means that they will not pay out-of-pocket expenses, or they may want additional explanation of general conflict of interest information disclosed to them through the informed consent process. This type of study-specific information should be readily available upon request, either through a secure Web site or a neutral third party within the program who can answer specific questions.

A third level of communication should be available to participants who are enrolled in an ongoing research protocol. Programs should make available a responsible, knowledgeable neutral third party to whom participants (or their families) can bring any questions or concerns regarding their experience in the study or with any member of the research team or institution. This individual should also be available to those involved in the research process who are not participants, such as investigators, co-investigators, or support staff and should be available to provide guidance regarding the appropriate channels for voicing concerns and the actions that will be undertaken to further evaluate and/or address a particular situation. Research participants, and every individual involved with the conduct of human research, should feel confident that their concerns will be taken seriously and that the program has an established and efficient mechanism for addressing them. In addition to an ongoing mechanism to hear stakeholder concerns, it may also be useful to establish a more structured forum through which participants have the opportunity to provide feedback to the protection program. For instance, a "Research Day" event in which past and current participants are invited to share concerns or complaints about their research experience can provide a proactive means to gain valuable input into program operations as well as an opportunity to further clarify program policies and oversight procedures (Zieve, 2002).

These communication and education processes can reassure the public that the protection program is open and approachable and help to allay concerns that decisions are made "behind closed doors" for the benefit of investigators, institutions, or companies, rather than for the protection of participants.

FUNCTIONS INTEGRAL TO THE PROTECTION SYSTEM

This chapter has focused on defining the purpose and structure of the HRPPP and the conditions necessary to ensure a viable system that will protect research participants. The remaining chapters will provide details about the four essential functions of a participant protection program—comprehensive protocol review; ethically sound participant-investigator interactions; ongoing safety monitoring; and quality improvement and compliance (see Figure 2.4). The following section will briefly outline each of these four functions, which may be carried out in a variety of ways within an organization's protection program, and refer the reader to the appropriate chapter for further information.

Comprehensive Protocol Review

The initial review of a protocol is one of the most powerful tools for protecting research participants, because when used appropriately, it can prevent problems before the research begins. The role of the IRB is to provide participant protection through the careful ethical review of protocols, both at the outset and during the progress of a research project.

In order to provide a comprehensive ethical review, every proposal should receive a rigorous scientific review by an appropriately expert panel. It is important to stress that the process through which any protocol is reviewed should be commensurate with the potential risks participants will face. For example, the design of clinical trials should be based on sound statistical principles, and issues such as sample size, stopping rules, endpoints, and the feasibility of relating endpoints to objectives. These factors are pivotal to a successful trial and should be included in the technical or scientific review process.

In addition, every protocol should be explicitly reviewed for potential financial conflicts of interest at both the individual (investigator and research staff) and organizational levels.[10] For those protocols in which po-

---

[10]Potential conflicts of interest of IRB members and DSMB/DMC members should also be assessed and, if necessary, appropriately managed by the relevant organization

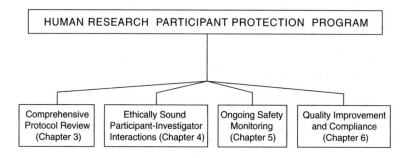

FIGURE 2.4   The Essential Functions of a Human Research Participant Protection Program

Four functions are fundamental to the protection of research participants and must be carried out by any assembled Human Research Participant Protection Program. These functions include comprehensive protocol review, ethically sound participant-investigator interactions, ongoing safety monitoring, and quality improvement and compliance.

tential conflict of interest is present, the initial in-depth determination regarding those conflicts and the development of any management strategies to deal with them should be conducted by a program element other than the IRB, which does not have the necessary resources or authority in this area. Therefore, this responsibility should lie with the research organization, and thus this aspect of the conflict of interest discussion is considered in Chapter 6.

In order to weave the three disparate aspects of proposal review together effectively (science, conflict of interest, ethics), the scientific and financial conflict of interest analyses for every project should be communicated in a clear and generally understandable format to the IRB for use in its comprehensive ethical deliberation and final assessment of the research protocol (see Chapter 3).

Ethically Sound Participant-Investigator Interactions

The interaction between the investigator and the participant is fundamental to the protection of research participants. Even the most elaborately and fully developed protection system will not work if the investigator does not adhere to ethical standards and obligations or if the research participant does not understand his or her responsibilities as a participant or give truly informed consent. In clinical trials, particularly those in which the investigator is also a treating physician, the need to assess participant understanding regarding the research nature of the study he or she is considering is especially important due to the pervasiveness of the therapeutic misconception (see Chapter 4). In addition, investigators should be aware of their own potential conflicts of interest and must disclose those with financial implications to the designated institutional body for assessment and any necessary management.

Informed consent is also fundamental to the ethical conduct of research. To fully respect participant autonomy, informed consent should be more than a signature on a form; it should be a *process* during which a structured conversation takes place to help the participant understand the study he or she may enter. In order to exercise their rights, participants should be prepared to ask questions about any aspect of the research that they would like to better understand and about their responsibilities as participants (see Chapter 4).

Ongoing Safety Monitoring

Ongoing oversight and monitoring of research is a critical program function. To be most effective, however, ongoing monitoring activities such as protocol review processes should be correlated to the level of risk posed to participants. In high-risk studies, regular, ongoing review is necessary to ensure that emerging data or evidence have not altered the risk-benefit assessment to the point that the risks are no longer reasonable. In addition, mechanisms are needed to monitor adverse events, unanticipated problems, and changes to a protocol and their subsequent incorporation into the informed consent process. Programs could better meet these responsibilities with improved federal guidance and funding and through some restructuring of the review and monitoring processes.

Research monitoring was foremost among the problems identified by Department of Health and Human Services (DHHS) Office of Inspector General (OIG, 1998a, 2000a). Because IRBs are already overwhelmed with their primary responsibility to comprehensively review the ethics of research proposals, they may not be the entity best able to carry out the specialized monitoring of research studies. The committee believes that research monitoring—including adverse event reporting, DSMB/DMCs, ombudsman programs, reporting mechanisms for concerns or complaints, and consent monitoring programs—should be defined as part of program activities but should not rest solely with the IRB component (see Chapter 5).

Quality Improvement and Compliance

As detailed in Chapter 6, assessing institutional, IRB, and investigator compliance and implementing a CQI program can help to ensure that a program is functioning adequately. The only mechanisms currently available for assessing such compliance include compliance assurances issued by DHHS and several other federal departments, site inspections of IRBs conducted by FDA, other types of site inspections for participant protection, and institutional audits. Some institutions have taken steps to establish ongoing mechanisms for assessing investigator and/or IRB compliance with regulations.[11] However, institutions vary considerably in their efforts and abilities to monitor investigator compliance, from those that have no monitoring programs to those that conduct random audits. Assessing the performance of investigators and all program entities is an important part of protecting research participants and should be considered a serious responsibility of each protection program.

SUMMARY

A number of core systematic and complementary functions are essential to the protection of research participants and can be provided through a protection program that ensures that the research is conducted ethically. The entity within the protection program that carries out each function may vary according to the specifics of the protocol, but it is essential that some component within the established program have the clearly delineated responsibility for each core function in every study. To accomplish these essential functions, those at the highest levels of organizations that participate in human research should ensure that explicit lines of authority and responsibility are established and that a culture of ethics is pervasive throughout the organization. In addition, the research organization should ensure that those conducting and overseeing research with humans have the appropriate ethical and regulatory knowledge and that continuing education programs and consultative services are available to supplement basic education. Sponsors are obligated to effectively partner with research organizations to provide adequate resources for all elements of protection programs. Protection programs should be structured so that information regarding their general operations and specific protocol-related activities is accessible in a format useful to the public and, in particular, to current and potential research participants. In addition, research organizations and sponsors should ensure that all functions are carried out by responsible parties in order to fully protect research participants.

---

[11]Albany Medical Center; University of California, San Diego; University of Pennsylvania; University of Texas Medical Branch; and the Fred Hutchinson Cancer Research Center have such quality assurance procedures in place.

3

Back to Basics:
Scientific, Conflict of Interest, and
Ethical Review of Research Protocols

Protecting the rights and welfare of research participants is based on respecting the relevant ethical principles that underlie such protection, including the principal of beneficence. *The Belmont Report: Ethical Principles and Guidelines for the Protection of Human Subjects of Research* states that "persons are treated in an ethical manner not only by respecting their decisions and protecting them from harm, but also by making efforts to secure their well being" (National Commission, 1979, p.2). In the context of research, individuals are sometimes placed at risk, and such risks should be carefully weighed against potential benefits, either to the individual or to society. The principle of beneficence incorporates the rules of "do no harm" and "maximize possible benefits and minimize possible harms" (National Commission, 1979, p. 6). The best means for assessing risks and benefits is through independent review of the proposed research by individuals who have no direct vested interest in its outcome.

THE NEED FOR RESEARCH ETHICS REVIEW BOARDS

As detailed in this chapter, Institutional Review Boards (IRBs) should be reshaped and reformed to serve the role for which they were originally intended—ensuring participant protection through the careful ethical review of research protocols. As such, IRBs are the cornerstone of a system in which other entities, such as research sponsors, also have obligations to protect research participants, for example, by ensuring that investigators and research staff have completed necessary education requirements. However, IRBs have come to shoulder an increasing share of these tasks in ways that were not originally intended. Because IRBs should be constituted to carry out their obligation to focus primarily on the ethical aspects of human protection issues, the committee suggests that protection programs consider changing the name of these boards to reflect this recommended fundamental shift in emphasis.

> **Recommendation 3.1: The Institutional Review Board (IRB), as the principal representative of the interests of potential research participants, should focus its full committee deliberations and oversight primarily on the ethical aspects of protection issues. To reflect this role, IRBs should be appropriately renamed within research organizations' internal documents that define institutional structure and policies. The committee suggests the name "Research Ethics Review Board (Research ERB)."**

Changing the name of an entity can be a useful way to signal important substantive change. In the United Kingdom and elsewhere, ethics review is carried out by what are typically called "Ethics Committees" or "Ethics Review Committees." The International Conference on Harmonisation uses the terminology "Independent Ethics Committee." In each case, the objective of these reviews is to ensure the ethical conduct of research and that participants' interests are fully recognized, represented, and protected. The committee therefore recommends moving away from the term "Institutional Review Board," which conflates institutional interests with those of participants and which may cause at least the appearance of an institutional conflict of interest.

Admittedly, the term IRB is now firmly embedded in the regulations and literature, and is likely to continue to be used despite its imperfect reflection of the function that the board is designed to serve. However, many research organizations in this country have given these bodies different names ("Committee on the Protection of the Rights of Human Subjects" or "Committee on Clinical Investigations")[1] that more accurately describe their appropriate functions, while empowering them to carry out the functions that have been assigned to IRBs by the applicable federal regulations.

This committee urges all research organizations (as well as free-standing IRBs) to signal their commitment to reform by changing the name of the bodies serving the functions of IRBs to "Research Ethics Review Board"

---

[1]In addition to these designations in use at the Duke University Medical School and the Albert Einstein College of Medicine, respectively, Johns Hopkins University also uses the terms "Joint Committee on Clinical Investigation" and "Committee on Human Research" within their medical school and school for public health.

("Research ERB"). The modifier "research" is intended to distinguish the body from the ethics review board commonly found in many hospitals, which is charged with providing advice and consultation on difficult issues related to health care delivery. Throughout the remainder of this report, the term "Research ERB" will be used when describing the idealized system of protections. The term "IRB" will be used when describing aspects of the current system.

The Research ERB should refer issues of institutional interest (e.g., risk management concerns, resolution of institutional or investigator conflict of interest) to the institution's management and/or compliance office (see Chapter 6).

THREE-PRONGED REVIEW

A central tenet in the protection of research participants is the independent review of research protocols to assess their scientific merit and ethical acceptability. It is also critical to consider whether conflicts of interest on the part of the investigator, the Research ERB, or the institution place research participants at undue risk. Thus, every protocol requires an autonomous analysis of several interrelated factors (scientific merit, ethical design, and potential financial conflicts of interest)[2] before it is deemed appropriate for investigators to enroll participants. Evaluation of each factor requires a specific knowledge base for sufficient assessment, both in depth and breadth. Thus, it is unrealistic to expect a single group of individuals to possess the requisite skills to competently carry out the many tasks needed to protect the rights and welfare of research participants.

> Recommendation 3.2: Research organizations and research sponsors should ensure that Human Research Participant Protection Programs utilize distinct mechanisms for the initial, focused reviews of scientific and financial conflicts of interest. These reviews should precede and inform the comprehensive ethical review of research studies by the Research Ethics Review Board (Research ERB) through summaries of the relevant findings submitted to the Research ERB for full board consideration.

---

[2]The committee acknowledges that nonfinancial conflicts of interest also pose potential threats to the integrity of study conduct. Some possible conflicts of this nature are discussed in Chapter 4, and the need for the research community to rigorously pursue policies to oversee and manage such potential conflicts is discussed in Chapter 6. In light of the need for further development of the policy discussion in this arena, the committee has largely concentrated its discussion with respect to the protocol review process on financial conflicts of interest.

In the United States, ethics review of federally funded research and of some sponsor-funded research (specifically, clinical trials of products subject to Food and Drug Administration [FDA] regulation) is generally conducted by IRBs, as specified in federal regulations.[3] The degree to which these bodies should and can explore the scientific merits of protocols has been a matter for impassioned debate since review of protocols by nonscientists was first suggested in the 1960s and 1970s (Levine, 1986; Moreno, 2001). Today, some observers assert that most IRBs as currently constituted do not routinely or sufficiently review scientific concerns, such as justification for sample size, eligibility criteria, or the qualifications of the investigator (Bohaychuk et al., 1998). Others believe that ethics and science review cannot and should not be separated because they are intrinsically tied (Freedman, 1987). In the United States, not *all* human research is routinely subjected to both scientific and ethical review. In some cases, particularly when no federal funds are used to sponsor the research, scientific review may not occur or may be conducted only cursorily by a group internal to the research organization. In other cases, ethics review may not occur if the research is not subject to the various federal regulations governing the conduct of research with human participants.[4] As stated in Chapter 2, the committee believes that all research involving human participants, regardless of site or funding source, should be subject to an independent review and a common system of protections (Recommendation 2.1).

The protection program should ensure that each research protocol receives objective *scientific* review, relying on input from content experts. These experts may be found, for example, within local scientific departments, external academic institutions, pharmaceutical companies, federally organized peer-review groups (i.e., the National Institutes of Health [NIH] or National Science Foundation [NSF] study sections), or FDA Review Divisions, and they should be sufficiently insulated from the interests of the investigator or the protocol. Program procedures should clearly articulate mechanisms for documenting such insulation and for the transmittal of the findings to the relevant Research ERB. The program should be subject to external audits (by FDA, NIH, or accreditation bodies) that verify, among other things, the appropriate degree of insulation of these functions and their operations.

Although some IRBs rigorously consider the scientific merits of proposed research, the extent to which they are aware of or consider potential financial conflicts of interest is not clear. In addition to scientific and ethical considerations, it is essential to ensure that potential financial conflicts of interest involving the investigator or the institution are identified, managed,

---

[3] 45 CFR 46.103, 21 CFR 56.103.
[4] 45 CFR 46, Subpart A, 21 CFR 50 and 56.

and, if possible, eliminated. This determination is especially critical if the conflicts pose possible risks to research participants.[5] In its 2001 report, the National Bioethics Advisory Commission (NBAC) suggested that IRB review of research studies is "one method for identifying and dealing with conflicts of interest that might face investigators" (2001b, p.58). However, NBAC concluded that "IRB review alone…is not sufficient to manage conflicts of interest, because the options available to IRBs to eliminate such conflicts are limited" (2001b, p.59). Indeed, given the burdens faced by IRBs in terms of work volume, expecting these boards, especially in large research organizations, to assume primary responsibility for such reviews is unrealistic (see Chapter 6).

Potential *financial conflicts of interest* of the investigator, Research ERB members, or the institution should be assessed by the organization's relevant conflict of interest oversight mechanism (Recommendation 6.5) and communicated to the Research ERB. As described in Chapter 6, the conflict of interest oversight body should determine whether financial conflicts should be disclosed, managed, or are so great that they compromise the safety or integrity of the proposed research. The conflict of interest body should communicate to the Research ERB its determination of potential conflicts relevant to protecting the rights and welfare of research participants, the rationale for its determination, and any recommended conflict management plan. Such communications could be verbal or achieved by providing the Research ERB chair or administrator a copy of the conflict of interest committee's final determination, if that conclusion suggests a conflict that poses greater than minimal risk to potential research participants. Some institutions "cross-fertilize" various review committees to maintain communication and promote awareness of the relevant issues within each committee's purview (Dretchen, 2001). The Research ERB should use this information to determine if and how participant protection could be negatively affected, whether the recommended conflict management plan is sufficient to ensure participant protection, what information pertaining to any conflict should be disclosed to participants through the informed consent process, and whether ongoing review is required in the event that the research goes forward.

By ensuring that properly constituted bodies review protocols for scientific merit and freedom from conflicts of interest, the Research ERB should be able to focus its efforts on assessing whether the protocol meets the *ethical* requirements as stated in the *Belmont Report* (National Commission, 1979) and the federal regulations.[6] Each program should ensure that

---

[5]For FDA-regulated products, the responsibility for managing investigator conflicts lies with the study sponsor (21 CFR 54).

[6]45 CFR 46.111, 21 CFR 56.111.

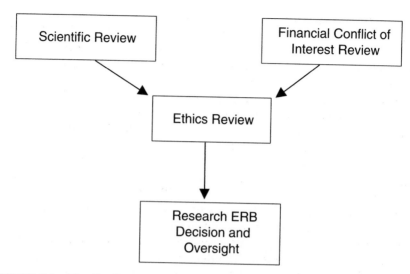

FIGURE 3.1   The Confluence of the Research Review Process

these reviews occur in accordance with established standards and are subject to a system of internal checks and balances.

Despite the need for the three distinctive reviews (science, ethics, financial conflicts of interest), their interrelated nature and their underlying considerations requires that a *single* body be vested with the explicit authority and accountability for the final determination regarding the ethical acceptability of research protocols. The committee believes that this body should be the newly designed Research ERB (Figure 3.1). Therefore, the focused reviews of scientific merit and the evaluation of potential financial conflicts of interest should feed into the ethics review process for each protocol, and the Research ERB should have the ultimate authority regarding participant enrollment.

ENSURING DISCRETE SCIENTIFIC REVIEW OF PROTOCOLS

Scientific and ethical reviews of research protocols are both essential because each considers different sets of questions and therefore each can yield different determinations. For example, a proposed study might be deemed scientifically sound and intellectually intriguing and yet pose significant or even intolerable risk of harm to participants. Conversely, the former Office of Protection from Research Risks (OPRR) wrote that "a proposal without scientific merit can on the surface appear to be ethically acceptable, but the fact that it will not produce new or usable data does not justify the use of human participants regardless of the level of risk" (1993). Furthermore, a scientifically meritorious study might be ethically conducted in one cultural context but not in another (NBAC, 2001a). Unquestionably, there are areas in which the two sets of considerations intersect, for example, in determining if inclusion/exclusion criteria are wisely chosen on scientific grounds and properly justified ethically. Each review process is likely to consider aspects of the other, but in general, greater benefit can result through separate, focused reviews.

For these reasons, programs should not rely solely on one review mechanism (e.g., the Research ERB) to conduct all aspects of ethical and scientific review of protocols.[7] When a Research ERB is called on to conduct the exclusive scientific review of a protocol, two primary problems can arise: 1) it can be distracted from intensive review of the ethical issues due to lack of time, or 2) it may lack the scientific expertise necessary to adequately assess the technical merit of a proposal (OIG, 1998a). An additional complication arises if the only resource available to the Research ERB to answer technical questions is the principal investigator (PI) who submitted the protocol— obviously not a disinterested party. In this case, the Research ERB would lack an appropriately independent technical resource who could address challenging scientific questions pertaining to the given protocol. The Human Research Participant Protection Program (HRPPP) should also ensure that any expert scientific panel is free of significant conflicts of interest.

Elements of Scientific Review

All protocols involving human participants should undergo an independent and rigorous scientific review to assess scientific quality, the importance of the research to increase knowledge, and the appropriateness of the study methodology to answer a precisely articulated scientific and, in some cases, clinical question. For example, the design of clinical trials should be based on sound statistical principles and methodologies, including sample size, use of controls, randomization, population stratification, stopping rules, and the feasibility of relating endpoints to objectives. Ensuring that the chosen study design minimizes bias and generates data that will answer the scientific question requires some understanding of the research process and the area under study (Spilker, 1991). These issues are pivotal to a successful study and

---

[7]The committee recognizes that there may be situations in which adequate content and ethics expertise can be assembled within one body, such as at a small institute with a focused research portfolio or a protection program formed to oversee a specific line of research. However, even in these instances, the science and ethics review functions should be understood to be distinct activities.

Box 3.1
Elements of Scientific Review

- Importance and novelty of the scientific question
- Strength of the scientific design and methodology
- Feasibility of the research as designed
- Appropriateness of the statistical analysis plan
- Estimate of the probability of meeting the enrollment goals
- Need for, and structure of, a Data and Safety Monitoring Board/Data Monitoring Committee (DSMB/DMC)
- Assessment of the thoroughness of the proponent's evaluation of the relevant literature and previous studies, if available
- Strength of the qualifications of the investigator to carry out the protocol and the facilities available to him or her
- Appropriateness of the inclusion/exclusion criteria
- Dissemination plan (to enrolled participants and through formal publication)

should be evaluated by a mechanism that is distinct from the ethical review process before participants are enrolled (see Box 3.1).

This mechanism should ensure that adequate technical expertise in the evaluation of the proposal occurs, which could be accomplished by using a separate committee(s) based on expertise, by using a subcommittee of the Research ERB augmented by others in the institution with specific expertise, or by using outside experts. The result of the scientific review should include the elements shown in Box 3.1; the result should be provided to the Research ERB.

There will always be some level of overlap between scientific and ethical reviews. Research ERB review should continue to include some consideration of a protocol's scientific merit; however, delegating the in-depth scientific review to an upstream mechanism should facilitate the Research ERB's more focused consideration of the ethical elements of particular protocols. One advantage of ensuring a distinct scientific review mechanism is the opportunity to identify protocols that are not yet suitable for Research ERB consideration. Such protocols should be returned with suggestions for revision to the author of the proposed research. This would help ethics review meetings maximize their time to focus on a thorough deliberation of the ethical considerations of fully developed, scientifically sound protocols. In rare and controversial cases, however (e.g., proposals to conduct embryonic stem cell research or xenotransplantation research), it may be appropriate to pursue the ethical consideration of a protocol before, or in conjunction with, the evaluation of its scientific merits.

Mechanisms for Scientific Review

It is the responsibility of the research organization directly overseeing the conduct of the research to ensure an adequate process for the scientific review of protocols. As with other components within protection programs, the scientific review process should be accountable to the highest authority within the research organization, and failure to conduct an independent, nonconflicted scientific review should be met with sanctions by that authority. Therefore, a mechanism for periodic audit of the scientific review process should be established.

A variety of mechanisms can be used to ensure independent scientific review. In fact, most protocols currently undergo some level of scientific review through existing mechanisms. Measures should therefore be taken to ensure that protocols not currently subject to technical review are funneled into existing or newly created mechanisms for this purpose (Box 3.2).

Research sponsored by established industrial entities typically undergoes rigorous scientific review (FDA, 2001c; Spilker, 2001). For example, protocols designed by pharmaceutical companies often go through numerous and prolonged iterations before ultimately being approved by an internal oversight committee of physicians and scientists. In large pharmaceutical companies, scientific review committees typically comprise medical directors, clinical scientists, safety managers, and regulatory affairs professionals, and these committees report to a high-level clinical executive within the organization. In addition, they often rely on other experts in areas such as pharmacology, toxicology, and pharmaceutical development for additional support. The committees are generally part of the clinical organization of the sponsor (e.g., in the Chief Executive Officer's office), rather than being placed outside it. This process is not entirely devoid of conflicts of interest, and care should be taken by companies to appropriately insulate their scientific review committees, perhaps by providing a charter that governs the committee's operations and allows the committee to be audited. The charter should also indicate the qualifications required of scientific review committee members.

If protocols involve investigational drugs, devices, or biologics, they must be submitted to FDA for regulatory review, comment, and approval; they can be rejected by the agency on scientific or safety grounds. FDA reviewers are also trained scientists and physicians versed in the pertinent therapeutic area and intimately familiar with issues of inclusion/exclusion, appropriate endpoints, and safety issues. Thus, comments provided to sponsors by FDA reviewers should be made available to the Research ERB to inform the final comprehensive assessment of a protocol.

Federally funded biomedical, social, and behavioral research protocols are typically subjected to a scientific peer review process by the funding

Box 3.2
Possible Mechanisms for Scientific Review

Academic-based research: A separate, internal committee with requisite expertise (such as departmental or GCRC [General Clinical Research Center] unit); a subcommittee of the Research ERB, perhaps augmented with others from the institution with appropriate expertise; external committees of experts (i.e., federal peer review mechanisms). Outside expert consultants should always be considered as a resource to remove the perception or the reality of conflicts of interest and to ensure a sound scientific review. Funding for scientific review should be assumed by the academic institution, which should also include auditing of the scientific review process within its overall quality assurance (QA) activities. Written assurance of the scientific review should be provided to the Research ERB.

Industry-sponsored research (for FDA-regulated products): Company Protocol Review Committee independent of the author(s) of the research protocol; applicable FDA Review Division. Both should provide written assurances to the Research ERB.

Privately sponsored research (not for FDA-regulated products): Protocol Review Committee (e.g., leaders in the applicable field) independent of the author of the research protocol and external to the research sponsor. The committee should provide written assurance to the Research ERB. May be funded by the research sponsor, but should operate at arm's length and according to a charter.

Federally funded research (NIH or equivalent): Protocol Review Committee independent of the author of the research protocol. Written assurance to the Research ERB should be provided (such as grant "pink sheets"). May be funded by the research sponsor, but should operate at arm's length and according to a charter. NIH or equivalent agency should have an audit mechanism to verify adequacy of the scientific review process.

Locally sponsored research (e.g., a university department using unrestricted grants): Departmental Protocol Review Committee independent of the author of the research protocol. Written assurance should be provided to the Research ERB. Should be subject to audit by institutional-level body.

agency. The guiding principles for the initial review of research project grant applications submitted to NIH are based on the Public Health Service Scientific Peer Review Regulations, which state that peer review groups are to make recommendations concerning the scientific merit of applications. The specific criteria used to assess the merit of research project grant applications vary with types of applications reviewed. However, the review by the scientific panel is expected to reflect existing codes adopted by disciplines relevant to the research or the collective standards of the professions represented by the membership. In addition, the evaluation is to take into consideration the investigator's response to six points relevant to the protection of human participants, ranging from the inclusion criteria to the protection of confidentiality to the minimization of risks and to obtaining informed consent (NIH CSR, 2001, 2002). No awards are made until all expressed concerns about human participants have been resolved to the satisfaction of NIH.

At NSF, proposals are assigned to the appropriate NSF program for acknowledgment. If they meet NSF requirements, they are submitted for review. All proposals are reviewed by a scientist, engineer, or educator serving as an NSF program officer and usually by 3 to 10 other individuals outside the organization who are experts in the fields represented by the proposal. Proposers are invited to suggest names of those they believe are especially well qualified to participate in the review and/or those they would prefer not participate. These suggestions may serve as one element of the reviewer selection process, at the program officer's discretion. Program officers may obtain comments from assembled review panels or from site visits before recommending final action. Senior NSF staff further review recommendations for awards (NSF, 2001).

Scientific review of a protocol should be particularly rigorous at the local level if the study will not be submitted for federal funding and/or will not be subjected to a peer review process similar to that of NIH or NSF. Scientific beliefs and biases, as well as competing interests by reviewers and the relationship of reviewers to investigators or chairs of departments, can affect the outcome of the review and should be considered in the selection of a scientific review mechanism. The responsibility for scientific review should not be left solely to a department chair, as he or she may lack sufficient time. The committee recognizes that it will not be practical or appropriate to subject every protocol to rigorous external peer review (e.g., a student-led research project in the social sciences). However, even in such cases, some level of internal scientific review should occur under the auspices of the departmental faculty based on a documented process that can be audited by an institution-level body.

Finally, when commercial Research ERBs are called upon to review research protocols, their standard operating procedures should provide the mechanisms to ensure that scientific review of proposed research occurs and that their primary function remains focused on the ethics review and the integration of the scientific and financial conflict of interest review elements pertinent to the research. Currently, most protocols reviewed by independent IRBs undergo intensive scrutiny by the same group for both scientific merit and ethical safeguards, with reliance on external content experts as necessary. For multisite studies, the protocol may be submitted to the IRB directly from the sponsor, often before investigator selection.

Considering the frequency of this practice, it is critical that the mechanisms for independent scientific review are defined and can be audited.

Departmental Responsibilities

Academic departments have a responsibility to establish and cultivate the highest standards in scientific conduct, including the treatment of those who participate in human studies. There are few, if any, investigators who are so senior and experienced that their proposed research cannot benefit from scientific review. In large institutions, departmental committees may already vet proposals before they are submitted to the IRB, perhaps serving as the formal scientific review mechanism. In smaller institutions, an inter-departmental review may occur. And in the case of graduate level research, the mentor or thesis committee may assume this responsibility.

Secondary gains from the use of this particular scientific review mechanism include an additional level of mentoring for new and junior investigators, continuing education of reviewers, a mechanism for monitoring and developing departmental research programs, and departmental investment in and responsibility for its research program and the consequent human participant protection needs. The organization's standards should become an integral component of the mentoring that senior investigators provide to less experienced investigators and reviewers. Furthermore, the departmental responsibility for fostering quality research among its members is representative of the accountability for research conduct and behavior at the highest levels of a research organization (Recommendation 2.2). In this way, the local leadership provided by a department facilitates the realization of an ethically rich and robust research culture.

Communicating with the Research ERB

If the targeted scientific review mechanism, in whatever form it may take, is to be optimally utilized, a summary of the results of the scientific review must be reported to the Research ERB before the focused ethics consideration occurs, and it should be reported in a manner that is understandable to nonmedical, nonscientific members. A written, signed report might include the following items:

- A determination that the importance of the scientific question is sufficient to merit the inclusion of human participants and the risks imposed upon them;
  - Comments on the strength of the scientific design and methodology;
  - An assessment of the practical feasibility of the research design;
  - An estimate of the probability of meeting the goals of enrollment;

- The need for a DSMB/DMC;
- Assurance that the relevant literature and previous studies, if available, have been taken into account by the PI and that, if necessary, experts in the field have been consulted;
- Comments on the qualifications of the investigator to carry out the protocol and the adequacy of the facilities available to him or her.

Depending on the review mechanism utilized, communication to the Research ERB could take the form of a distinct summary specifically prepared for the Research ERB, or it might be possible to use existing forms, such as the NIH grant review summary (the "pink sheet"), if the information listed above is included. The goal is to facilitate a quick and responsive system of review capable of resolving most scientific issues with the investigators before the protocol is considered by the full Research ERB.

FINANCIAL CONFLICTS OF INTEREST AND PROTOCOL REVIEW

As stated in Chapter 2, Research ERBs should not bear the primary responsibility for identifying and managing financial conflicts of interest, as they lack the necessary resources, expertise, or authority to do so (AAMC, 2001; Glass and Lemmens, 1999; NBAC, 2001b; NHRPAC, 2001). However, the most important function in assessing potential conflicts of interest (financial or nonfinancial) in human research studies is determining whether bias or overly optimistic promises of potential benefits are clouding risk assessments. Therefore, the Research ERB should retain a central role in determining whether financial conflicts of interest have the potential to affect participant safety, and, if necessary, how participants should be informed of any resulting risk (see Chapter 6 discussion).

Investigator Conflicts of Interest

In recent years, pressure has been building to require investigators to disclose financial conflicts of interest to the IRB, so that it is aware of any potential conflicts when a protocol is reviewed (DeRenzo, 2000). However, simply disclosing conflicts to the IRB is insufficient (Cho et al., 2000; Lo et al., 2000; NBAC, 2001b). Independent conflict of interest review by another entity within the program is essential to ensure that such review is given appropriate attention, that any necessary conflict management plans are implemented, and that the relevant aspects of the review and management plan are communicated to the Research ERB for its ethics review (see Recommendation 6.5). This separate conflict of interest review should focus on whether an investigator's or an institution's financial interests in the proposed research are inappropriate; the results of this review need to be communicated to the Research ERB.

The role of the Research ERB with respect to financial conflicts of interest is to assess the determinations made by the research organization's conflict of interest mechanism with specific regard to participant protection. The Research ERB is responsible for the ultimate determination of a conflict's acceptability in terms of participant protection, and it also should determine how information about the conflict should be presented to the participant through the informed consent process (DHHS, 2001a; NBAC, 2001b). Simple means of obtaining further information also should be clearly made available to potential participants (see Chapter 2). If the investigator has a financial interest or, in the case of medical studies, is the participant's primary caretaker, then the investigator should not be the sole person involved in the informed consent process. A number of institutions already have established financial disclosure procedures regarding the consent form. However, the effectiveness of these procedures or their protective contribution has not been determined (AAMC, 2001; DHHS, 2001a).

Although public attention and consequent reports and guidelines have focused on financial conflicts of interest, conflicts are not limited to the potential for pecuniary gain. In fact, the desire for professional advancement, fame, or the desire to make a scientific breakthrough can present very strong conflicts of interest (Angell, 2000; Kirchstein, 2000; NBAC, 2001b; NHRPAC, 2001; Spilker, 2001). These desires also have been cited as motivating factors in clinical research, and are an inherent part of the research environment (IOM and NRC, 2002). In 1978, the National Commission for the Protection of Human Subjects of Biomedical and Behavioral Research noted that "...investigators are always in positions of potential conflict by virtue of their concern with the pursuit of knowledge as well as the welfare of the human subjects of their research" (1978, p.1). The Association of American Medical Colleges addressed the issue in its 1990 report: "Such conflicts become detrimental when the potential rewards, financial or otherwise, cause deviation from absolute objectivity in the design, interpretation, and publication of research activities, or in other academic and professional decisions" (1990). In addition, subconscious biases and preconceptions may lead to a flawed informed consent process. These conflicts, although less quantifiable than those with financial implications and not subject to conflict of interest committee financial reviews, should be considered by the Research ERB during the review of research involving human participants. (Potential nonfinancial conflicts of interest of investigators are discussed further in Chapter 4.)

Research ERB Conflicts of Interest

Research ERBs themselves can also have conflicts of interest at multiple levels. Critics have charged that academic IRBs, by virtue of their constitution and location, are too close to the scientific community whose research they review and that their role has shifted from protecting research participants to protecting the research institution (Annas, 1991; Francis, 1996). Eventually, as the HRPPP system continues to evolve, it may be desirable for Research ERBs to become structurally independent, without any institutional links to academic centers or other research organizations. Although the process of forming independent IRBs has already begun,[8] substantial restructuring of the present system undoubtedly will take several years. In the meantime, it is essential for Research ERBs within academic centers to protect and maintain their independence within organizational structures in order to reduce the risk that participant protections will be compromised by institutional interests. To signify the importance of this realignment, the committee encourages academic centers and other constituencies in the research community to begin to structure their IRBs as "independent" review boards rather than "institutional" review boards in addition to renaming the board, as suggested in Recommendation 3.1. Such a change in vocabulary will not by itself eliminate the potential for conflict when research organizations utilize internal Research ERBs within their HRPPPs. However, it may encourage the development of structural mechanisms that would insulate Research ERB operations from institutional power structures as the broader discussion concerning the appropriateness of moving to a system that utilizes completely unaffiliated and wholly independent Research ERBs develops.

Beyond the structural relationship of Research ERBs to research organizations, conflict of interest can occur at the individual member level. Members of these bodies, particularly when the board is located at an academic research institution, may have ties to the researchers whose proposals they are reviewing; they may have concern for an institution's financial well-being and reputation; or they may have an excessive faith in science that could be harmful to human participants if potential consequences are overlooked. One possible way to address this problem is to ensure that the Research ERB has sufficient representation of members from the nonscientific and noninstitutional communities (NBAC, 2001b; Levinsky, 2002; also see Recommendation 3.5). An increase in the percent-

---

[8]In addition to commercial IRBs, there are also examples of academic centers or regional research facilities coming together to form IRB consortia. Well-known examples of academic consortia include the Multicenter Academic Clinical Research Organization (MACRO) and the Biomedical Research Alliance of New York (BRANY).

age of unaffiliated members serving on review boards may also help address the concerns regarding the ability of Research ERBs to make decisions without regard for the potential institutional ramifications.

However, outside representation is not enough to counter conflicts of interest—or the perception of such conflicts—that may affect the review of research. In addition to appropriate recusals at each meeting, Research ERB members should submit a disclosure statement once each year to the chair (and if it exists, to the organizational conflict of interest committee). This statement should include information about financial and nonfinancial biases including but not limited to professional relationships or competing scientific projects. If even remotely relevant, these potential conflicts should be shared with the Research ERB (as a committee or with the chair), or the board member should state that a potential conflict of interest exists and recuse her- or himself from the discussion and from voting on a particular protocol, as required in federal regulations.[9]

Similar problems could arise in the case of proprietary Research ERBs (i.e., established by a company to review its own research). However, in these instances, the issues are exacerbated by the explicit purpose of a company to make a profit. For the most part, these conflicts can be addressed in a manner similar to those of academically based review boards. Lemmens and Freedman argue that "this appearance of conflict [in proprietary IRBs] makes it crucial to require public scrutiny and access to information on how IRB members are protected from corporate sanction, whether they have secure positions...and whether they have any other financial interests in research undertaken by the company" (2000, p.567). These precautions should enhance the independence of the Research ERB within the company—essential to preserving the board's judgment and the public's trust.

Independent Research ERBs (i.e., noninstitutional or commercial boards), although avoiding the conflict of being located within an institution, have a more obvious conflict—they are paid for their review by an interested party (e.g., an investigator, a sponsor, a contract research organization [CRO], or an institution) and depend on these contracts to remain viable. But paradoxically, the financial issues that suggest the potential

---

[9]45 CFR 46.017(e); 21 CFR 56.107(e). In addition, a bill recently introduced by Degette and Greenwood proposes to amend the Public Health Service Act to include specific language with respect to conflict of interest and IRBs [A Bill to Amend the Public Health Service Act with Respect to the Protection of Human Subjects in Research. H.R. 4697. 107th Congress, 2nd Sess. (2002)]. The proposed H.R. 4697 states, in part, "each member of the Board has disclosed to the institution served by the Board, and such institution has disclosed to the Board, any actual conflicts of interest, or interests that create the appearance of a conflict of interest...."

conflict of interest also provide more resources than are available to academic committees, resources that, in fact, allow the independent review boards to perform robust reviews (Thacker, 2002). Individual member conflicts can be addressed as described earlier, but a further concern is involved if the independent board members, who are paid for their services, have a vested interest in approving research and facilitating friendly relations with sponsors to ensure their own income (Lemmens and Freedman, 2000; Thacker, 2002). Moreover, if a given review board does not satisfy a client, the client can end the business relationship and go "IRB shopping."

In addressing these concerns, independent boards point out that they are paid regardless of the review outcome and that business management aspects should be, and often are, completely separated from the review function (Jacobs, 2001; Thacker, 2002). A recent FDA proposal for rulemaking aims to counter the IRB shopping concern somewhat by requiring sponsors and investigators to inform boards of any prior reviews (FDA, 2002a; Lemmens and Thompson, 2001; OIG, 1998c).[10] In addition, independent Research ERBs must adhere to the federal regulations governing human research; if a board was censured by the Office for Human Research Protections (OHRP) for failing to perform its duties or was cited by FDA for compliance violations, it would lose credibility within the research community, adversely affecting its income and possibly its entire business.

ETHICS REVIEW: CLARIFYING THE ROLES AND RESPONSIBILITIES OF RESEARCH ERBS

Independent review of proposed research by Research ERBs to determine ethical acceptability should provide a comprehensive ethical assessment of protocols from the perspective of the local community and the institution. However, despite the central role of these review boards in the federal regulations and the research review process, their ability to keep pace with the enormous volume of work and the high-quality services expected of them has been in question for some time (AAU, 2001; GAO, 1996; Levine, 2001a; NBAC, 2001b; OIG 1998a, 2000a).

The Research ERB's role is to review human research proposals that have passed scientific review to ensure that they comply with federal and institutional policies regarding the ethical treatment of research participants throughout a project. The board should focus solely on the protection of research participants and should consider itself an advocate for these volunteers. It should refer issues of organizational interest (e.g., institutional conflicts of interest, adequate reimbursement, or risk management

---

[10]Proposed legislation also currently contains language directed at disclosure of this practice.

concerns) to organizational management or the appropriately designated office among the program elements (see Chapter 6). In addition, it should consider to what extent and in what manner conflict of interest information should be communicated to potential participants if that information might influence the investigator's, institution's, or participant's assessment and judgment about the risks and potential benefits of the proposed study. In general, Research ERBs are responsible within the protection program for the functions listed in Box 3.3.

Box 3.3
Research ERB Functions Within the Protection Program

- Reviewing scientifically validated protocols for compliance with ethical tenets and relevant regulations;
- Assuring that all procedures minimize risks of unwarranted harm to participants;
- Assuring compliance with all regulations involving human research participants;
- Assuring appropriateness of inclusion and exclusion criteria on ethical grounds;
- Reviewing and approving informed consent forms and processes;
- Conducting post-approval monitoring of ethics compliance by the investigator, commensurate with level of risk;
- Conducting ongoing review of the protocol and protocol amendments to ensure continued ethical compliance;
- Performing review of serious and unexpected adverse events (including DSMB/DMC reports);
- Reviewing recruitment strategies for research participants (e.g., advertisements, recruitment letters, financial or other inducements);
- Reviewing organizational conflict of interest determinations for relevance to participant protection concerns;
- Reviewing complaints related to ethical treatment of human participants in research;
- Reviewing and approving procedures for protecting confidentiality in the collection, processing, analysis, dissemination, and storage of data; and
- Reviewing whistleblower complaints about ethical treatment of participants, followed by recommended actions to institution executives, OHRP, or FDA as appropriate (see Chapter 6 for further discussion about compliance).

Research ERBs should *not* be expected to perform the following tasks:

- monitor safety and establish data and safety monitoring plans or boards;
- comprehensively review conflict of interest;
- investigate allegations of scientific misconduct;

- investigate publication-related disputes and claims;
- address indemnification and contract issues;
- review radiation or isotope safety, biohazards, or recombinant DNA-specific issues;[11]
- review material transfer agreements;
- conduct QA or quality improvement (QI) for the program as a whole; or
- establish ethical training programs for investigators.

Although these functions are important in the protection of research participants, they should be addressed by other program units or collaborating units within an organization (e.g., Office of Technology Transfer for Material Transfer Agreements, see Chapter 6).

In addition, training is an institutional responsibility, not that of the Research ERB (see Chapter 2). Similarly, ongoing oversight of investigator compliance with applicable professional standards, such as Good Clinical Practice, is a responsibility of the organization that employs the researcher and makes him or her available to conduct the research. The organization should establish an audit function for nonminimal risk research that flags violations and violators and reports its findings to the organization and to the Research ERB for remedy and communication with any sponsor as appropriate (see Chapters 5 and 6 for monitoring and QA discussions).

Finally, it is not the Research ERB's responsibility to adjudicate issues regarding institutional liability, drains on institutional resources, or public relations. The committee emphasizes that the Research ERB is one element of a protection program; the organization responsible for the conduct of the research (in some cases, private sponsors) should subsume or appropriately delegate these distinct functions.

Improving Protections Through Appropriate Levels of Review

In recent years, the protocol review responsibilities of IRBs have received more focused attention at the national level (ACHRE, 1995; GAO, 1996, 2000; NBAC, 2001b; OIG 1998a,b,c,d,e; 2000a,b,c), and recent reports have highlighted the significant workload borne by the IRB system (AAU, 2001; AAUP, 2001; Bell, et al., 1998; GAO, 1996, 2000; NBAC, 2001b; OIG 1998a, 2000a). As the sheer diversity and volume of research studies have increased and IRBs have been asked to assume more and more

---

[11]Not included in this category are radiation studies that require IRB review under the FDA Radioactive Drug Research Committee regulations [21 CFR 361.1(d)(q)].

responsibilities, proposals have surfaced to relieve these boards of some of their more mundane and less controversial tasks. The intent of these proposals is to enable IRBs to focus on protocols that pose the greatest risks, and their recommendations often emphasize the need to establish policies that allow boards to conduct reviews in a manner commensurate with the nature and level of the risk involved and that allow senior staff to grant approval for studies that are clearly of minimal risk (NBAC, 2001b). In fact, the federal regulations provide several mechanisms by which certain kinds of research involving no more than minimal risk can be expeditiously reviewed;[12] however, the fear of liability and the absence of clear federal guidance have caused some boards to hesitate to adopt such mechanisms.

> **Recommendation 3.3: The Office for Human Research Protections, with input from a broad spectrum of research disciplines and participant groups, should coordinate the development of guidance for risk classification.**

A defined process for assigning levels of review commensurate with levels of risk is needed to help rationalize and systematize program functioning and to ensure that participants receive appropriate protection. Guidance incorporating specific examples regarding the interpretation of risk levels would be most useful to the research community.

Determining level of risk is central to ensuring that risks are minimized to the extent reasonably possible and that adequate protections are in place. It also provides the framework on which ethics review is based. The definition of "minimal risk" in the regulations[13] is difficult to grasp and operationalize; examples that help to clarify this term are available in medical studies, but are seriously lacking in social and behavioral science studies (see Appendix B).

OHRP notes that some investigators fail to report studies that are more than minimal risk to IRBs (OHRP, 2000). The current culture of IRB review emphasizes local autonomy in making these decisions, but the current system, due to a lack of sufficient guidance and an environment of regulatory fear, has caused many boards to take few chances in independently determining the level of review required. In 2001, NBAC recom-

---

[12] 45 CFR 46.110, 21 CFR 56.110.

[13] 45 CFR 46.102(i) and 21 CFR 56.102(i): "*Minimal risk* means that the probability and magnitude of harm or discomfort anticipated in the research are not greater in and of themselves than those ordinarily encountered in daily life or during the performance of routine physical or psychological examinations or tests." 45 CFR 46.303(d): "*Minimal risk* is the probability and magnitude of physical or psychological harm that is normally encountered in the daily lives, or in the routine medical, dental, or psychological examination of healthy persons."

mended that "Federal policy should require research ethics review that is commensurate with the nature and level of risk involved" (2001b, p.41). However, a more refined formal stratification of studies, with guidance nuanced to match the different strata, is needed for protection programs. For example, a sample survey involving the risk of disclosure of information about a sensitive topic (e.g., sexual behavior, illicit drug use) raises different issues than would an experimental study of a medical intervention that is not life threatening (e.g., a moderate exercise program).

Research with humans can range from second-stage analysis of existing datasets, to anthropological studies of communities, to psychological research involving deception, to experiments involving potentially life-threatening interventions for serious illnesses in vulnerable populations. A major challenge facing any HRPPP is determining how to appropriately and efficiently manage this variety of activity. Although the same ethical principles apply to participant protection regardless of the methodologies employed, a "one size fits all" approach to the review and oversight of heterogeneous studies can cause inefficiency and frustration, which unacceptably diminish a program's capacity to provide adequate protection.

Inefficiency results when excessive attention is paid to studies that involve minimal risk. Frustration results when the implementation of minor modifications to a minimal risk study is delayed because the protocol must be returned to the review board or when investigators are overruled by boards with limited understanding of the research context. The contrary result is that overwhelmed boards may not pay sufficient attention to high-risk studies that warrant careful and ongoing monitoring (NBAC, 2001b; OIG, 1998a,d).

Over the past few years, IRBs have strived valiantly to grapple with these issues, but the high volume of reports citing problems as well as discussions with the IRB community suggest to the committee that considerable inconsistency remains in how IRBs address these issues and whether they are being handled successfully.[14]

The committee therefore offers one possible scheme for explicitly recognizing the variations that can be expected during review, which involves dividing human research studies into three categories that might be labeled categories 0, 1, and 2:

- Category 0 studies are exempted from regulatory oversight.
- Category 1 studies should be submitted to Research ERB review, but are deemed eligible for expedited review.
- Category 2 studies require full Research ERB review.

---

[14]The committee gathered this and other information during two conference calls; one with IRB members and another with investigators. See Appendix A, "Methods," for more information.

Clinical trials could be stratified further according to whether or not they include a DSMB/DMC that conducts interim assessments of whether to terminate or continue a trial (see Chapter 5). Although less explicitly defined by the Common Rule,[15] this distinction has clear implications regarding how research participants are protected; thus, it seems useful to divide Category 2 studies in two subcategories:

- Category 2A studies receive full Research ERB review but no DSMB/DMC review.
- Category 2B studies receive full Research ERB review and monitoring through a DSMB/DMC or other mechanism.

Two additional key questions pertain to the current state of stratification:

- How effective and consistent is the current stratification of studies? That is, do investigators and Research ERBs have sufficient guidance to make the right decisions about which stratum is appropriate for any given study?
- Is the current system of stratification adequate, or would a more refined form of staging be useful?

Systematic empirical evidence regarding these questions is lacking and needs to be developed, perhaps by using inter-rater reliability studies that compare the disposition of similar protocols across sets of review boards. Based on anecdotal evidence and testimony to the committee, it seems likely that current stratification practices vary widely and leave much to be desired (AAUP, 2001; Investigator conference call;[16] NRC, 2001). Whatever the cause, the protection system is undermined by the too common occurrence of some boards exempting a study from review as allowed in the regulations,[17] while other boards require review. Similarly, the granting of expedited review as allowed under the regulations[18] is also practiced inconsistently. Previously, NBAC found these variations even among federal agencies that are signatories to the Common Rule (NBAC, 2001b). Review boards lack clear guidance about how to make these assessments and do not have sufficient educational materials available to assist in these determinations, which are key to ensuring adequate levels of protection.

The level of scrutiny of research proposals involving human partici-

---

[15]45 CFR 46, Subpart A.
[16]See Appendix A for more information.
[17]45 CFR 46.101(b), 21 CFR 56.104.
[18]45 CFR 46.110, 21 CFR 56.110.

pants needs to be calibrated with the degree of risk, to ensure that studies involving minimal risk are handled efficiently and studies involving high risk receive the careful attention they require. However, board members generally have little guidance for weighing the risks and benefits of research, as classifications of studies by level of risk currently lack refinement and consistency. Further, the fear of being found "noncompliant" by regulators has led boards (and programs) to be overly conservative in utilizing the flexibility available to them within the current mandates. While there is on-going work to devise practical methods for determining risk (Barnbaum, 2002), this issue is of such importance that this committee, as well as the Committee on National Statistics/Board on Behavioral, Cognitive, and Sensory Sciences and Education panel, believes federal intervention and guidance is warranted (see Appendix B, Recommendations 7 and 8). Therefore, the committee recommends that OHRP engage representatives of the scientific, participant, and policy communities in activities designed to develop illustrative and practical guidance for risk classification.

These activities could be used as means to move the interaction between research organizations and regulators from a focus on the punitive aspects of compliance toward a proactive conversation that emphasizes continuous improvement in the participant protection system (see Chapter 5 for further discussion).

Research Ethics Review Board Focus on Informed Consent

Recommendation 3.4: Forms signed by individuals to provide their legally valid consent to participate in research should be called "consent forms" rather than "informed consent forms." Research Ethics Review Boards should ensure that the focus of the informed consent process and the consent form is on informing and protecting participants, NOT on protecting institutions.

The ethical foundations of research protections in the United States can be found in the three tenets identified in the *Belmont Report*: respect for persons, beneficence, and justice (National Commission, 1979). To assure that these principles are followed, two protections are considered fundamental to the ethical conduct of research involving human participants— informed consent and independent review by an IRB. Indeed, IRB review has traditionally included an assessment of the protocol informed consent procedure and its documentation.[19] However, the committee believes it is important to distinguish between the processes in place to facilitate in-

---

[19]45 CFR 46.116-117, 21 CFR 56.111.

formed decision making and the instrument for obtaining legally valid consent (the consent form). Because the facilitation of decision making is what enables potential participants to make informed and autonomous choices, the ethics review process should be reformed to emphasize this goal as paramount by ensuring that the process (as well as the content) of informed consent is based on an exchange of information and ongoing dialogue. This conclusion is based on two trends that were described anecdotally to the committee during its meetings, as well as on the experiences of committee members themselves (Levine, 2001b; Sugarman, 2001).

First, traditional informed consent often does not appropriately inform and empower the participant, because the information in the consent document increasingly serves institutional rather than participant needs. In other words, consent forms have been hijacked as "disclosure documents" for the risk management purposes of research organizations. In the event of a negative outcome and legal action, the plaintiff is generally the individual participant (or his agent), and the defendant is the research organization where the research was conducted. For this reason, heavy pressure is exerted on those organizations to build waivers into the consent form for all possible negative outcomes as a means of self-protection and/or risk management (Annas, 1991). The effect on the participant, however, is that the consent document can become of marginal relevance to his or her protection during the research study (see Chapter 4), and it may be highly technical and overly detailed. The paradox is that the mechanism for allowing participants to protect themselves from risks inherent to a specific protocol has become intermingled with the mechanism that institutions utilize to protect themselves from a different set of risks, with the interests of the institution often overwhelming those of the participant. The role of the Research ERB in this process should be as an advocate for the participant, not the institution.

The committee and others have formulated examples of methods to address this problem. One involves "layered approaches"—an initial simple and clear statement accompanied by one or more increasingly detailed explanations of core elements of consent that may be studied to the degree desired by potential participants (NAPBC, 1996; NBAC, 1999). Another approach would be to place information regarding legal and business matters, such as indemnification agreements, which represent "disclosure documents" and which are clearly distinct from the protocol-specific consent form, in attached appendixes.[20]

---

[20]The International Conference on Harmonisation Good Clinical Practice Guideline states, "None of the oral and written information concerning the trial, including the written in-

Whatever approach is taken, the goal is to encourage simplification of the consent form as part of a program's QI efforts, to urge accreditation agencies and federal regulators to acknowledge the legitimacy of seeking such improvements, and to encourage the toleration of deliberate variation in the strategies employed to assure protection (including alternative methods for providing information within the informed consent process and for obtaining legal consent—e.g., videos or Web-based tools).

In biomedical research there is the potential for the therapeutic misconception to contribute to a participant's failure to understand the issues presented to them through the informed consent process (Appelbaum et al., 1982; Churchill et al., 1998; King, 1995). In their 1982 paper, Appelbaum and colleagues introduced this term to focus attention on the problem that many participants do not always understand the differences between research and treatment. In fact, many participants think that by participating in a research protocol, they are receiving treatment designed by a physician with their best interests in mind, when in fact the work is driven by the demands of the research protocol.

The Research ERB should take responsibility for ensuring that participants are voluntarily participating in research and that they understand the uncertainty of potential benefits. However, Research ERBs face a dilemma when participation in a trial provides to individuals health care services that are otherwise unavailable to them, particularly in instances in which the risks are minimal.[21]

Research ERBs should ensure that consent forms contain study-specific information relevant to a potential participant's decision to enroll, including information related to the nature of the study, the level and nature of its risks, reasonable expectations of benefit(s), alternatives to the research, clarification that this is research—not treatment, relevant investigator or institutional conflicts of interest, and opportunities for recourse in the event of problems during the course of the study. Research ERBs should require that disclosure language regarding liability, indemnification, and business agreements be removed from the consent form altogether, or at a minimum, be moved to an appendix in order to clearly distinguish the informed consent discussion from risk management information. Furthermore, accord-

---

formed consent form, should contain any language that causes the subject or the subject's legally acceptable representative to waive or to appear to waive any legal rights, or that releases or appears to release the investigator, institution, the sponsor, or their agents from liability or negligence" (ICH, 1996, 4.8.4).

[21]As noted in Chapter 1, such situations raise complex ethical and policy questions that are beyond the scope of this committee to fully consider. However, they should be pursued by appropriate groups to provide guidance to Research ERBs.

ing to revisions announced for the Rule implementing the Health Insurance and Portability Accountability Act of 1996 (HIPAA), Research ERBs may also utilize protocol consent forms to ensure that the appropriate provisions for protecting participant privacy and confidentiality are described to potential volunteers (see Chapter 7 for further discussion regarding the impact of HIPAA requirements). However, such additional language is contrary to the committee's goal of simplifying consent forms.

Finally, the Research ERB should emphasize that the act of obtaining informed consent from a potential research participant should be interactive and ongoing and that obtaining written "informed consent" is tangential to the *process* of informed consent and merely provides a mechanism to document and record that communication with the participant regarding relevant considerations to enrollment in a protocol has taken place.

Research Ethics Review Board Membership, Qualifications, and Voting System

The effectiveness of the review process depends on the experience and commitment of board members. Reviewers should be able to make complex judgments that depend on an elaborate scientific and intellectual calculus that requires both the ability to assess the ethical appropriateness of the research design and methodology and an awareness of the important elements that affect the ability of potential participants to refuse or consent to enroll. Board members should be especially well grounded in ethics and community values, given their primary function of assessing a scientifically validated protocol in terms of its ethical soundness. In addition, board membership must be diverse, representing scientific and nonscientific, institutional and noninstitutional interests.[22] Recruiting individuals who can meet all of these needs presents a major obstacle for many programs. Attempting to create the "perfect" Research ERB is a challenge that consumes much of the time of board chairs and administrators and creates a great deal of frustration (IRB conference call).[23]

Current federal regulations require that each "IRB have at least one member who is not otherwise affiliated with the institution and who is not part of the immediate family of a person who is affiliated with the institution."[24] The regulations also require that each IRB include "at least one member whose primary concerns are in scientific areas and at least one member whose primary concerns are in non-scientific areas."[25] However,

---

[22]45 CFR 46.107, 21 CFR 56.107.
[23]See Appendix A, "Methods," for more information.
[24]45 CFR 46.107(d), 21 CFR 56.107(d).
[25]45 CFR 46.107(c), 21 CFR 56.107(c).

it is not clear that these current requirements and practices regarding board membership adequately serve the system.

> **Recommendation 3.5: The Research Ethics Review Board composition and the qualifications of its chair in particular should reflect its unique and preeminent responsibility to provide a thorough ethical review of proposed research studies. At least 25 percent of its membership should be reserved for unaffiliated members and those who can provide non-scientific perspectives.**

While all members should have a core body of knowledge, a critical mass of the membership (i.e., a sufficient number of members to influence the tenor of the discussion), either scientific or nonscientific, should possess a specialized knowledge of human research ethics (see Figure 3.2). In addition, the goal of research organizations should be to assemble a board with at least 25 percent of its membership not affiliated with the institution, not trained as scientists, and able to represent the local community and/or the participant perspective. The committee encourages the Research ERB community to work toward developing common goals and content for Research ERB member training, so that within five years, certification programs might be available to demonstrate the initial and continuing qualifications of members who serve within participant protection programs.

Currently, the regulatory language and guidance that describe the criteria for meeting the definition of an unaffiliated member, for determining how long such members should serve and under what circumstances they may be removed, or for determining what payment should be provided for members who are otherwise not affiliated with the institution are insufficient (NBAC, 2001b). Also, nonscientific, unaffiliated members can represent either the community being studied or the community in which the research will take place. However, it is sometimes not clear whose interests such members represent and if one individual can represent more than one community (Hogg, 2001; MacQueen et al., 2001).

In order to address the lack of guidance, NBAC recommended that

> Institutional Review Boards should include members who represent the perspectives of participants, members who are unaffiliated with the institution, and members whose primary concerns are in nonscientific areas. An individual can fulfill one, two, or all three of these categories. For the purposes of both overall membership and quorum determinations 1) these persons should collectively represent at least 25 percent of the Institutional Review Board membership and 2) members from all of these categories should be represented each time an Institutional Review Board meets (2001b, p.64).

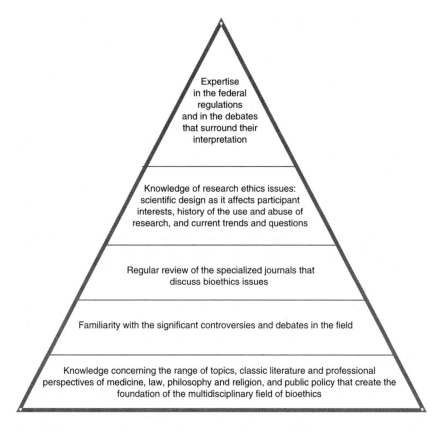

Expertise
in the federal
regulations
and in the debates
that surround their
interpretation

Knowledge of research ethics issues:
scientific design as it affects participant
interests, history of the use and abuse of
research, and current trends and questions

Regular review of the specialized journals that
discuss bioethics issues

Familiarity with the significant controversies and debates in the field

Knowledge concerning the range of topics, classic literature and professional
perspectives of medicine, law, philosophy and religion, and public policy that create the
foundation of the multidisciplinary field of bioethics

FIGURE 3.2   Content Knowledge Intrinsic to Human Research Ethics

The requisite expertise, or "specialized knowledge," which the committee believes should be available to (or preferably found within) the membership of a Research ERB can be broken down into various levels of familiarity with the topics listed above. The depth of knowledge necessary in the particular areas correlates to the position of the issue within the pyramid, moving from the base to the top tier.

The committee agrees that the composition of the Research ERB should reflect its ultimate function as the ethical review body for human research protocols. Science and ethics expertise should be appropriately balanced with each other and with noninstitutional member perspectives. Review boards could better avoid conflicts by including a greater proportion of individuals who are unaffiliated with any of the institutions/firms involved in the research study.

Research ERB Voting System

Modern IRBs have tended to become larger as members have been recruited to reflect the broad range of scientific expertise needed to conduct informed scientific review of a diverse array of research protocols (OIG, 1998a). Consequently, some deliberations have the potential to be dominated by a scientific voice, leading to a corresponding reduction in ethics-centered reflection and the possible marginalization of the perspectives of nonscientific members (Cho and Billings, 1997; Peckman, 2001). Under the committee's proposed refocusing of the ethics review, responsibility for the initial in-depth scientific review would lie elsewhere, enabling the Research ERB to focus on its primary functions of providing ethical review of proposed research and integrating the scientific and financial conflict of interest reviews. Consistent with this mission, the most important roles of the board chair are to constitute a proper and balanced membership, facilitate open discussion, and promote consensus. In fact, it is not required or always the case that board chairs themselves be trained physicians or scientists (Jacobs, 2001).[26]

> **Recommendation 3.6: A Research Ethics Review Board's deliberative process should aim for consensus. If consensus cannot be achieved, approval of a protocol should require favorable votes by three-quarters of the voting members.**

If the membership of the Research ERB is modified to reflect the increased number of unaffiliated and non-scientific perspectives as suggested in Recommendation 3.5, but a simple majority voting procedure remains in place, no actual mechanism or basis for change will have been established and only the appearance of change will have been created. Such a scenario would tend to divide the deliberative body, encourage power blocks and leave the less powerful perspectives in the minority. Therefore, an alternative to standard parliamentary process is needed.

Seeking consensus can be a way of acknowledging, exploring, and managing conflict and is a process that would facilitate the full expression of the minority perspective(s) and provide the basis for substantive discussion and debate. It also requires chairs who are skilled in techniques of mediation and conflict resolution. The process of facilitating consensus requires skills that include listing the players/parties who represent competing interests, characterizing their stakes and goals, identifying and maxi-

---

[26]In New Zealand, the chair of the health research ethics board must be a "lay person." Similarly, the United Kingdom requires that either the chair or vice chair be a lay person (Bastian, 1994).

mizing the options that might be employed to accommodate competing interests, and reaching agreement on this new solution.

The committee acknowledges that sometimes mediation and the search for consensus will fail and that at some point a vote may need to be taken. The committee therefore recommends that the Research ERB adopt super-majority rules stating that no protocol will be approved unless it has the affirmative endorsement of at least three-quarters of the voting members present. A vote of unanimity would be unworkable and would effectively give a veto to a single dissenting committee member, while allowing a simple majority to approve a protocol in the face of substantial minority opinion to the contrary poses too much risk of suppressing respectable and responsible ethical opinion.

Research ERB Member Education

The need to educate board members has been discussed by every major national body charged with the review of human research protections, with each clearly stating the need for additional resources and educational programs (ACHRE, 1995; National Commission, 1978; NBAC, 2001b; President's Commission, 1983). In addition, a 1998 survey documented strong support for increased board member education (Bell et al., 1998).

Training programs at the national, regional, or institutional level could provide education to Research ERB members about the required core body of knowledge (Box 3.4 expands this point with a biomedical focus). Although the specific content will vary based upon the portfolio of the Research ERB, the basic elements will remain constant. Currently, Public Responsibility in Medicine and Research (PRIM&R) offers a course known as "IRB 101" to train board members. PRIM&R, in cooperation with OHRP, also has produced a CD-ROM version of "IRB 101." NIH offers a computer-based training course[27] designed for NIH board members but also accessible to the public. In addition, some universities include ethics training in research design and history of science courses.

The inclusion of the perspectives of individuals not affiliated with a particular research organization in all decision-making and oversight bodies, particularly the Research ERB, is a vital component of any protection system. Specialized training for these members can help maximize their contribution to the process.

Such training could include the following:

---

[27]Available at ohsr.od.nih.gov/irb_cbt.

Box 3.4
Basic Knowledge for Research ERB Members

Background: Ethical perspectives on the research enterprise, history of human research, current structure and funding of research, identifying who conducts and pays for research, setting the research agenda, methodological issues, current regulatory structure and the Common Rule.

Foundation Knowledge: An introduction to clinical medicine, basic science, epidemiology, introduction to ethical principles, concepts, and issues, and skills, such as reading scientific literature and research protocols.

Methodological Issues: Identifying the elements of research design, thinking about statistical power without statistical or mathematical training, the use and abuse of the placebo model, randomization before or after consent, and adequate use of animal models and competent persons before investigations with vulnerable or incapacitated persons.

Difficult Design Questions: Questions of placebo arms in general, in psychiatry protocols, and as required by the FDA for review when effective treatment exists; testing of "me too" drugs when effective treatment exists and when the desire is for a more or a less expensive treatment; stratification of subjects and treatments; use of children, fetuses, or prisoners, whose involvement in research is governed by a specific sub-set of federal regulations; investigations with incapacitated persons whose use in research is subject to state law and regulation and to institutional policy in the absence of clear federal policy.

Conflicts of Interest: How to think about the relationship of institutions, investigators, and participants in light of the monetary and status benefits that institutions and investigators can expect from the research, and how to manage and minimize possible conflicts.

Cultural Competency: How to understand the design issues that will either encourage or discourage participation by persons of color and other vulnerable populations that have a history of being suspicious of the research enterprise.

Reviewing Research Proposals—The Intellectual Calculus: Determine if a proposal presents an important question; identify who is included and excluded and why—women, children, racial minorities, prisoners, and other vulnerable populations; the risk-benefit calculus; informed consent; conflicts of interest; confidentiality; monitoring and review.

Overarching Issues: International research, genetic and stem cell research, AIDS research, research with children, research in the name of national security.

The Responsibilities of Research ERB Members: Ethics review, protocol assessment, research participant advocacy, accountability, community perspective.

- A detailed description of the process of research, the identity and roles of all who are involved, and the components of a research study;
- A description of the process within a specific institution, including scientific review and conflict of interest review;
- Rules of scientific ethics (and broader theories of ethics as well).

It is preferable that these training programs be designed, funded, and owned by consumer or community oriented nonprofit organizations. However, collaborations of such organizations with scientific trade associations or research organizations might also be sufficient to provide these programs.

Several programs developed by consumer groups provide intriguing models for supporting and training unaffiliated members on Research ERBs or any other research oversight committee, such as programs developed for medical specialty boards by the Citizen Advocacy Center or those targeted to the research setting by Project LEAD (Leadership, Education, and Advocacy Development) and the National Alliance for the Mentally Ill (CAC, 1994; Cowdry, 2001; Dickersin et al., 2001; Hinestrosa, 2001; NAMI, 2001; Swankin, 2001).

Certification of Research ERB Professionals

Certification for Research ERB members (and investigators) has been a problematic issue, in part because they are predominantly scientists and traditionally belong to subspecialty professional organizations. However, IRB administrators are now being certified by the Council for Certification of IRB Professionals; through the National Association of IRB Managers; and as Certified IRB Professionals, through the Applied Research Ethics National Association in conjunction with the Professional Testing Corporation. The committee supports these efforts because they encourage the development of professional staff who can facilitate the ethics review function of the Research ERB.

ORGANIZING AND INTEGRATING THE REVIEW PROCESSES

In this chapter, the committee has proposed that separate and independent scientific review and conflict of interest review mechanisms should be available to the Research ERB, and that relevant findings from those reviews should be communicated to the Research ERB to inform its comprehensive ethical assessment. It is the responsibility of the program to ensure that this process occurs. Under this new vision, Research ERBs would review the research protocol, the written and signed findings of the scientific review and financial conflict of interest review bodies, and the oral reports given by members of these bodies as appropriate. In the final stage, the Research ERB would integrate this information and determine the acceptability of the proposed research. A critical factor in making this three-pronged review process successful is to ensure that it is not unduly extended, complicated, or confused by these improvements. Participant interests are not served if research protocols are unnecessarily delayed. Therefore, in establishing review mechanisms, it is important to remain responsive to incoming applications by aligning submission and meeting dates for the preliminary reviews with the Research ERB schedule. Furthermore, communication between investigators and the review structure should continue to originate with the Research ERB office, except in instances of identified problems at the initial review levels, in order to prevent duplication of effort and avoid confusion resulting from overlapping and possibly contradictory messages to investigators about a protocol's status. Likewise, efforts should be made to align and consolidate other administrative procedures within the HRPPP—e.g., the creation of one master application for the submission of protocols to all appropriate review bodies.[28] If the functional integration of review activities is to successfully improve protection, it must be mirrored by a similar integration of administrative activities.

Review of Multisite Studies

In addition to ensuring coordination and communication between the various review groups, special consideration should be given to protocols conducted at more than one site, and possibilities for alternative review mechanisms should be considered.

Recommendation 3.7: The review of multisite trials should be streamlined, as allowed by current regulations. One primary scientific review committee and one primary Research Ethics Review Board should assume the lead review functions, with their determinations subject to acceptance by the local committees and boards at participating sites.

The rapid growth of multisite studies, particularly in the clinical trials arena, brings a new complexity that challenges the ability of review committees to meet their responsibilities efficiently and effectively. Multisite protocol review has become a cumbersome and labor-intensive process, because in most cases each research organization's board considers the

---

[28]For example, Children's Hospital Regional Medical Center in Seattle has devised a combined electronic application for the purposes of the General Clinical Research Center Advisory Committee and the IRB. In this instance, the electronic format will enable investigators to complete relevant information and avoid irrelevant questions, through a series of drop boxes. The form will be posted at www.seattlechildrens.org/research after October 2002.

same protocol; performs the same risk assessment; examines the same, or similar, consent form; and later reviews the same, often voluminous, set of adverse event reports. In addition, multisite review can introduce considerable variability into the approvals and/or required modifications to study design or disclosure language, which actually detracts from participant protections. At best, it is an inefficient use of time and money for the review boards, investigators, and sponsors. The time involved in these reviews could be better spent attending to the participant protection needs of other studies or, in the case of the investigator, interacting with participants.

In general, the review of multisite studies by each organization participating in a study does not significantly increase the level of protection provided to research participants or enhance the scientific design of the protocol. In fact, this repetitive review can be detrimental to the protection of the other research participants within a program, as the review board is unable to provide the needed time, resources, and expertise to thoroughly evaluate other protocols.

Current federal regulations and guidance for IRBs contain provisions for the sharing of oversight responsibility with institutions in which regular collaboration takes place—including the ceding of authority for the reviews.[29] In 2001, NBAC recommended that alternatives be considered for multisite review, including the use of central or lead review boards (2001b). In a multisite project, the sites could designate an independent Scientific Review Committee (SRC) and Research ERB or could designate one of the SRCs and Research ERBs as the "primary SRC and Research ERB." The organization that has primary responsibility for obtaining the assurances should also assume the responsibility for acting decisively should violations occur, including termination of the study or the site and/or reporting violations and violators to authorities. In FDA-regulated trials, it should not be assumed that the industry sponsor has primary responsibility for the program; it would be preferable for the medical institutions involved to share that responsibility, since they are most directly and closely involved with the research participants. In addition, determinations regarding potential financial conflicts of interest should be forwarded to the lead Research ERB by the appropriate entity (i.e., the party responsible for the oversight of an investigator's role in a project). Sponsors and federal regulators should encourage such collaboration and centralization, and local committees should reserve the right to refuse the primary review body's determination for serious safety concerns and unique local requirements.

Under this system, the opportunity and responsibility for locally appropriate oversight would continue to be intrinsic to protocol review, and

---

[29]45 CFR 46.114, 21 CFR 56.114.

some institutions might insist on being involved in the review process for reasonable instances of indemnification and confidentiality. The committee believes, however, that flexible approaches might provide helpful alternatives to reduce redundancy that does not enhance participant protections. Effective use of communication tools, such as the use of protocol Web sites that would enable local Research ERBs to follow the lead Research ERB's progress, will be fundamental to successful collaboration.

Sharing Responsibilities: Alternative Review Models

Models exist in the United States for sharing program responsibilities among collaborating institutions and their Research ERBs—for example, MACRO and BRANY.[30] Similarly, the United Kingdom relies on regional committees for review of multisite research, and Denmark handles multisite studies by assigning the review responsibility to a lead committee (Alberti, 2000; Holm, 2001). These approaches can reduce duplicative workload and assure that reviews take place in settings that can bring to bear the appropriate scientific and ethical expertise. For example, complex protocols may involve consulting with biostatisticians, epidemiologists, and clinical specialists who might not be available at some individual sites.

The ability to distribute costs could also place a regional program in a better position to provide the resources and infrastructure needed for various functions, such as maintaining qualified monitors for higher-risk research involving human participants. Furthermore, by ceding certain responsibilities to a regional unit, local programs could direct their efforts and resources to the remaining single-site studies for which they are responsible. This could be particularly useful to research organizations that have few resources, including small academic centers and community hospitals.

In addition, regional or centralized review could provide a cost-effective alternative to smaller institutions and study sites that cannot afford to maintain a sufficiently comprehensive program onsite. Such organizations, for example, may find it difficult to sustain Research ERBs with the associated increased costs for training, monitoring, and, should it become a standard of practice in the community, accreditation preparation and the asso-

---

[30]MACRO is a collaboration between Baylor College of Medicine, University of Alabama at Birmingham, the University of Pennsylvania School of Medicine, Vanderbilt University, and Washington University School of Medicine. See ccs.wustl.edu/macro/aboutmacro.htm for more information. BRANY focuses on sites near New York City. The Alliance serves more than 100 sites in multiple states, from New Jersey to Hawaii. For more information, see www.brany.com.

ciated fees. Possible examples include smaller hospitals, community-based organizations, local health agencies, and CROs.

Regional programs/Research ERBs offer a solution to another set of problems encountered by boards today—the difficulty of recruiting and maintaining active and involved members. Many recent reports have noted the problems of heavy workloads, lack of professional or personal reward for committing the time needed to do the work, problems of ascertaining and managing conflict of interest within small organizations that may have a limited choice of potential board members, and a host of similar problems (IRB teleconference;[31] Levine, 2001a,b; Moreno et al., 1998; OIG 1998a). Of course, regionalized approaches would need to include an equitable fee or honorarium structure to cover the expected services of board members and of expert consultant reviews needed in specialized topic areas and would need to extend liability insurance coverage to all involved in the process (see Chapter 6).

Utilizing regional Research ERBs would also alleviate the potential conflict of interest inherent to the use of internal review boards. To encourage institutions conducting or sponsoring research to develop shared arrangements or use regional programs and to make Research ERBs more comfortable with ceding authority (but not ultimate accountability), adequate communication between local and regional programs will need to be assured. Research organizations should be kept abreast of the status and progress of studies, adverse events, media coverage, and other matters relevant to the organization, while keeping the reporting burden reasonable for the regional programs. Obviously, such a scenario could draw on the experience of the independent IRB review model.

RESOURCE NEEDS

The most important aspects of the review process depend on the experience and commitment of those who conduct the reviews. The processes of protecting human participants, which require skill, learning, wisdom, and sufficient practical experience to make complex judgments, are not tasks that can be assigned exclusively to junior faculty members or unskilled researchers. Time and focus are needed to accomplish these tasks, and if their difficult and demanding nature is to be taken seriously, the members—and not just the administrative staff—of scientific review groups and Research ERBs should be compensated for their efforts. This compensation may be monetary, may support academic promotion, or may provide release time from other duties. If the ethical review of research involving human participants is to be adequately conducted, appropriate resources

---

[31]See Appendix A, "Methods," for more details about the teleconference.

should be committed to the process. These considerations apply equally to those involved in scientific review, financial conflict of interest review, and ethics review of proposed research.

Need for a Common Body of Knowledge

Recommendation 3.8: The Office for Human Research Protections and the National Human Research Protections Advisory Committee should convene conferences and/or establish working groups to develop and disseminate best practices, case presentations, and conference proceedings for use by local protection programs and their Research Ethics Review Boards.

Intellectual and educational resources are as important as financial resources in ensuring protections. The current protection system emphasizes local control and archiving of collective wisdom in the decision-making process for approving human research protocols. A more systematic literature and "case presentation" approach is needed for educational purposes and to promote consistency and high-quality decision making within Research ERBs. The lack of consistency among boards regarding, for example, the interpretation of the definition of minimal risk or investigator education requirements, can lead to contradictory—and often unproductive—directives to investigators that detract from time interacting with participants and overseeing research staff (investigator teleconference).[32] Steps should be taken to improve the consistency of review board practices and regulatory interpretations through the dissemination of best practice guidelines; consensus conferences involving board chairs, investigators, ethicists and participant groups; and eventually, the building of a rich database of case dispositions analogous to case law in the legal arena. Such activities could also be useful in the exploration of complex ethical situations, such as research with children. The National Human Research Protections Advisory Committee (NHRPAC)[33] has begun to address this void within the research review community through working groups focused on social and behavioral sciences and research with children.[34] However, their work alone cannot be expected to meet this need.

The availability of such materials would assist Research ERBs and other review bodies in making difficult decisions by aggregating institu-

---

[32]See Appendix A, "Methods," for more information.

[33]As this report went to press, it was reported that DHHS had disbanded NHRPAC (Weiss, 2002). Committee discussion and recommendations directed to NHRPAC should now be directed to any future advisory body constituted to address participant protection issues.

[34]See ohrp.osophs.dhhs.gov/nhrpac/nhrpac.htm for further information about the National Human Research Protections Advisory Committee.

tional experiences and creating precedent cases. Although it is anticipated that the continued development and implementation of accreditation programs will contribute to the dissemination of best practices, this mechanism cannot substitute for the recommended deliberations at the national level. OHRP and NHRPAC, with input from the FDA to ensure that issues particular to drug, biologic and device research are incorporated, should initiate such efforts forthwith.

SUMMARY

The adequate review of research to ensure that human research participants are protected involves the evaluation of several factors that require specific expertise. The IRB structure should be redefined and renamed the "Research ERB" to assert its mandate to conduct ethics reviews on protocols on behalf of those who will eventually be enrolled in studies. However, the newly configured Research ERB cannot be expected to carry out all of the specialized tasks required of a comprehensive protection program. Therefore, when appropriate to the research risks and context, scientific and financial conflicts of interest review should occur through distinct mechanisms that feed into and inform the Research ERB's comprehensive ethical review of research.

In order to carry out the responsibilities that should be under the purview of the Research ERB, all members should have core knowledge regarding human research ethics. In addition, at least 25 percent of the body's membership should have no affiliation with the institution, not be trained as scientists, and be able to represent the local community and/or participant perspectives. To ensure that no study goes forward if a substantial portion of the Research ERB objects, no protocol should be approved absent three-quarters of the voting members' agreement.

One of the primary responsibilities of the Research ERB is the review of consent forms and the informed consent process. The board should ensure that the consent forms convey information relevant to the participant's decision about whether to enroll and limit, or preferably delete, any language that would serve only to protect the institution.

Robust, ethical review by the Research ERB could be enhanced by better employing risk-stratification, allowing boards to deal with minimal risk studies efficiently and devote more attention to high-risk studies. The review of multisite protocols could be streamlined by designating lead scientific review and ethics review committees, whose judgments would be subject to acceptance by the local review boards (this would include the sharing of conflict of interest determinations with the lead Research ERB). A common body of knowledge and guidance should be developed at the national level to assist review boards in their deliberations and promote consistency among the research oversight community.

4

The Participant-Investigator Interface

Before further considering the oversight mechanisms that would best protect research participants, it is useful to step back to the initiation of a research study and consider the relevant roles, responsibilities, and interactions of the primary parties: the investigator, who asks a scientific question, and the willing individual, who consents to help the investigator answer the question. Both parties have preconceived expectations of what this relationship will be like and how the exchange between them will proceed. For a productive partnership to occur, i.e., one that results in answering the research question, it is important for both the investigator and the participant to understand and fulfill their respective responsibilities.

This chapter discusses how protections should be incorporated into research from the moment a research question is conceived to the point that individuals are recruited and provide their informed, voluntary consent to proceed. A qualified, properly trained investigator and an informed participant together provide the best opportunity for maximizing participant protections, as the most elaborate protection system imaginable will not work if the investigator does not carry out his or her ethical duties and the research participant does not knowingly and willingly agree to participate.

Efforts to ensure participant protection should begin with the preparations of investigators. After a research question has been posed and a protocol developed and reviewed, the investigator should seek individuals who are willing to participate in the research, a process that hinges on obtaining the potential participant's informed consent to enroll in a study. The committee believes that there is a need to improve and standardize the approach to the informed consent process, which underpins the relationship between researcher and participant. Because many groups are currently reviewing various aspects of informed consent and because its complexity requires far more scrutiny than this committee can undertake, the topic is addressed only briefly in this report, as a central element of protection that should be conducted properly and scrutinized by the protection program. An appropriate informed consent process is an exchange between the researcher and the potential participant that is structured appropriately for the research design, the protocol risks, and the participant community in which the study is carried out.

Finally, the roles and responsibilities of research participants are addressed, as well as the need to include the participant perspective within the protection program and to provide basic educational material to potential participants on the general nature of research and the protection program itself.

PREPARATION OF THE INVESTIGATOR AND PROTOCOL DESIGN

The federal regulations do not speak specifically to the knowledge and expertise of the investigator, although they do require that the "IRB shall be able to ascertain the acceptability of proposed research in terms of institutional commitments and regulations, applicable law, and standards of professional conduct and practice."[1] In addition, the necessary qualifications and professional obligations of clinical investigators are defined within the *Guideline for Good Clinical Practice* developed by the International Conference on Harmonisation (1996, Section 4). The committee suggests that there are common responsibilities incumbent to any investigator who engages participants in research studies, regardless of the scientific discipline or methodology (see Box 4.1).

Regardless of the expertise of the investigator, a poorly designed human research protocol is unethical. If the data cannot be validated or replicated, research participants have been exposed to risk or have volunteered their time for no useful purpose. Thus, research that requires enrolling participants should be conducted only by properly trained individuals.

The question posed by the research protocol should be of sufficient scientific importance to justify the use of human participants and valuable

---

[1]45 CFR 46.107(a), 21 CFR 56.107(a).

Box 4.1
Responsibilities of the Investigator

From the time informed consent is provided until a study is completed, the research investigator plays a pivotal role in assuring participant safety. In some cases,
the investigator will have posed the initial research question and will therefore be
responsible for the overall research design. In other situations, the investigator may
have received a completed research protocol from a sponsor or another investigator.
In either case, the investigator is responsible for ensuring that the protocol is properly conducted. The investigator's responsibilities include the following:

- receiving appropriate training and credentials to properly perform or supervise
  all procedures required for study conduct;
- maintaining training in the ethics and regulatory requirements of human experimentation;
- ensuring that the research protocol is scientifically and ethically sound;
- submitting proposals to appropriate bodies for scientific and ethical review before the initiation of the research protocol;
- disclosing potential conflicts of interest to appropriate parties;
- ensuring that participation is voluntary and informed and that the informed consent process is effective and active throughout the duration of the study;
- conducting the study in accordance with the approved protocol;
- submitting for review amendments to the protocol that arise during the conduct
  of the study;
- ensuring that appropriate safety monitoring and continuing review activities
  take place for the protocol;
- acknowledging and reporting protocol violations, errors, and problems to appropriate parties, such as the Research ERB, regulatory agency, or research sponsor,
- reporting research results in a responsible manner; and
- when appropriate, communicating research results to participants or participant communities.

social resources.[2] As discussed in Chapter 3, the merit of the scientific
question should be established by peer review, or an equivalently rigorous
mechanism before comprehensive ethical analysis by the Research Ethics
Review Board (Research ERB).[3] Issues to consider include whether the

---

[2]The committee does not mean to imply that there is an absolute standard with which to
judge scientific importance. Well-qualified and intentioned individuals will disagree about the
level of importance or novelty inherent to the question posed by a specific protocol. Many
late Phase 3, Phase 4, and student-conducted research projects may be ethically designed and
scientifically sound, yet offer relatively small advancements in knowledge. The key determination to be made is whether a research study contributes sufficiently to the greater good to
justify the resources consumed.

[3]Recommendation 3.1 calls for "Institutional Review Boards" (IRBs) to be named and
referred to within research organizations by a title reflective of their focus on the ethics underly-

answer to the scientific question will advance knowledge and contribute to the general good, whether the necessary literature searches and background studies have been done, and whether the safety of participants is clearly being considered by the investigator. In a well-designed study, the objectives are defined, the methodology is sound, and the statistical approaches are appropriate to analyze the data and obtain results. The key to ethical protocol design is choosing an approach that addresses the scientific question being asked, the intervention being tested, and the group of participants involved, while at the same time minimizing the risks to the participants. In addition, the final data analysis should provide results that are valid, replicable, and not explained by chance (Saunders et al., 2001).

In designing a protocol, especially a clinical experiment, there should be true uncertainty in the medical community about the value of a particular intervention, a state called "equipoise" (Day and Altman, 2000; Freedman, 1987; Lilford and Jackson, 1995). Equipoise has been defined as the point at which a rational, informed person would express no preference between two (or more) available treatments (Lilford and Jackson, 1995). The results of any trial should be free of bias, which can be caused by flaws in the study design. In clinical trials, bias refers to the tendency of any aspect of the methodology or the interpretation of data to lead to conclusions about the effects of an intervention that are systematically different from the truth, but bias can occur in any type of human research endeavor (FDA, 2001b). Ensuring that the chosen study design avoids bias and generates relevant data is an integral characteristic of clinical research, with a growing literature accumulating to address this point (Gallin, 2002; Meinert and Tonascia, 1986; Sackett, 1983; Spilker, 1991).

If the proposed study will utilize control groups, additional ethical considerations arise, many of which are critically important from the perspective of the participant. Control groups permit investigators to determine whether an observed effect is caused by the experimental intervention being tested or by other factors, such as the natural progression of the disease, observer or participant expectations, differences in the baseline condition of participants, or other treatments or effects (FDA, 2001b). Observing an appropriately selected control group allows the investigator to ascertain what would have happened to study participants had they not received the test intervention or, in clinical situations, what would have happened had they received a different treatment that is known to be effective (FDA, 2001b). In recent years, use of placebo-controls has been

---

ing participant protection activities. The committee has adopted the term "Research Ethics Review Board" (Research ERB) for this purpose. Therefore, Research ERB refers herein to the committee's idealized protection program, and IRB to descriptions of the current system.

controversial (Weijer et al., 2002). Although the placebo-controlled, randomized, double-blind clinical trial is an authoritative and widely accepted standard for new drug evaluation, some have argued that it is not always ethical to use placebos when a better alternative drug is already available (Freedman et al., 1996). In situations in which the best scientific design is not ethically acceptable, it may be necessary to reconsider the primary research question and to choose one for which an ethically acceptable design can be proposed, or it may be necessary to accept the fact that ethical constraints can create limitations to obtaining scientific knowledge (Levine, 1998; NBAC, 1998; NBAC, 2001a).

Another important design issue with ethical implications is the selection of the population to be studied. For example, in the early phases of drug development, research participants are selected from a small subgroup of the patient population in which the drug eventually may be used (CPMP, 1995). This is done to maximize the opportunity to observe specific clinical effects. By the time the experimental intervention enters Phase 3 trials, the characteristics of enrolled participants should more closely mirror those of the intended users.

Determining sample size is another important component of protocol design and planning. Although many methods and statistical models have been developed to calculate appropriate sample size, the number of participants in a study always should be large enough (but no larger than necessary) to provide a reliable answer to the question(s) posed.

Protocol Development

The diverse origins of research proposals influence how their designs emerge and how the protection of research participants is ensured. Clinical studies by industry are undertaken to evaluate one of their products and develop it for Food and Drug Administration (FDA) approval. Large pharmaceutical companies and contract research organizations usually have clinical departments with professional staff who design protocols in association with biostatisticians. Only after the research design, inclusion and exclusion criteria, outcome measurements, statistical powering, monitoring plan, and all other details are determined and approved by FDA and a Research ERB can the recruitment of the first subject begin. The sponsor (the holder of the investigational new drug exemption) is responsible for selecting only investigators qualified by "training and experience" to carry out the project.[4]

---

[4]21 CFR 312.53(a).

Thus, in order to protect potential research participants, any proposed investigator should, through his or her training, professional commitment, and moral judgment, be able to review what has been done prior to his or her involvement and either accept it, urge modification, or decide he or she cannot be part of it. Faculty members in academic health centers or private physicians may be asked to undertake research initiated in this way.

In contrast, the typical project initiated by an academician is more often motivated primarily by a scientific question rather than by drug development. For biomedical studies, a drug may be involved, but more likely as a probe or perturbation to the system than as an element of proving efficacy and market potential. The investigator in this case is likely to be seeking support from the National Institutes of Health (NIH) or a foundation (or drug company), but the study will not have the elaborate developmental and group participation described for industry. Similarly, NIH will not be monitoring each step of preparation, but will first be involved when a grant application is submitted. The individual investigator is therefore responsible for arranging the same features of research design referred to above and for considering the elements of participant protection.

It should be clear that the investigator working on his or her own to develop a human research protocol needs extensive education and preparation for that role. This is the subject of further discussion below.

Research Ethics Education Goals

The different perspectives between investigators from distinct fields are less important than their commonalities. Anyone studying human beings requires mentoring that is grounded in the science of the discipline, the integrity of research, and the ethics of human investigation. For this reason, the committee believes that formal education, for which numerous programs are now available, with a measured learning achievement should be required of all investigators. The committee does not endorse any single approach, but believes that the research organization should establish standards by which investigators' initial preparedness, their continuing education, and their adherence to institutional policies and procedures can be assessed. However, it is critical that federal agencies require such education as a basic precondition for carrying out research (Box 4.2) and encourage others research sponsors to do the same.

Educational opportunities within a research organization may include attending seminars, workshops, or Internet-based training. These programs should offer continuing education credits and, when appropriate, a certificate of completion. Topics can be derived from a variety of sources,

Box 4.2
Requirements and Regulations for Education

National Institutes of Health: In 2000, NIH initiated the requirement that investigators submitting grant applications or contract proposals must complete an educational program on the protection of research participants (NIH, 2000b). The NIH statement stressed the responsibility of institutions to ensure that their clinical investigators and Institutional Review Board (IRB) members receive adequate education and training.

Food and Drug Administration: FDA requires that sponsors select investigators who have appropriate education and training to oversee the conduct of a clinical trial, and the investigator, by signing Form FDA 1572, commits to ensure the sound and ethical conduct of research, including compliance by his or her institutional IRB and research staff [21 CFR 312.53(a)].

Department of Veterans Affairs (VA): Since 2001, the VA has required that all principal investigators, co-principal investigators, and co-investigators submitting research proposals to an IRB and Research and Development Committee provide documentation of participation in an educational program, which must be renewed every three years (Feussner, 2001).

Office of Research Integrity (ORI): ORI has embarked on a similar education requirement for personnel receiving federal funds to do research (DHHS, 2000a). However, the policy is now under the President's regulatory review plan that suspends implementation of this policy pending additional review. A final ruling on this policy will affect the educational requirements of ORI for clinical investigators (IOM and NRC, 2002).

The International Conference on Harmonisation (ICH): ICH addresses the need for investigator education as a part of Good Clinical Practice in its E6 Guideline. Principle 2.8 states, "Each individual involved in conducting a trial should be qualified by education, training, and experience to perform his or her respective task(s)"; educational requirements also are listed under the investigator guidelines (ICH, 1996).

including faculty, literature searches, professional organizations, consumer groups, and the IRB Forum (formerly mcwirb).[5]

Additional possibilities include providing support for off-site programs, annual meetings, and tuition reimbursement. A formal mentoring

---

[5]The IRB Forum is designed to provide a platform for conversations among IRB professionals, via e-mail, about ethical, regulatory, and policy issues involved in research with human participants. Although the forum is not directed at investigators per se, issues commonly arise that would be useful to investigators. The Web site for the group is www.irbforum.org.

program for both young investigators and junior staff also should be considered.

A number of colleges and universities are now offering both under-graduate and graduate degree programs in clinical investigation and re-search methodology.[6] Although most are open to anyone interested in pursuing advanced studies in clinical research, a few programs focus spe-cifically on faculty at academic institutions interested in pursuing a career in clinical research.

Assessing the Knowledge and Competency of Individuals

In order to assess the knowledge base and competency of personnel, research organizations could encourage participation in certification pro-grams and institute a basic core competency program within the institution for all currently employed and newly hired investigators and staff who are directly involved with the conduct of human research. Several institutions (such as NIH, Emory University, and the University of Rochester) currently require that investigators and "key personnel" complete a program of in-struction and, at some sites, pass a written test that documents basic com-petency to conduct a research study. These institutions should be encour-aged to collect and share data on their educational program interventions. In addition, adherence to institutional policies and federal laws and regula-tions governing human research and research integrity should be part of each faculty, staff, and student's annual performance evaluation. Sanctions for nonadherence and unethical behavior should be unequivocal and effec-tive. Acknowledgment or incentives for consistent performance and excep-tional ethical conduct and leadership may also be useful to stimulate the appropriate research culture.

An individual's knowledge and observance of regulations and ethical considerations should be measurable and sustained. Although the commit-tee strongly encourages, at a minimum, the pursuit of formal education by investigators, all Research ERB members, and administrators (see Chapter 2), content understanding should be documented for those who are re-quired to complete education programs. Updated documentation of the understanding of current policies and practices should be obtained periodi-

---

[6]Albert Einstein College offers a two-year clinical research training program, resulting in a master of science (MS) degree (www.aecom.yu.edu/crtp/); Northwestern University Graduate School offers an interdisciplinary MS degree in clinical investigation (www.northwestern.edu/graduate/academic/clin-investms.html); and the George Washington School of Medicine and Health Sciences offers an MS in Clinical Research Administration (learn.gwumc.edu/hscidist/DE/Program_DE_cra.htm).

cally, perhaps every three years. In order to be effective, rewards and sanctions should be concrete and consistent, and educational and behavioral endeavors promoting the safety of human research should be closely linked to the institution's program promoting research integrity.

As a measure to demonstrate competence in the design and conduct of ethically sound research, the National Bioethics Advisory Commission (NBAC) recommends that all investigators, Institutional Review Board (IRB) members, and IRB staff should be certified prior to conducting or reviewing research involving humans. Certification requirements should be appropriate to research roles and to the area of study. The federal government should encourage organizations, sponsors, and institutions to develop certification programs and mechanisms to evaluate their effectiveness. Federal policy should set standards for determining whether institutions and sponsors have an effective process of certification in place (NBAC, 2001b, p.48-49). The committee concurs that it is the responsibility of the research organization to establish the level of initial and continuing instruction appropriate for individuals with different responsibilities.

This committee's previous report, *Preserving Public Trust: Accreditation and Human Research Participant Protection Programs*, addressed the utility and potential value of an accreditation program for Human Research Participant Protection Programs (IOM, 2001a). Similar arguments regarding a move toward quality improvement (QI) and stimulating attention to weaknesses can be made for the certification of individual investigators. Certification would increase the likelihood that program principles would be followed by

- systematizing the body of knowledge that any investigator would be expected to have,
- providing an external mechanism to attest to the investigator's knowledge and understanding,
- stimulating periodic re-review and updates by investigators seeking recertification,
- reassuring stakeholders and potential participants that research is conducted appropriately, and
- recognizing the skilled research practitioner and screening out the unprepared investigator.

Investigators would be more likely to seek certification if offered an incentive, such as an increased likelihood of qualifying as a study site in multisite studies, or a disincentive, such as exclusion from federally funded or regulated investigations. The committee believes that certification of investigators is a promising approach that deserves immediate and careful study and deliberation at the national level by the research community, federal policy makers, and professional associations before implementation in a formal or mandatory manner.

Relevant Potential Conflicts of Interest

As an investigator conceives research questions and designs a study to answer those questions, there are multiple points at which unintentional self-interest may bias his or her decision making. The consideration of potential conflicts of interest at this very early stage in the research process is important, as early decisions may significantly affect participant protections provided down the road.

Formulating the research question, for example, may seem to be straightforward if the main considerations are perceived to be only scientific in nature. However, the importance of the research question should demonstrate sufficient possibility of adding to the fund of useful knowledge in order to consider involving volunteers. Merely adding to a company portfolio or to the publications on an investigator's curriculum vitae, for example, are not useful expenditures of human capital, let alone sufficient reasons to subject research participants to the risks inherent in any research protocol (including instances in which no physical or psychological harm would result). The issue in these cases is a simple balance between the participant's interests and those of the investigator or institution.

Personal biases and conflicts also can emerge during protocol development. For example, the addition of a placebo arm in a drug study may enable the investigator to use fewer participants, and thus obtain results (and a publication) more quickly than a comparison with an existing drug. However, such a design may or may not be in the best interests of participants, and participants' rights should trump scientific considerations.[7]

Conflicts of interest could also lead an investigator to seek out a population simply because it is easy to reach or to seek out individuals because they consciously or subconsciously feel pressure to volunteer. An example is the recruitment of employees, students, or trainees who are in any way associated with the investigator. Rigorous scientific review and appropriate training in the ethics of research with humans can often prevent or identify trouble spots before damage is done. Furthermore, strong organizational leadership and the promotion of a culture based upon ethical norms (as

---

[7]The committee notes that reducing the number of participants who should be exposed to protocol risks in order to sufficiently answer a scientific question also serves overall participant protection needs. The point in this instance is that individual participants' rights should not be sacrificed in doing so (Katz, 1993).

discussed in Chapter 2), possibly complemented by appropriate accreditation standards, could help to avoid or manage such conflicts.

For this reason, disclosure is the cornerstone of financial conflict of interest guidelines and regulations (AAMC, 2001; AAU, 2001; DHHS, 2001a; NBAC, 2001b; NHRPAC, 2001; 42 CFR 50, subpart F; 21 CFR 54). Investigators should understand their obligation to disclose potential financial conflicts of interest to the institution, as required by federal regulations.[8] The Public Health Service and National Science Foundation require that investigators disclose payments of $10,000 or more and more than 5 percent ownership in any single entity, while FDA requires investigators to report, among other things, payments of $25,000 beyond the cost of research and equity interests valued at more than $50,000 in sponsor companies. Research organizations, and particularly Research ERBs, should be apprised of the potential conflicts of interest of researchers, their staff, spouses, and dependents, before research is approved. As discussed in Chapter 3, conflicts relevant to research with human participants should be communicated to the Research ERB as a component of the protocol review.

At the conclusion of a research study, investigators should have sufficient control of data and publication to ensure that objective information is shared with the public (Blumenthal, 2001; Bodenheimer, 2001; Davidoff et al., 2001; Yamada, 2001). Sponsor input that limits investigator control over research design and data can create a serious conflict that can be precluded by the institution's role in the approval of contractual agreements.

Payments to the investigator conditioned on particular research results should not be allowed, and payments to investigators for participant enrollment should be allowed only under limited circumstances, according to the American Association of Medical Colleges (2001). Likewise, the American Medical Association states in its ethical code that "offering or accepting payment for referring patients to research studies (finder's fees) is unethical" (Council on Ethical and Judicial Affairs, AMA, 2000). Some associations, advisory groups, and government agencies have further declared that investigators and staff responsible for the informed consent process, patient selection, monitoring, management, or data analysis should have no financial stake in a trial (ASGT, 2000; DHHS, 2001a; NHRPAC, 2001). This committee agrees that finder's fees constitute a serious conflict of interest and should not be allowed for anyone directly responsible for enrolling participants and that individuals who have been identified as having a conflict of interest should not be allowed to carry out functions that could be compromised by their conflicting interest. Further consideration is given in Chapter 6 to financial conflict of interest issues.

---

[8] 42 CFR 50 subpart F; 21 CFR 54, 312, 314, 320, 330, 601, 807, 812, 814, 860.

THE INFORMED CONSENT PROCESS

Once a protocol has been developed, reviewed, and approved for scientific and ethical acceptability, the investigator must recruit individuals to participate in the research. The voluntary informed consent of the individual is a central element of participant protection. In addition, the informed consent process is a critical means by which investigators can establish the trust and confidence of participants. As such, informed consent can influence and shape long-term relationships with the study population and the general public (Getz and Borfitz, 2002).[9]

Since the publication of *The Belmont Report: Ethical Principles and Guidelines for the Protection of Human Subjects of Research* (*Belmont Report*) and the report on IRBs by the National Commission for the Protection of Human Subjects of Biomedical and Behavioral Research in 1978, informed consent and IRB review have served as the primary procedural safeguards in human research in the United States (National Commission, 1978, 1979). The centrality of informed consent to the research process was reiterated in a 1982 report by the subsequent President's Commission for the Study of Ethical Problems in Medicine and Biomedical and Behavioral Research, which identified informed consent as an "ethical imperative" to distinguish it from and raise it above the de minimus nature of law or regulation (1982b, p.2).

The continued importance of informed consent as a moral imperative is reflected in the attention it has received as a subject of research on the effectiveness of human research safeguards. A vast literature on informed consent has emerged in recent decades (Erb and Sugarman, 2000; Sugarman et al., 1999, 2001). Indeed, informed consent has been an ongoing subject of investigation by federal advisory committees (the Advisory Committee on Human Radiation Experiments, NBAC, the National Human Research Protections Advisory Committee), bioethics centers, and individual scholars (Faden and Beauchamp, 1986; Moreno et al., 1998; Sugarman, et al., 1999).

However, the safeguards necessary to protect informed consent have been undermined in recent years by several factors, including the advancing complexity of science, threats to privacy, the conflation of institutional risk management with disclosure in consent forms (see Chapter 3), conflicts of interest, the inadequate time available for in-depth consideration of protocols by many IRBs, and the lack of investigators and reviewers sufficiently

---

[9]The committee refers to consent by participants themselves in this section. All of the conclusions and recommendations are meant to cover situations in which the participant's decision-making capacity is not impaired and situations wherein disclosures are made to surrogate decision-makers who are authorized to consent on behalf of the participant under the applicable federal regulations and state laws.

trained in biomedical, behavioral, and public health ethics. Other parts of this report discuss the role of the program in promoting informed consent by participants (Chapters 3). This section addresses the *process* of assuring informed participation at the level of interactions between the investigator and the participant.[10]

The Concept of Informed Consent

The meaning of the phrase "informed consent" has become distorted over the last two decades as concerns of institutional risk managers have overwhelmed the patient-centered spirit of the Common Rule. In the committee's view, the intent of this analysis is to recover the original concept of informed consent by disentangling the strands of meaning now woven together under that label, identify and preserve those parts of the current practice needed to empower participants, and rejuvenate and nurture a participant-centered process.

> **Recommendation 4.1: The informed consent process should be an ongoing, interactive dialogue between research staff and research participants involving the disclosure and exchange of relevant information, discussion of that information, and assessment of the individual's understanding of the discussion.**

The ethical ideal of informed consent, grounded in the philosophical concept of autonomy, represents a departure from the paternalistic traditions of medicine revealed in the Hippocratic text, in which physicians were told to direct their commitment to the health and well-being of their patients, but were not instructed to foster their independence of thought or individual choice. In the Hippocratic text, physicians are exhorted to keep patients from "harm and injustice"...not to give a "deadly drug"... and to "come for the benefit of the sick" (Temkin and Temkin, 1967).

In the late 1950s and the 1960s, however, judges began to propose in court opinions that one of the duties of the physician was to share sufficient information or "reasonable disclosure" with the patient so that the patient could choose among available medical options.[11] In addition to the idea of

---

[10]The committee acknowledges that there are substantial complexities surrounding the informed consent process in international settings, particularly in developing countries (NBAC, 2001a). However, sufficient treatment of these challenges is beyond the scope of this committee, and the discussion herein is therefore limited to domestic research carried out in U.S. research facilities.

[11]*Canterbury* v. *Spence* (1969) held that part of the physician's overall obligation to the patient was a duty of "reasonable disclosure" regarding the choices and options for therapy that would make the inherent and potential dangers of the alternatives apparent.

professional duty was the developing legal concept of self-determination. In *Schloendorff* v. *Society of New York Hospital* (1914), Judge Cardozo stated that "Every human being of adult years and sound mind shall have the right to determine what shall be done with his own body...." This idea of liberty or self-determination evolved to include decisions about choices in medicine.

Concurrent with the legal development of these concepts, the higher profile of medical ethical analysis and the various rights movements, including the patient rights discussions, led to an ongoing discussion in medicine about the doctor-patient relationship. The result of that discussion, in the context of the legal opinions and scholarship, was the general agreement that paternalism was no longer appropriate as the guiding philosophy of medicine and physician practice. The physician was exhorted to discuss, deliberate, and share with the patient so that this relationship could provide the basis for individually appropriate patient choice.

Finally, in the specific context of research, the iterative set of federal regulations and the related multinational documents made clear that the informed and voluntary consent of the capable research participant was the norm for legally and ethically valid informed consent. Unfortunately, however, this ideal has been trampled by the research power structure and the ... onstrated by sponsors and ... t as one that provides for ... earch participant has fallen ... ument to be signed by the ... or site to comply with the ... research, these documents ... oses, prognoses, treatment ... treatments, the risk of no ... to provide care even in the ... icy of the sponsoring insti- ... be compliance with regula- ... the articulation of every ... nt complaint can be coun- ... d been informed and had ... guistic sophistication, and ... e not conducive to increas- ... m the patient-participant.

Informed consent should never be focused merely on a written form, which constitutes only a fragment of the process. A structured conversation between the participant and a member of the research team should occur when it is required by the nature of the research, as it usually is in research involving significant risks (Box 4.3). From a purely ethical standpoint, the purpose of the written form is to document and record that the ethically

---

Box 4.3
Informed Consent as a Structured Conversation

Items that should be discussed with participants face-to-face:
1. Participant is being asked to consent to a research study
2. Purpose of the study
3. Procedures involved in the study
   • Procedures that differ from ordinary treatment (e.g., randomization, double blind, fixed protocol, placebo, wash-out periods)
   • Procedures that resemble ordinary treatment
4. Nature and extent of risks/disadvantages
   • Risks/disadvantages that derive from research procedures (e.g., no guarantee of getting active treatment in placebo-controlled study)
   • Risks/disadvantages associated with the treatments provided
5. Nature and extent of possible benefits
   • Possible benefits that derive from research procedures (e.g., generalizable knowledge about the participant being studied)
   • Possible benefits that derive from the treatments provided
6. Alternatives to participation in research, including availability of treatments used in the study in ordinary clinical settings

Items that should be described in a consent form and that participants should have an opportunity to review before agreeing to participate in the study:
1. Procedures for assuring confidentiality of information obtained about the participant
2. Relevant investigator or institutional conflicts of interest (on the assumption that direct conflicts have been precluded)
3. Opportunities for recourse in the event of perceived mistreatment or injury
4. Information regarding compensation and medical treatment in the event of injury (in greater than minimal risk research)
5. Person(s) to whom questions can be directed

---

relevant information has been discussed. However, whatever role it may play in relation to potential legal liability, a signed form is not sufficient evidence of an ethically valid informed consent.

Informed Consent as an Ongoing Process

Emerging data show that informed consent is most effective as an evolving process, as opposed to a static, one-time disclosure event and/or signing of a consent form. Jeremy Sugarman, an expert on informed consent and the ethics of research involving humans, advised the committee during his testimony that informed consent should be considered an inherent component of the research process itself (not an adjunct exercise) in the form of an ongoing conversation that occurs at each research encounter or before each intervention (2001). Ideally, the disclosure of information during the informed consent process takes place as a bilateral process involving an exchange of questions and answers between a research participant and a research investigator. This interplay is an important and potentially challenging process, as it requires the person obtaining consent to gauge the appropriate level of language and technical detail suitable for the participant's understanding (Atkinson, 2000; Coulter, 1999).

Conceptually, informed consent should be construed as an evolving decision making process, rather than as simple "permission." This model of "ongoing conversation and decision making" allows for reinforcement of previously disclosed information, introduction of new information, and respect for autonomous participant decision making. The act of obtaining *written* consent is tangential to the *process* of informed consent and merely provides a mechanism to document and record that ethically relevant communication has taken place.

Particularly in instances of clinical research, investigators face many difficulties in communicating to potential participants the complex set of procedures, side effects, long-term risks, trade-offs relative to alternatives, and other information relevant to study participation. This task is not impossible, however. The challenge is to spend the necessary time and resources to prepare the appropriate language and ensure that communication truly occurs.

Role of Consent Forms

In current practice, so-called informed consent forms are best characterized as consent forms (see Recommendation 3.4). Additional documents (or appendixes to the basic consent form) that contain the boilerplate language directed at the legal protection of the institution rather than informing participants represent disclosure documents. These documents make little contribution to the process of communication and mutual understanding that is central to obtaining ethically valid informed consent. In contrast, the term "informed consent" should refer to the interactive process of education, discussion, and support that permits the potential participant to understand the options and apply a personal scale of values and preferences to those options in order to reach a decision about enrolling in a study.

The present convention, adhered to by investigators and followed by IRBs, is to review the consent form as the mechanism used to obtain informed consent, which is not sufficient as a process of involving and empowering the participant and promoting participant understanding. In the future, it should be up to the research organization's attorneys to decide whether the consent form and the disclosure documents are legally adequate; that is not the job of the Research ERB (see Chapter 6). Instead, the Research ERB should be expected to review the consent form to determine if it meets the federal standard and to decide whether a shorter, more accessible document might be used as a blueprint for the ensuing conversation with potential participants and as an aid to promoting understanding and choice. If a shorter form were offered, it might be useful to refer the participant to the sections in the full consent form that elaborate on the items in the short form. This would permit the participant to grasp the major procedures and their attendant risks, benefits, and alternatives and then explore them in greater depth. This process would facilitate understanding rather than impede comprehension, which, unfortunately, is often the result of the present use of lengthy consent forms.

Accomplishing the goal of real understanding as a precondition to a meaningful decision to participate will require a sea change in Research ERB and investigator perception and practice. Based on anecdotes and committee member experience, some investigator-participant exchanges are limited to answering questions such as, "What do you think I should do?" Such impoverished interactions utterly fail to link the skill and wisdom of the practitioner with the questions and concerns of the participant.

Disclosure of the nature of the study and its procedures, risks, benefits, and alternatives is a central pillar of the informed consent process. However, although it is necessary, it is not sufficient to support a process with real integrity. Disclosure information, presented comprehensively without overwhelming detail, is a pivotal aspect of the informed consent discussion, as without it potential participants will not have an adequate basis for decision making. Therefore, the committee encourages the development of innovative mechanisms (including written, electronic, or video instruments) to genuinely inform participants and promote understanding as well as record the interaction between the research staff and the potential participant.

In addition to this knowledge, the research professional's experience, perspectives, opinions, and recommendations are essential. Indeed, it might be more appropriate to label the process "advised consent" rather than "informed consent." This change would accommodate the interactive and supportive nature of the ideal process that assumes that information is the starting point of a discussion that alternates between participant questions and investigator responses and that helps participants understand the abstractions of benefit and risk in the context of a specific research situation and his or her personal needs and medical history.

An ideal informed consent process might use a brief document to present the basic material first and then offer the potential participant the opportunity to pose additional questions, as well as sufficient time to consider a more comprehensive document that may also be provided. It should always be stated in the case of nontherapeutic research that the project is research and not therapy. Appropriate help should be available to assist the participant in assuring that he or she understands the relevant issues and receives answers to all questions. In addition, special attention to the informed consent process should be provided for participants with language barriers, diminished capacity, and known vulnerabilities—both to facilitate informed consent and to avoid denying special groups access to human studies.

The Therapeutic Misconception

As mentioned in Chapter 3, in clinical research, informed consent often does not produce an appropriate understanding of the nature of research in participants because of the pervasiveness of the "therapeutic misconception" (Appelbaum et al., 1982; Churchill et al., 1998; King, 1995). The therapeutic misconception refers to the misunderstanding of the differences between research and therapy or treatment; that is, many think they are receiving treatment designed by a physician with their best interests in mind, when in fact the treatment they receive is driven by the demands of a research protocol.

Despite the provision of meaningful disclosures, participants who are ill are often motivated to participate in research by their hope for a therapeutic benefit and their belief that this is why they have been offered participation. At least one study has found that it is no accident that patients hold this belief, because their physicians also have somewhat unrealistic expectations of the therapeutic benefits their patients may receive during research (Daugherty et al., 1995). That study also found that 85 percent of patients decided to participate in a Phase 1 trial for a cancer drug exclusively for reasons of possible therapeutic benefit; the other 15 percent enrolled on grounds of either physician or family advice. None enrolled primarily for altruistic reasons, although 6 percent mentioned some altruistic reason as a secondary consideration (Daugherty et al., 1995).

It can be difficult for patients who are seriously ill or injured and thus who regard the investigational product itself as a potential lifesaving therapy to separate research considerations from possible therapeutic benefit. And, in some cases, access to an experimental protocol might, in fact, provide access to high-quality care that otherwise would likely not be available (Wayne, 2001). Participation in a clinical trial might be the only way that some individuals, particularly minorities, disadvantaged populations, and those with rare disorders can gain access to medical care (Gifford et al., 2002). Whether this situation is unduly manipulative is uncertain, but it is true that those who are seriously ill often see the investigational process as their only hope for therapy, even though an investigational product is not itself a therapy, and commonly other options exist (Daugherty et al, 1995). The availability of other options, however, is meaningless to a potential participant who believes that the investigational therapy he or she is considering may be considered by at least some experts to be a plausible therapy and therefore a reasonable option.

Considering these complexities, investigators should not abrogate their responsibility to ensure that participants are voluntarily participating in research and that they understand the uncertainty of the potential benefits. Although investigators often face a dilemma when participation in a trial provides otherwise unavailable health care services to individuals, particularly in cases in which the risks are minimal, he or she should remember that the persistence of the therapeutic misconception fundamentally undermines the achievement of meaningful informed consent.

The Need for Research on Informed Consent

A great deal of research has been conducted on the nature and adequacy of various consent procedures in the research and clinical contexts (Sugarman et al., 1999). Some research that has focused on the value of various educational approaches and materials (brochures, videotapes, information sheets) finds that the use of such materials enhances comprehension (Agre et al., 1994; Benson et al., 1988; Fureman et al., 1997). However, several reviews have been conducted regarding the readability of consent forms that have found in general that reading levels are too high to achieve broad comprehension (Briguglio et al., 1995; Grossman et al., 1994; Hochhauser, 1997). Other studies have focused on the ability of individuals to comprehend and remember complex probabilistic information and the effects of health status on comprehension and retention of information. In general, research has shown that in clinical research, both patients and providers place little weight on the value of informed consent (Lidz et al., 1983). Most see it as either a legal document or as a "contract" that is signed once information has been exchanged. And in one study, Getz and Borfitz noted that one out of seven participants reported that they did not even read the consent form before giving their consent (2002). This phenomenon once again highlights the need to distinguish the informed consent process from the consent form and for investigators to take an active role in ensuring that consent is voluntary and informed.

The need for further research and evaluation of the informed consent process became abundantly clear from the committee's investigation of the literature and from the testimony of experts and research participants. Such research should be funded by federal agencies as well as private research organizations, and institutionally based QI programs should include the local effectiveness of informed consent processes as part of a comprehensive and iterative evaluation of protection programs (see Chapter 6).

The solicitation of informed consent would be strengthened by the measures urged in this report, including the establishment of an ethically based protection program; the education and certification of all senior personnel involved in studies; the settlement of institutions' legal concerns in a process distinct from human studies' approval; the evaluation, disclosure, and management of individual and institutional conflicts of interest; the requirement for in-depth scientific review before Research ERB consideration of human studies issues; and an increase in unaffiliated membership on review boards. However, the central feature of ensuring that the informed consent process occurs and is effective lies in the commitment to this effort of the investigator and every member of the research team.

Heeding the Collective Rights and Interests of Participant Communities

The concept of "community" in the context of research has been discussed for some time and became part of official federal policy when FDA and NIH published new rules for the waiver of consent in emergency research (FDA, 1996; NIH, 1996). The new rules included the protection of consultation with the community, public disclosure of the study design and attendant risks before its commencement, and public disclosure of study results when completed. Other studies, particularly in genetics research and those involving controversial topics (e.g., behavior, violence) have also raised concerns about whether and how communities can be consulted before and during research and, in fact, whether there are any circumstances in which "community consent" can be contemplated or required.

The notion of community consultation increasingly is viewed as beneficial to participants, to investigators, and to the integrity of the study design (Dresser, 2001). It is especially critical when the investigator is not a member of, or is unfamiliar with, the community that is the focus of or the host for the research. However, the idea of "community consent" has been problematic for several reasons, but largely because of the difficulty involved in defining communities. Communities are defined by social and ethnic group boundaries, which are highly permeable and fluid. Individuals rarely reside fully in one group over time and place and often belong to more than one community. In addition, communities are more often socially rather than biologically constructed, and individuals self-define their communities.

Furthermore, identifying the spokesperson(s) for a particular community or ethnic group for the purpose of obtaining a community or group's consent to a research study is especially problematic. Although community spokespersons are important, they are also power brokers guarding the interests of their group and may have different perceptions of research than those individuals they attempt to represent. In a 2001 report on the ethical issues involved in international research, NBAC made two recommendations regarding community involvement and consent that are broadly applicable:

> Researchers should consult with community representatives to develop innovative and effective means to communicate all necessary information in a manner that is understandable to potential participants. When community representatives will not be involved, the protocol presented to the ethics review committee should justify why such involvement is not possible or relevant...

> Where culture or custom requires that permission of a community representative be granted before researchers may approach potential research participants, researchers should be sensitive to such local requirements. However, in no case may permission from a community representative or council replace the requirement of a competent individual's voluntary informed consent (2001a, p. vi, recommendations 3.5 and 3.7).

The committee endorses the NBAC recommendations. Investigators and Research ERBs have a significant responsibility and great latitude to make adjustments to protect groups or communities as appropriate, but many may not be well equipped to exercise this responsibility. Investigators and Research ERBs can involve individuals and communities in making decisions about relevant protocols and the development of consent forms that are understandable to them. As such, investigators and Research ERBs should be informed, knowledgeable, and sensitive to the research aims of community-based studies and the communities involved in these studies.

Steps to increase researchers' accountability and responsibility to communities might include requiring them, in their grant proposals, to justify their selection and definition of communities; to demonstrate sensitivity to the possible community implications of their research where appropriate; and to anticipate potential group harms. Research ERBs can make recommendations to investigators regarding actions that could be taken to educate and inform the community about the research and to enlist their support in enrolling individuals into the study. Research ERBs could also suggest ways to communicate research results back to the community. Reciprocally, communities should participate in reviewing such research.

Public advisory groups at NIH and research institutions could play an important role in reviewing applications for research projects involving communities, recommending funding priorities and ensuring appropriate community representation and protection of community rights.

ROLES AND EXPECTATIONS OF
RESEARCH PARTICIPANTS

Once a study is approved to begin recruiting participants, the protection system should immediately begin to protect the rights and welfare of potential participants. When individuals agree to participate in a project, they will be faced with a number of new roles and responsibilities. By being more assertive and protective of their own rights, participants can improve protections—not only for themselves, but also for others—and improve the quality of the research to which they are contributing. A more active participant role can help to balance the power between the investigator and toward the participant.

Federal regulations and international guidelines refer to "human subjects" of research rather than to "participants" in research, language that distinguishes the person being studied from the investigator and signals an asymmetry of power. The regulations aim to "protect" the rights and welfare of participants, with the underlying premise that those being studied are vulnerable when their interests conflict with those of science or of the investigators and that when such conflicts arise, the human rights of the participants trump the scientific interests of investigators and their research organizations.

This concept of protection, however, is not entirely consistent with an alternative framework that views research as a good in itself. Advocates of this framework, which include prospective "human subjects," have come to regard access to research as a right (Batt, 1994; Epstein, 1996; IOM, 1994a, 1999; Love, 1995; Merkatz and Summers, 1997). Thus, the historical and somewhat mythical basis of the investigator/subject relationship in which the individual volunteers out of altruism and despite risks is being supplanted by a new reality in which research participants sometimes demand access to trials, are often backed by an advocacy movement, and are ready to confront the research enterprise when mistakes are made or injustices arise.

The Role of the Individual Research Participant

Research participants are a diverse group of individuals who enter into the research setting for a variety of reasons and who play important roles in the research process. A participant in one study may be a seriously ill patient deciding among experimental treatments under the guidance of a health care professional. In another study, a student of journalism might be interviewing prominent business figures, and the "subject" may be considerably more powerful than the investigator. Those who respond to a survey may have only glancing contact with any investigator. Even within the confines of a phase 1 clinical trial testing dose and toxicity, the person participating in the trial may truly be the healthy "subject," or a desperately ill patient who views participation in the trail as a potential means of extending life.

Despite the perceived possibility of serving as a "guinea pig,"[12] the public has not lost faith in the goals of biomedical research, nor in researchers; substantial majorities of those questioned in a recent survey of participant attitudes about research favored clinical trial participation in most instances presented to them (Harris Interactive, 2002), and more individuals than ever are currently enrolled in studies. However, research participants do express concerns regarding their ability to fully interpret risks based on the information provided to them. They report uncertainty about whether their access to information about protocols is sufficient to facilitate their independent and informed decision making through the informed consent process. And, they want open access to research that may be relevant to their conditions or interests.

> Recommendation 4.2: Decisionally capable participants should understand their potential role in any study in which they enroll, the rationale underlying that study, and importantly, what is required of them to prevent unanticipated harm to themselves and to maintain the scientific integrity of the study.

Comprehension of participant responsibility within a study is essential, because failure to adhere to a protocol may expose the participant to unanticipated harm, invalidate the study, and expose other research participants to unnecessary risks, all of which can undermine a study's future benefits to others.

Research participants should be assisted in expanding their knowledge about the clinical research process by being offered educational materials and by being encouraged to ask questions of the investigator or other members of the research team. This is particularly important for studies involving greater than minimal risk and those protocols enrolling patients rather than healthy volunteers. Furthermore, participants should be encouraged to read the consent form thoroughly and write down questions for the investigator, if they are able. Participants should be provided the time to take the document home and to discuss the study with family, friends, or their personal physicians. If they do not understand any portion of the consent form, they should be provided the opportunity to request assistance from a representative or advocate in this process or to ask the investigator to further clarify the information. Participants should never sign the consent form unless they believe that they understand its content

---

[12]Lemonick and Goldstein, 2002.

and feel comfortable with their decision. The informed consent process may require multiple discussions between the participant and the investigator.

If the study involves an investigational product, efforts must be made to ensure that the participant understands the proper usage, dosage, storage, maintenance (in the case of a device), and disposal of the product before the trial begins. Further, a participant should appreciate that he or she is responsible for following these directions throughout the trial, as well as reporting any change in symptoms or overall health as quickly as possible to an investigator or his or her representative. It should be clearly explained that a participant must inform the investigator if he or she seeks medical care during a study, or if at any time during a study he or she cannot comply with the protocol requirements or does not want to continue participation. Participants have the right to (and should) ask for educational materials regarding the protocol and to ask questions of the investigator, including those relating to findings that result from the study. A list of questions and concerns that individuals might have regarding their potential participation in any research study is provided in Box 4.4.

Individuals who enroll in a research study should fully intend to comply with its requirements as explained to them at the time of enrollment. The decision to enroll in research is a serious commitment and individuals that enter a study with the intent to change treatments if they do not like their treatment assignment, or those that know they are not likely to complete the study should not enroll. In either case, the study and its analysis would be negatively affected, and more significantly, these individuals may cause undue harm to themselves or other participants.

The Need for the Participant Perspective Within the Protection Program

If the research enterprise is to remain relevant to the public, it should incorporate the realities and interests of research consumers, including those of potential research participants and the general public. As the examples of the HIV/AIDS and breast cancer activist initiatives to influence research agendas and policies demonstrate, the mutual education of participant communities and investigators can be a powerful tool in advancing research goals (Dresser, 2001). It has been noted that the perspectives of scientific professionals regarding research participation are likely to differ significantly from those of the general public. Therefore, effective processes are needed to ensure that the perspectives and views of the average individual are part of the research oversight system (Bastian, 1994). Meaningful participation in research does not include tokenism or the appointment to oversight committees only of individuals who are known to be friendly to an institution or to the research system generally. Rather, input to and

Box 4.4
What a Participant Might Want to Know

Potential Benefits and Harms
- If I am ill, will this research help me?
- What are the risks to me?

Protecting Participant Interests
- What are the realistic alternatives to study participation?
- What is involved? What will I have to do?
- Who will be in charge of my care? Can I see my own doctor?
- Are checks and balances in place to protect my safety?
- How was the research reviewed and approved?
- Will I be charged anything or be compensated for my participation?
- How can I end my participation if I change my mind?
- What will happen to me when the study is over? Will I be told the results?

Study Design and Leadership
- Who designed the protocol?
- Is the protocol well designed?
- Is the investigator competent?
- Why is this research important?
- Who else is involved in this research?
- Was anyone in the advocacy community involved in the design or review of the research?

Conflict of Interest, Study-related Controversy
- Is the study controversial?
- Has anyone conducted this study already, or one like it?
- Who will benefit financially if this works? What's in it for the investigator?

Institutional Oversight
- Whom do I contact to express concerns or obtain information?

NOTE: The information in this box was supplemented by elements described in the Department of Veterans Affairs' booklet, *I'm a Veteran: Should I Participate in Research?* (VA, 2002).

regarding the protection program should be sought from those who are prepared to probe and at times challenge conventional research practices (Dresser, 2001). A degree of skepticism regarding such practices serves to stimulate and enhance discussion and is vital to creating a robust and responsive protection program.

The justifications for including public voices within research oversight mechanisms have been delineated in the literature and include principles also expressed by this committee, such as the need for openness in the system to promote public trust, the need to provide a sufficient level of unaffiliated and nonscientific perspectives in the decision making processes, the need to ensure the ethical implementation of research in a manner consistent with relevant community values, and the need for accountability (Andejeski, 2002; Bastian, 1994; Dresser, 2001; Swankin, 2001). As noted in *Preserving Public Trust*, "those participating in research are also in the best position to appreciate their wants and needs as a practical matter" (IOM, 2001a, p. 41). The committee further believes that whenever possible, a broad and diverse constituency should inform the perspectives of participant representatives, in order to supplement their individual perspectives with the cumulative experience of the larger group.

The presence of a support structure external to the research organization could be another advantage of the consumer-informed model for participant representation. For instance, public members and consumer representatives on health care licensing boards, governing boards, and advisory bodies have access to objective support from the Citizen Advocacy Center. This nonprofit organization provides research, training, technical support, and networking opportunities "to help public members make their contributions informed, effective, and significant" (CAC, 2002). The establishment of a similar organization for unaffiliated Research ERB members might provide a neutral (i.e., nondisease or research-centered) source for the training and support of participant representatives. In the absence of such an organization, the committee encourages consumer groups to expand their efforts to provide educational programs to their members. Additionally, the committee encourages research organizations to pursue partnerships with local organizations such as patient organizations, religious organizations, and community centers in order to identify individuals with the skills and potential to become effective Research ERB members. Such partnerships should include the development of policies that will encourage and facilitate increased participation in the protection program by unaffiliated members (e.g., holding Research ERB meetings during the evening so that unaffiliated members do not have to miss work to attend) (Rand Reed, 2001).

Basic Research Education Needs

Before enrolling in any research study, potential research participants should be provided with basic information regarding the research process, including the implications of the experimental nature of the individual projects that they may be considering. Several groups have developed materials directed at providing this information to potential participants in biomedical research (Centerwatch, 2001; NCI, 1998; VA, 2002). In the cited examples, a description of the research process is provided using lay terminology (e.g., "What Are Clinical Trials?"), along with a discussion of the review process and oversight structure. A list of questions potential participants should ask investigators, similar to those listed in Box 4.4, is also provided. More in-depth discussions of similar topics recently have been published by both Centerwatch and ECRI (formerly the Emergency Care Research Institute) (ECRI, 2002; Getz and Borfitz, 2002). For clinical trials, the Council for Public Representatives at NIH has recommended that each research site provide a list of "Frequently Asked Questions" for any individual considering participation (NIH COPR, 2001). The committee encourages further expansion and dissemination of these materials through multiple formats (including Web-based tools) in order to facilitate the engaged and meaningful participation of research volunteers.

As discussed in Chapter 3, individuals asked to serve in an oversight capacity within protection programs as a participant or community representative should be provided with the background knowledge and tools to fulfill this role. For example, unaffiliated members of Research ERBs should be provided with educational opportunities regarding the history of research, the need for ethical review, the methodology of research design, the federal regulations governing research, the role of advocacy for participants, and the processes for protocol review, as well as information on how to assess risk and consider possible benefits and the group dynamics pertinent to Research ERB deliberations.

Existing programs may serve as useful models for educating research participants about the research process. For example, Project LEAD, a project of the National Breast Cancer Coalition, includes language and concepts critical to understanding scientific research in clinical medicine, basic science, and epidemiology (Dickersin et al., 2001; Hinestrosa, 2001). Beneficial skills to develop through such programs might include those related to leadership, the critical appraisal of scientific literature, and those involved in understanding how research decisions are made. All of these skills can increase a participant representative's confidence to ask questions and to share his or her perspective on technical issues (Hinestrosa, 2001).

SUMMARY

Although research protocols are developed in many different ways, ultimately, a professional investigator is responsible for the conduct of the research and the relationship with the involved participants. This individual should work within the culture of a protection program that maintains the highest ideals of justice, beneficence, and respect for persons. To discharge his or her responsibility, the investigator should be trained in the methods and values of human research in addition to the technical aspects of a protocol. The research organization through which he or she is engaged in the project should ensure that only qualified investigators are given the privilege of doing research with human beings.

The voluntary informed consent of research participants is essential for ethically sound research involving humans. In order to ensure that participants provide truly informed consent, the informed consent process should be interactive and ongoing, rather than focused on the signing of a written consent form. Research staff should ensure that participants understand the risks and benefits of the study as well as their responsibilities as participants.

Participants can play useful roles in the generation of new research ideas, in the evaluation of protocols for their impact on patients, and in guaranteeing a participant-focused review, particularly by serving on Research ERBs. In addition, potential research participants should be aware of the responsibilities necessary to maintain compliance with a protocol in order to prevent harm to themselves or the invalidation of the study. In this sense, participants have an important social responsibility that is as critical to the validity of human research as the scientific design itself.

5

Improving Protection Through Oversight and Data and Safety Monitoring

To advance the continuing safety of individuals who volunteer to participate in research, the Human Research Participant Protection Program (HRPPP) ("protection program" or the "program") is responsible for systematically collecting and assessing information about the conduct of human research activities within its purview. Research involving humans is a data- and labor-intensive activity, from the inception of a protocol through its implementation to final completion and reporting of results. Ongoing review and monitoring is necessary to ensure that emerging information obtained from a study has not altered the original risk-benefit analysis. Yet in 1998, the Department of Health and Human Services (DHHS) Office of Inspector General (OIG) wrote that Institutional Review Boards[1] (IRBs) do not adequately conduct ongoing reviews and that, in general, such reviews are "hurried and superficial" (OIG, 1998a,b). In addition to complying with the regulatory requirements for IRBs to conduct ongoing monitoring and review,[2] additional efforts are needed so

---

[1]Recommendation 3.1 calls for "Institutional Review Boards" (IRBs) to be named and referred to within research organizations by a title reflective of their focus on the ethics underlying participant protection activities. The committee has adopted the term "Research Ethics Review Board" (Research ERB) for this purpose. Therefore, Research ERB refers herein to the committee's idealized protection program, and IRB to descriptions of the current system.

[2]45 CFR 46.109(e); 21 CFR 56.109(f).

that protection programs can improve the oversight and monitoring of ongoing studies.

Mechanisms should be in place to track protocols and study personnel and provide assurances that data are valid and are collected according to professional standards. These tasks should be accomplished in a way that safeguards participants' safety, privacy, and confidentiality within the system. Protection measures should be monitored by various means at all levels of oversight—from the government to the research organization to the investigator—to ensure that informed consent has been properly obtained and that all adverse events have been identified and promptly reported by the investigator to the appropriate institutional body, sponsor, and federal agency(ies). In turn, investigators and participants require assurances that the process is being handled responsibly by the protection program, that federal rules are being applied, and that those charged with these responsibilities have been appropriately trained.

Although regulations and guidance are available from both the National Institutes of Health (NIH) and the Food and Drug Administration (FDA) to direct IRBs, investigators, and sponsors in reporting and evaluating adverse events, confusion remains. Moreover, other entities not considered in the federal regulations, such as Data and Safety Monitoring Boards/Data Monitoring Committees (DSMB/DMCs), are beginning to play an increasingly important role in safety monitoring (DeMets et al., 1999).

In 2001, the National Bioethics Advisory Commission (NBAC) stated that "For the purpose of continuing review, IRBs should focus their attention primarily on research initially determined to involve more than minimal risk" (2001b, p.112). NBAC reasoned that in research involving high or unknown risks, "the first few trials of a new intervention may substantially affect what is known about the risks and potential benefits of that intervention" (2001b, p.112). For minimal risk studies, NBAC stated the following:

> Continuing review of such research should not be required because it is unlikely to provide any additional protection to research participants and would merely increase IRB burden. However, because minimal risk research does involve some risk, IRBs may choose to require continuing review when they have concerns. In these cases, other types of monitoring would be more appropriate, such as assessing investigator compliance with the approved protocol or requiring reporting of protocol changes and unanticipated problems. Although such efforts might fail to detect some protocol problems, the resource requirement inherent in conducting continuing reviews for all protocols and the distraction of the IRB's attention from riskier research do not justify devoting a disproportionate amount of resources to continuing review (2001b, p.112).

This committee concurs with NBAC's conclusion and thus focuses in this chapter on a discussion regarding recommendations to require and improve safety monitoring of all higher-risk studies, particularly clinical trials.

> **Recommendation 5.1: Research organizations and Research Ethics Review Boards should have written policies and procedures in place that detail internal oversight and auditing processes. Plans and resources for data and safety monitoring within an individual study should be commensurate with the level of risk anticipated for that particular research protocol.**

This chapter addresses the following topics surrounding the protection program's responsibilities for oversight and data and safety monitoring:

- government, industry, and local oversight;
- internal tracking mechanisms;
- data and safety monitoring within the program;
- the role of the Research ERB;
- data security;
- privacy and confidentiality provisions;
- reporting information to participants;
- communication among program components; and
- resource needs.

(Box 5.1 provides definitions for many of the terms and acronyms used throughout this chapter.) However, not all research with humans requires this level of intensive monitoring and safety review.

GOVERNMENT REGULATION OF RESEARCH

Through federal regulations, the government has established a system of protections for research participants that involves requirements for minimizing risk and monitoring the safety of studies that are under way. Seventeen federal agencies and departments adhere to the Common Rule (45 CFR 46, Subpart A), which is a set of identical regulations codified by each agency that applies to human research conducted or sponsored by the agency. In addition, FDA has its own regulatory authority over research involving "food and color additives, investigational drugs for human use, medical devices for human use, biological products for human use being developed for market, and electronic products that emit radiation" (21 CFR 50,56). The mechanisms by which oversight is generally conducted are described below. This system of protections, however, applies only to research that is federally funded by an agency that is subject to the Common Rule or that is subject to FDA review and approval.

Box 5.1
Terms Commonly Used in This Chapter

510(k) Notification: A marketing submission to FDA providing evidence that a medical device is "substantially equivalent" to a currently marketed device. A 510(k) clearance, not an approval, is granted for marketing these devices. Medical devices requiring a 510(k) clearance rather than a Premarket Approval (PMA) are typically lower-risk medical devices and devices that are substantially equivalent to devices that have been on the market since 1976 (pre-amendment devices). These devices also do not require an investigational device exemption for conducting clinical studies.

Audit: A systematic and independent examination of study-related activities and documents to determine whether those activities were conducted and the data recorded, analyzed, and accurately reported according to the protocol sponsor's standard operating procedures (SOPs), Good Clinical Practice (GCP), and the applicable regulatory requirements.

Biologic License Application (BLA): An FDA submission for marketing approval of specified biotechnology products such as products manufactured by recombinant DNA technology and monoclonal antibody products. A BLA is submitted to FDA's Center for Biologics Evaluation and Research (CBER).

Common Rule: The colloquial name for 45 CFR 46, Subpart A, the Federal Policy for the Protection of Human Subjects. This regulation conslidates requirements or IRB review and informed consent to participate in human subject research. It pplies to any DHHS-funded research conducted on human subjects as well as hat funded by 15 other agencies. FDA has proWmulgated its own regulations (21 CFR Parts 50 and 56) for FDA-regulated research, which closely mirror the Common Rule. Both sets of regulations apply when research is FDA-regulated and federally funded (wholly or partially).

Continuing Review of Research: The concurrent oversight of research on a periodic basis by an IRB. In addition to the at least annual reviews mandated by federal regulations, reviews may, if deemed appropriate, also be conducted on a continuous or periodic basis.

Data and Safety Monitoring Board/Data Monitoring Committee (DSMB/DMC): An independent data monitoring committee that may be established by the sponsor to assess at intervals the progress of a clinical study, the safety data, and the critical efficacy endpoints, and to advise the sponsor whether to continue, modify, or stop a study. The terms Data and Safety Monitoring Board, Monitoring Committee, Data Monitoring Committee, and Independent Data Monitoring Committee are synonymous.

OR

A committee of scientists, physicians, statisticians, and others that collects and analyzes data during the course of a clinical trial to monitor for adverse effects and other trends (such as an indication that one treatment is significantly better than another, particularly when one arm of the trial involves a placebo control) that would warrant modification or termination of the trial or notification of subjects about new information that might affect their willingness to continue in the trial.

(continued)

Box 5.1   Continued

Federalwide Assurances (FWA): Under federal regulations, an approved Assurance of Compliance must be in place for any institution that is engaged in federally funded human subject research. This written Assurance of Compliance documents the research institution's understanding of and commitment to comply with federal standards for the protection of the rights and welfare of the subjects enrolled in that research. For research funded by DHHS, these standards are found in 45 CFR Part 46. Assurances are awarded and monitored by the DHHS Office for Human Research Protections (OHRP). In December 2000, OHRP issued a plan to require each institution engaged in research activities, either on its own or as a subcontractor, to hold its own FWA. A single FWA would cover all research conducted at that institution. The FWA would be renewed every three years, and compliance would be monitored by OHRP. A revised version of the FWA was issued in March 2002.

Form FDA 483: Written documents describing objectionable practices observed during an FDA inspection of a sponsor, IRB, or research site.

Good Clinical Practice (GCP): A standard established by the International Conference on Harmonisation (ICH) for the design, conduct, performance, monitoring, auditing, recording, analyses, and reporting of clinical studies that provides assurance that the data and reported results are credible and accurate and that the rights, integrity, and confidentiality of study subjects are protected. (E6 is the relevant guideline.)

Investigational New Drug Application (IND): Refers to the regulations in 21 CFR 312. An IND that is in effect means that the IRB and FDA have reviewed the sponsor's clinical study application, all the requirements under 21 CFR 312 are met, and an investigational drug or biologic can be distributed to investigators.

Monitor or Monitoring: The act of overseeing the progress of a clinical study and of ensuring that it is conducted, recorded, and reported in accordance with the protocol, SOPs, GCP, and applicable regulatory requirement(s).

New Drug Application (NDA): An FDA submission for marketing approval of new drugs. An NDA is submitted to FDA's Center for Drug Evaluation and Research (CDER).

Premarket Approval (PMA): An FDA submission for marketing approval of new medical devices that impart significant risk. A PMA is submitted to FDA's Center for Devices and Radiological Health.

Product License Application (PLA): An FDA submission for marketing approval of all other CBER-regulated products except those that require a BLA. This includes but is not limited to blood products, vaccines, and allergenic extracts.

Standard Operating Procedure (SOP): A document that specifies all the operational steps, acceptance criteria, personnel responsibilities, and materials required to accomplish a task.

NOTE: Most definitions are adapted from the International Conference on Harmonisation; Good Clinical Practice: Consolidated Guideline (E6) Glossary (ICH, 1996).

Other mechanisms and authorities also are in place to monitor and oversee the research enterprise. For example, in 1992 the Office of Research Integrity was consolidated within DHHS and charged with overseeing investigator misconduct and prevention activities in DHHS-funded research, except for those investigators that fall under the jurisdiction of FDA. Investigative and oversight units of the Executive Branch and Congress have the authority to oversee various aspects of the research enterprise and report on its status. In addition, agencies that sponsor research reserve the right to revoke, suspend, or terminate funding if the research grantee or contractor is in violation of federal policy. Actions also can be taken at the recommendation of an agency's Office of Inspector General, and Congress reserves the right to intervene through the budget process or its investigatory powers.

These activities at the federal level provide an overarching system of protections that are operationalized, implemented, and responded to by research institutions and programs. A central role of these agencies is the provision of monitoring and oversight. However, the two leading agencies responsible for regulating the bulk of human research in the United States—the DHHS OHRP and FDA—should do more to harmonize regulatory requirements in these areas; share the results and findings of oversight activities; and provide useful guidance for investigators, research institutions, and HRPPPs to facilitate the enhancement of protection functions.

Monitoring by the Office for Human Research Protections

DHHS is the federal agency in which the bulk of clinical research and its oversight occurs. Eighty percent of federally funded research with human participants is conducted by one DHHS agency, NIH (NBAC, 2001c). NIH was also the original home of the major regulatory office in this area—the Office of Protection from Research Risks (OPRR), which was created in 1972 within NIH and charged with the protection of research participants involved in all DHHS-funded research, including NIH's intramural and extramural research programs. In June 2000, OPRR was replaced with OHRP, which was moved out of NIH and charged with protecting human research subjects in biomedical and behavioral research across DHHS and other federal agencies that follow the Common Rule (DHHS, 2000b). Thus, OHRP monitors compliance with regulations that specifically address IRBs, informed consent, vulnerable populations, and other issues directly related to the protection of participants as addressed in the federal regulations. Data verification, however, is not included in OHRP's direct mandate.

OHRP operates on a system of Written Assurances of Compliance, in which the institution assures its compliance with the regulations. The office revised its assurance process for domestic institutions in December 2000, replacing the previous Single and Multiple Project Assurances (SPAs and MPAs) with a Federalwide Assurance (FWA).[3] OHRP conducts periodic oversight evaluations "for cause," based on "all written allegations or indications of noncompliance with the HHS Regulations derived from any source" (Koski, 2000).

If OHRP finds an institution to be noncompliant, it can suspend all or a portion of its research activities at the institution and revoke its MPA/FWA. Between 1990 and June 2000, OPRR issued 40 Determination Letters to institutions and organizations citing violations of their MPA and in some cases suspended research activities until violations were addressed (NBAC, 2001b). Between July 2000 and May 2002, OHRP issued 289 Determination Letters.[4] This increase in the number of Determination Letters is due in part to increased surveillance activity on the part of OHRP, but also reflects the volume of research currently being conducted and the increased instances of noncompliance identified nationwide.

Other OHRP initiatives include a new system for IRB registration, a quality improvement program directed to research organizations, and the sponsorship of the Award for Excellence in Human Research Protection.[5] The latter two initiatives are particularly significant, as they represent a shift in the manner that OHRP and its predecessor agency, OPRR, have traditionally conducted business. Although ensuring compliance through monitoring and site visits is essential to maintaining the integrity of the system, to maximize its impact, OHRP should expend more resources on facilitating the work of protection programs to meet compliance goals. One way to do so is through informing the research organization of the outcome of its compliance assessment and by more proactively assisting programs in meeting regulatory requirements.

DHHS should provide additional resources to OHRP to build its capacity to develop useful guidance and facilitate educational and problem-solving activities to better complement its regulatory compliance mandate.

---

[3]In March 2002, revised language for the FWA agreement was issued by OHRP. This language can be reviewed at ohrp.osophs.dhhs.gov/humansubjects/assurance/fwas.htm.

[4]Included within the count of 289 Determination Letters are instances in which a single institution received multiple letters. OHRP maintains determination letters from July 2000 forward at ohrp.osophs.dhhs.gov/detrm_letrs/lindex.htm.

[5]The Award for Excellence in Human Research Protection was established by the Health Improvement Institute. OHRP and DHHS are the funding sponsors for the award, which acknowledges three different categories of excellence. For more information, see www.hii.org. Friends Research Institute has also instituted an award for research ethics. For more information, see www.friendsresearch.org/award.html.

In addition, OHRP should continue to advance its activities to emphasize an oversight system based on routine surveillance and proactive performance improvement (see, for example, Recommendation 3.8) rather than concentrating solely on compliance investigations and reporting of noncompliance and suspected violations.

Regulatory Requirements for Continuing Review

The federal regulations at 45 CFR 46.109(e) require that "an IRB shall conduct continuing review of research covered by this policy at intervals appropriate to the degree of risk, but not less than once per year, and shall have authority to observe or have a third party observe the consent process and the research." Regular, continual review is necessary to ensure that emerging data or evidence have not altered the risks or potential benefits of a study in such a way that risks are no longer reasonable.

The conduct and adequacy of such reviews have been considered erratic and ineffective for some time. A 1975 study of 61 institutions conducted for the National Commission for the Protection of Human Subjects of Biomedical and Behavioral Research (National Commission) found that half of the IRBs seldom or never reviewed interim reports from investigators (Cooke and Tannenbaum, 1978). The National Commission recommended, at a minimum, annual continuing review for research studies involving more than minimal risk or vulnerable populations (1978). In 1981, the President's Commission for the Study of Ethical Problems in Medicine and Biomedical and Behavioral Research concluded that "many IRBs do not understand what is expected in the way of 'continuing review'...[and] the problems manifested in these studies clearly need attention" (1981, p.47). In 1998, the DHHS OIG found that IRBs "conduct minimal continuing review of approved research" and that the reviews are "hurried and superficial" (OIG 1998a,c). In 2001, NBAC wrote that "Because the federal regulations are incomplete in describing what should be considered in continuing review, it is understandable that IRBs do not always conduct appropriate review. Thus, additional guidance is needed" (2001b, p. 112). This committee concurs with the NBAC statement and encourages OHRP to pursue the necessary activities to meet this need.[6]

---

[6]The committee commends OHRP for issuing such guidance on July 11, 2002 (ohrp.osophs. dhhs.gov/humansubjects/guidance/contrev 2002.htm), although the committee did not have the opportunity to review or assess the guidance.

Monitoring by the Food and Drug Administration

Recommendation 5.2: The Food and Drug Administration and the Office for Human Research Protections should notify the research organization(s) under whose jurisdiction a study was conducted of any deficiency warnings as well as any responses to such warnings. The research organization should share this information with the relevant Research Ethics Review Board (Research ERB). Likewise, monitoring reports prepared by or for sponsors that identify serious violations should be submitted to the principal investigator and the designated Institutional Review Board of record. In multicenter trials, these reports should be submitted to the central Research ERB, if applicable. All such communications should occur in a prompt and timely fashion.

The most extensive system of data and safety monitoring exists in the area of clinical trials subject to FDA review and approval. FDA inspects investigators, IRBs, and occasionally sponsors, to verify compliance with GCP. FDA does not have the resources to inspect every investigator and thus is more likely to focus inspections on those entities that enroll large numbers of participants. Foreign as well as U.S. investigators are subject to inspection, but U.S. investigators are more likely to be scrutinized.

The 1962 Kefauver-Harris Amendments to the Federal Food, Drug and Cosmetic Act[7] promulgated new regulations to improve protections for persons involved in clinical research investigations. In addition to proving efficacy, sponsors were expected to monitor the progress of studies, and investigators were required to maintain case histories for enrolled participants that included reports of serious adverse events.

In 1977, a distinct oversight unit within FDA was formed to provide ongoing surveillance of clinical research investigations. The Bioresearch Monitoring Program audited the activities of clinical investigators, monitors, sponsors, and nonclinical (animal) laboratories. It was intended to ensure the quality and integrity of data submitted to FDA for regulatory decisions, as well as to protect research participants.

The regulations that permit FDA to consider the validity of data submitted to it are contained in 21 CFR 312 and 21 CFR 812. In 1981, FDA published final regulations at 21 CFR 50 and 56 that cover the protection of human subjects and IRBs and were intended to complement the regulations issued the same year by DHHS (45 CFR 46). Thus, FDA inspects data to ensure their validity in support of an application, as well as the protec-

---

[7]Federal Food, Drug, and Cosmetic Act of 1938. P.L. No. 75-717, 52, Stat. 1040, as amended 21 U.S.C. 31 et. seq.

> **Box 5.2**
> **Results of Food and Drug Administration Inspections**
>
> From June 1977 through January 1994, FDA performed 3,092 onsite inspections and discovered that 56 percent of these sites had problems with consent forms. Other deficiencies included the following: 29 percent of the sites had not adhered strictly to the protocols; 23 percent kept poor records; 22 percent were unable to properly account for the drugs they had dispensed; 12 percent had problems with their IRBs; and 3 percent were missing a significant number of their records. Still, during this same interval, extremely serious problems—including those that led to barring of investigators from conducting clinical studies—had decreased from 11 percent of total trials to 5 percent (Cohen, 1994).
> Figure 5.1 depicts the number and category of form FDA 483: "Inspectional Observations" deficiencies issued to clinical investigators who have performed studies under an IND. The data reflect clinical investigator inspection files that are closed with a final classification by FDA.

tion of the individuals from whom the data were collected. FDA may also audit the IRB of record for an inspected study, as well as investigate consumer complaints or reports from whistleblowers. If FDA finds that an investigator is noncompliant, he or she can be disqualified from future studies.

FDA inspections of clinical investigators generally are conducted after the trial is completed and a new drug application has been submitted for review (Box 5.2). NBAC has noted that

> Most FDA inspections of investigators are conducted after the trial is complete. Thus, any detected violations of regulations to protect research participants are found after the point when participants in the particular trial could have received adequate protection. However, the inspections are helpful in improving compliance of investigators and, therefore, protection of participants in future research (2001b, p.52-53).

However, a significant gap in this oversight exists in situations in which a sponsor elects not to submit an application to FDA [NDA, PMA, BLA, PLA, and 510(k)] due to the toxicity or ineffectiveness of the candidate compound or medical device, because the termination of a trial before the submission of an application for approval will eliminate the trigger for an FDA inspection.

To improve the Research Ethics Review Board's (Research ERB's) capability to oversee participant protection, the committee recommends that any monitoring report for studies under a board's purview be shared with that board. This would not affect ongoing oversight, but would alert a Research ERB to potential problems. It would be essential for the Research

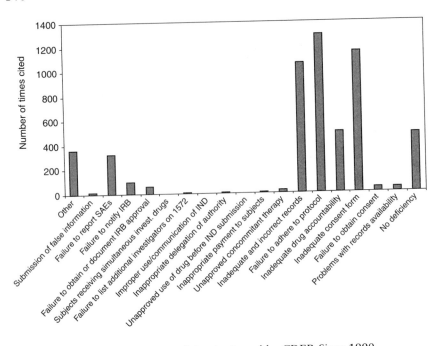

FIGURE 5.1   Form FDA 483 Deficiencies Issued by CDER Since 1990
   NOTE: This table is based upon data from 483s issued in connection with FDA
audits of human investigational drug studies. The analysis for the table was conducted by Center for Clinical Research Practice utilizing a listing of 483s issued
over a span of 10 years (ending in January, 2002) by Center for Drug Evaluation
and Research (CDER) and compiled by CDER (available at http://www.fda.gov/
cder/regulatory/investigators/default.htm). The information does not include data
from the Center for Devices and Radiological Health or the Center for Biologics
Evaluation and Research.

ERBs to also see the investigator's response to the deficiency warning (and
that of the research organization, as applicable), as the response often sheds
light on the inspection findings and clarifies how future problems can be
averted.
   Types of Deficiency Warnings to be shared would include Letters of
Determination and 483s, including those applying to manufacturing problems. Warning letters should be sent or at least copied to the head of the
research organization for distribution to those who need to know (e.g., the
Research ERB), as is the practice for industry Chief Executive Officers; and,
again, investigator's responses also should be forwarded.

Responsibility of Research Sponsors

A report issued by the Drug Research Board (DRB) of the Division of Medical Sciences of the National Research Council supported FDA's approach to monitoring, which sought to place the burden of responsibility for clinical investigations on the research sponsor (Kelsey, 1991). The DRB agreed with FDA that the sponsor should assume responsibility for 1) the clinical competency of its investigators; 2) the adequacy of the facilities being used for the clinical investigations; and 3) the investigators' understanding of the nature of the drug under investigation as well as the obligations that go with undertaking the investigation of that drug.

The DRB affirmed the sponsor's responsibility to ensure through periodic site visits the accuracy of the data, the adequacy of the research records, and adherence to the protocol. The DRB also affirmed the responsibility of a sponsor to terminate studies as deemed advisable, relate adverse effects of drugs discovered in animals to potential effects in humans, and ensure that participant consent was obtained and institutional review undertaken. Finally, the DRB recommended that FDA should not be responsible for active monitoring, but rather should monitor on an occasional basis and when there is reason to question data. It is not surprising, therefore, that the program for ensuring data validity became known as "monitoring the monitor" (Kelsey, 1991).

According to the regulations, "A sponsor shall select a monitor qualified by training and experience to monitor the progress of the investigation."[8] In FDA-regulated studies, data validity monitoring is conducted routinely by 1) industry monitors during site visits who conduct ongoing review of research data and 2) DSMB/DMCs engaged to look at safety data independently, with participant protection as their priority. Sponsors of FDA-regulated studies monitor all their investigators regularly (or at least they should).

Sponsors regularly monitor investigator compliance with GCP and with specific study protocol, including the degree of participant protection achieved. Many sponsors transfer this obligation to "monitors" who are employed by contract research organizations (CROs) and are therefore once removed from direct contact with the investigator site. The sponsor, however, does see the site visit monitoring report and remains ultimately responsible for the quality of the data and the conduct of the study.

---

[8]21 CFR 312.53.

Contract Research Organizations

In 1987, FDA recognized CROs as regulated entities, and provided that authority for the conduct of a study could now be delegated by a sponsor to a CRO.[9] Sponsors are expected to verify the accuracy of reports submitted by a CRO in support of a marketing application, thereby holding sponsors accountable for entities acting as their proxy.

In 1988, FDA published guidelines encouraging sponsors to enact policy that provides for monitors to make frequent site visits, review investigators' adherence to their protocols, ensure that investigators communicate as necessary with the IRB of record, and ensure that records are properly kept (FDA, 1998). Pharmaceutical companies, or a CRO acting on behalf of the sponsor, generally send monitors to visit each participating site every 6 to 10 weeks to monitor the progress of the study, verify the accuracy and completeness of data submitted in case report forms, and assess investigator compliance with regulations and GCP.

The Need for Collaboration and Harmonization of Federal Monitoring Activities

Although FDA retains its enforcement authority for participant protections in FDA-regulated drug, biologic, and medical device clinical trials, it is hoped that the increased centralized oversight provided by OHRP will lead to more consistent and effective guidance in human participant protections across federal agencies. In addition, the agencies should collaborate on providing useful guidance for investigators and protection programs. Finally, the entire research community would benefit from knowing annually the results and conclusions of federal inspections conducted each year. This would provide a basis on which programs could improve compliance and incorporate federal findings into their quality assurance and improvement programs (see Chapter 6).

Recommendation 5.3: Federal oversight agencies should harmonize their safety monitoring guidance for research organizations, including the development of standard practices for reporting adverse events.

Harmonization is required regarding 1) safety monitoring needs at various levels of risk (e.g., high-risk research such as gene transfer studies that are likely to require frequent monitoring) and 2) a baseline level of monitoring/chart audits that would be acceptable to ensure compliance at

---

[9]21 CFR 312.52 (52 FR Mar 19, 1987 amended 52 FR 23031 June 17, 1987).

each risk level. In turn, each program should specifically address its internal monitoring and auditing processes for protocols at the various risk levels.

The appreciation and recognition of adverse events is particularly important in the context of clinical research, specifically in early phase clinical trials when little is known about the action of a test compound during initial exposure in humans and the determination of the safety profile is a critical marker. Indeed, the recognition and reporting of adverse events, coupled with appropriate intervention strategies, may constitute the most important function for research personnel in protecting research participants from harm and the population at large from subsequent exposure to a toxic or dangerous device or agent. Postmarketing surveillance and continued reporting of adverse events, as occurs through the MedWatch mechanism established by FDA, is particularly critical for drugs that receive approval on FDA's fast-track mechanism.

Although the exact magnitude of adverse events in the general population and in clinical trials in particular is unknown, the incidence of adverse drug experiences related to the investigational and subsequent therapeutic use of drugs and biologics is an important health concern. These events may be attributable to a variety of factors, including inappropriate prescription of the drug(s) by physicians (e.g., improper dosing or inattention to drug interactions). In the research context, both FDA regulations and the Common Rule require that adverse events be reported.[10] The Common Rule requires that adverse events be reported to the IRB of record, and FDA regulations contain requirements for the reporting of adverse events during all phases of product development as well as some post-approval reporting requirements. IRBs report that they are inundated with adverse event reports, but are provided with little guidance on how to analyze or make sense of them (NBAC, 2001b; OIG 1998a,b). In 1998, the DHHS OIG found that investigators were often frustrated and confused about what to report and to whom, and many were required to report adverse events separately to sponsors, NIH, the IRB, and FDA (OIG, 1998a,b). Complex and fragmented regulations contribute to a system of monitoring that is ripe for error. As well described by NBAC in 2001, adverse event reporting mechanisms should be immediately addressed to harmonize and simplify reporting requirements and timelines and to improve safety (2001b). NIH's requirements, which differ from those of FDA and are not clearly linked to the regulatory language, contribute to significant confusion on the part of investigators. FDA's definitions also are not entirely clear (for example, regarding investigational drugs versus devices). However, its system for

---

[10]45 CFR 46.103; 21 CFR 312.56(c)-(d); 21 CFR 812.46(b)(1)-(2).

adverse event reporting is developed well beyond that of any other agency and is also the most widely used by investigators conducting clinical trials of FDA-regulated products.

Issues that require clarification by and harmonization among federal agencies include 1) the definition of an adverse event, 2) report format, 3) report recipients, and 4) reporting time lines. A standard reporting algorithm would be extremely useful and could greatly enhance compliance.

Finally, understanding basic pathophysiology and pharmacology is required for a full appreciation of the nature, cause, and diagnosis of an adverse drug reaction. Training in these areas should be offered as part of an institution's ongoing continuing education program for relevant research staff, as only research staff that have the appropriate training and education should be evaluating research participants for adverse events. Clinical investigators should receive specific instruction about assigning a causal relationship of an adverse event to the drug, biologic, or device under investigation; Research ERBs should be provided guidance on how to interpret and respond to such reports; and clinical trial participants should be instructed on how to recognize and report adverse events to study personnel.

> **Recommendation 5.4: The Secretary of the Department of Health and Human Services should issue a yearly report summarizing the results of research oversight activities in the United States, including Office for Human Research Protections (OHRP) and Food and Drug Administration (FDA) findings from inspections conducted during the previous year. OHRP and FDA should issue joint and regular statements containing the type of content currently found within "FDA Information Sheets."**

FDA's Office for Good Clinical Practice could spearhead this initiative to provide joint information regarding inspection findings from OHRP and FDA. Direct collaboration with OHRP should be strengthened, and the FDA office could be jointly staffed by both agencies. A set of recommendations to improve human participant protection compliance based upon inspection findings could provide valuable guidance to protection programs.

OVERSIGHT BY FEDERAL RESEARCH AGENCIES

Although at least 16 federal agencies support research with human participants, DHHS is the largest federal sponsor of research involving human subjects (NBAC, 2001c). In FY 1999, NIH supported nearly 83 percent of all federally funded research in the United States (NBAC, 2001c). As such, NIH is the federal agency most involved in monitoring activities and is the focus of the following section.

National Institutes of Health

Recommendation 5.5: When protocols warrant high levels of scrutiny because of risk to the participant, National Institutes of Health-sponsored clinical trials (intramural, extramural, and cooperative study groups) should be monitored with the same rigor and scrutiny as trials carried out through an investigational new drug application.

NIH Centers and Institutes are responsible for the oversight and monitoring of participant safety and data integrity for all NIH-sponsored clinical trials (intramural and extramural). In 1967, the National Heart Institute commissioned a report that recommended specific structural and operational components for NIH-sponsored cooperative trials (Heart Special Project Committee, 1967). Known as the Greenberg Report, it called for committee oversight, including the establishment of an Advisory and Steering Committee, protocol chair, and data coordinating center, and a mechanism for independent interim analysis of accumulating data that could call for premature study termination when warranted. DSMB/DMCs are the modern expression of this committee and are now routinely established for Phase 3, multisite clinical trials employing interventions that could pose a potential risk to participants. NIH policy further mandates a data and safety monitoring plan (DSMP) for all Phase 1 and 2 clinical trials (NIH, 2000a).

Research participant protections in the NIH extramural program are monitored by OHRP and FDA (if a research protocol involves an FDA-regulated product) through the relevant research organization's HRPPP. Activities of the intramural program are monitored by the NIH Office of Human Subjects Research, which oversees the multiple IRBs that sit for the various Institutes and the training of NIH clinical investigators. NIH's Office of Biotechnology Activities oversees gene transfer clinical trials through its management of the NIH Recombinant DNA Advisory Committee, which ensures additional safeguards on the conduct of gene transfer clinical trials.

The committee endorses NIH's requirement for DSMPs for all clinical trials, and further supports its extension to all studies involving more than minimal risk. However, the committee believes additional guidance is needed regarding what is expected of such plans. As appropriate, guidance provided by FDA and ICH for monitoring of investigations could be applied to federally funded studies (FDA, 1998; ICH, 1996). Further guidance is also needed regarding how to fund the DSMP requirement and how to assure compliance with established plans.

To meet this need, NIH could initiate an internal program based on FDA compliance program guidance or require that institutions conduct such reviews as a condition of receiving funds.

DATA AND SAFETY MONITORING BY THE PROGRAM

Data and Safety Monitoring Plans

Federal regulations require that protocols submitted under an IND include detailed descriptions of the "clinical procedures, laboratory tests, or other measures to be taken to monitor the effects of the drug in human subjects as to minimize risk."[11] As mentioned above, NIH is now requiring that all Phase 1 and 2 clinical trials have a DSMP.

Data Validity and Safety Monitoring

The practice of establishing data validity and safety monitoring is most firmly established in drug, biologic, and device studies subject to FDA review and approval. Data submitted to FDA in support of a marketing application must be complete, accurate, and verifiable, as the eventual safety of millions of people rests on the accuracy and integrity of data collected regarding a product's efficacy and toxicity profile. Although behavioral studies conducted to test a hypothesis do not expose individuals to an investigational drug, device, or biologic, they nevertheless draw conclusions that could affect the lives and health care of millions. These data should therefore also be verified and the methods of collection monitored to ensure data validity and participant protection. The frequency and breadth of these monitoring activities should be proportional to the degree of risk assumed by the participant, as determined by the Research ERB.

The investigator is responsible for ensuring that any study conducted is scientifically sound and implemented according to standards of ethical conduct and, as appropriate, GCP, by a trained and knowledgeable research team. It is the responsibility of the research organization to ensure that policies and SOPs are written and updated for study conduct and participant protection. The research organization should ensure that these policies and procedures are followed by all individuals conducting research under its jurisdiction. Mechanisms to ensure compliance include monitoring and auditing activities that should be ongoing and independent of the investigative site.

Monitoring the data generated and the research activities associated with the conduct of a protocol involves many distinct activities, including but not limited to the following:

- assuring adherence to the approved protocol and amendments;
- verifying that all participants provided informed consent before the institution of any study-related procedures;

---

[11]21 CFR 312.23.

- reviewing records to confirm protocol eligibility;
- reviewing records to determine compliance with the protocol and study intervention;
- properly storing, dosing, dispensing, and tracking investigational agents;
- verifying that data submitted are supported by source documents (paper or electronic);
- reporting adverse events to the Research ERB and sponsor completely and in a timely manner;
- ensuring that changes in the protocol are submitted and approved by the Research ERB before implementation; and
- ensuring the confidentiality of participant data.

The Role of the Research ERB in Safety Monitoring

Most institutions are familiar with risk assessment vis-à-vis the liability exposure of the organization. However, the principles of risk in clinical research need to be applied from the perspective of the participants and their exposure to risk, whether that risk is imposed by an investigational agent or through a breach of confidentiality. Determination of risk to a study participant would thus be a reasonable yardstick for allocating resources and personnel for program monitoring activities. General guidance in this area could be provided by the Research ERB at the time of initial review. Suggestions for risk assessment could include high-, medium-, and low-risk categories with monitoring resources focused primarily in the high-risk area, leaving medium- and low-risk studies subject to selective monitoring activities.

The Research ERB could assign a risk category to each study reviewed, and this assessment would provide oversight guidance for the program. Studies classified as "high-risk" would require more intensive and frequent monitoring of data and compliance with human participant protections. A random sample of medium-risk studies would provide random checks within the system and serve as an educational opportunity to instruct research staff. Less-than-minimal-risk studies would not require onsite visits, just as they often are not subject to continuing review by the Research ERB.

Monitoring the Consent Process

The informed consent process is fundamental to an effective participant protection system, and, therefore, the integrity of this process should be monitored over the course of a study. As previously discussed, it is the responsibility of the Research ERB to review and approve the original consent process and consent form presented to participants. In addition, once a study is under way, the Research ERB should monitor whether changes are required in the informed consent process based on the emerging study data.

The Research ERB could utilize a variety of mechanisms to ensure that informed consent is an ongoing, dynamic process that is responsive to participant needs and emerging data that could alter the ethical aspects of the study. Examples include the following:

- video presentations of informed consent,
- selected monitoring of consent by Research ERB staff,
- administering portions of the consent document through the Research ERB, and
- appointing an ombudsman for participants.

In performing the monitoring function, the Research ERB staff should focus on protection issues specifically centered on the consent process, recruitment practices, and adverse event reporting activities. The Research ERB office could function as an ongoing educational resource for these particular program activities.

Role of the Program in Data Monitoring

Investigators and institutions should take a proactive role in ensuring the validity and integrity of the data generated at each investigative site. Principal investigators (PIs) should assume the overall responsibility for the ethical and scientific conduct of research activities as individual participants are recruited, enrolled, and followed during a study by appropriately educated and trained research staff. For clinical trials, SOPs and procedures that are based on regulations and GCP should be adopted and applied throughout the research organization (ICH, 1996).

Institutional monitors could focus on source document verification, protocol adherence, and regulatory compliance, which would include chart reviews, regulatory file documentation, and case report form verification with source documents. Individuals not employed by the PI or directly involved with the conduct of the study should perform the monitoring functions.

DATA AND SAFETY MONITORING BY AN INDEPENDENT BODY

Recommendation 5.6: All studies involving serious risks to participants, enrolling participants with life-threatening illnesses, or employing advanced experimental technologies (e.g., gene transfer) should

assign an independent Data and Safety Monitoring Board/Data Monitoring Committee.

The committee believes that all studies involving more than minimal risk should include a DSMP for review by the Research ERB.[12] However, as trials increase in size and levels of potential risk—Phase 3 and 4 studies—more than a plan may be needed to enhance safety. Studies involving life-threatening illnesses generally secure a DSMB/DMC to perform interim analyses to evaluate toxicity and treatment outcomes as part of the overall trial design.

If the data strongly suggest a beneficial effect, harmful effect, or the probability that the study objective will not be addressed, the DSMB/DMC could recommend early termination of the trial, to protect the enrolled participants from prolonged exposure to an ineffective or harmful drug or intervention.

An interim analysis should determine if the study has met the scientific and ethical criteria established in the protocol to terminate it prematurely or allow the study to proceed to its planned completion. Whichever statistical methods are applied to testing outcome data during an interim analysis, the interpretation of the results is a complex process. To accomplish this interpretation in an unbiased and scientifically sound manner, the use of an independent DSMB/DMC that includes an appropriate mix of expertise has become an established norm for trials funded by industry and those funded by the federal government.

The primary responsibility of the DSMB/DMC should be to protect study participants from exposure to an inadequate or harmful intervention or continued participation in a futile study. In order to meet these goals, the membership of the DSMB/DMC should reflect its stated mission. Clinicians expert in the field of study, in combination with a statistician, epidemiologist, ethicist, and participant representative who have no vested interest in the findings of the board, are appropriate DSMB/DMC members. One model for the establishment of appropriate DSMB/DMCs would be the disease-specific boards that are currently active in clinical trial areas such as AIDS, cancer, cystic fibrosis, and cardiovascular disease. The targeted nature of these boards helps the individuals serving as members to develop the necessary level of expertise in the specific pathophysiology and safety concerns relevant to the disease. The nature of disease-specific "standing boards" such as these DSMB/DMCs also facilitates the necessary education activities that should occur if DSMB/DMCs are to fulfill their ethical obligations.

---

[12]It is also noted that further guidance regarding expectations, oversight, and funding for data and safety monitoring plans is needed from the relevant agencies.

According to a predetermined schedule based on projections for participant accrual, the DSMB/DMC meets to monitor the study's overall progress and conduct interim analyses on treatment outcomes and toxicity data. At first, all toxicity and efficacy data may be considered without regard to treatment group. If further refinement of the review is needed, the data can be segregated into blinded treatment groups. The identity of each treatment group is disclosed only if absolutely necessary for a final decision.

Most DSMB/DMCs meet during both open and closed sessions. During the open session, the DSMB/DMC may meet with representatives of the data coordinating center, sponsor, FDA, and study chair. A summation report of the study's progress is presented by the sponsor or its representative that focuses on operational issues, including recruitment, data management, and protocol design. During the closed session, the DSMB/DMC members review and discuss the study data. The board may recommend early termination, continuation of the study as planned, or continuation with modifications to the original protocol design and/or operational procedures.

To maintain its independence and confidentiality, the interim data that involve treatment outcome should be available only to DSMB/DMC members. It is also critical that any action by the board not be released in advance of an official report to investigators or the press. Unofficial or erroneous statements may dramatically affect the ongoing enrollment and integrity of the clinical investigation.

Recent Guidance from the Food and Drug Administration

In November 2001, FDA issued draft guidance entitled "Guidance for Clinical Trial Sponsors: On the Establishment of Clinical Trial Data Monitoring Committees" (2001a). According to FDA, the sponsor is responsible for ensuring that the DSMB/DMC operates under appropriate SOPs, and the guidance document offers some FDA perspective on criteria for establishing a DSMB/DMC, including committee composition, conflict of interest considerations, and other general considerations.

DSMB/DMCs should be convened according to guidelines provided by FDA when the study is under FDA purview, and according to NIH guidelines when a study is federally funded. In general, the size and composition of the DSMB/DMC may vary, but DSMB/DMCs should include appropriate expertise (e.g., clinical, scientific, statistical, and ethical). In addition, DSMB/DMC members and the DSMB/DMC as a whole should be independent from sponsors, investigators, and institutions.

NIH is the logical agency to take a strong lead in developing additional DSMB/DMCs, because it has had significant experience with this process.[13]

---

[13]Since 1979, NIH policy has been that "each Institute and Center should have a system for

NIH also should develop funding mechanisms to expand such programs to ensure DSMB/DMCs have adequate resources for performing their protection functions.

COMMUNICATING THE RESULTS OF DATA AND SAFETY MONITORING

FDA regulations require that sponsors review all information relevant to the safety of a drug from any source, including epidemiological or clinical studies and animal toxicology data. This also covers domestic and foreign reports for both investigational and approved drugs and both published and unpublished reports. The sponsor is also required to file an IND safety report with FDA and all participating investigators within a specified timeframe when the adverse experience associated with the use of the drug is both unexpected and serious or when animal studies of mutagenicity, teratogenicity, or carcinogenicity demonstrate a potential risk for human subjects.[14] The regulations further require that "significant new findings developed during the course of the research which may relate to the subject's willingness to continue participation will be provided to the subject."[15]

The regulations do not specify when or how the sponsor or investigator should inform subjects no longer participating in a study about reports of serious clinical or animal adverse events associated with a drug or biologic. Although traditionally the consent form has stated that participants will be informed of new findings, generally it is not stated when and how this information should be communicated.

For active participants, the ongoing consent dialogue between the investigator and participant would provide the ideal venue for informing participants of new information that may affect their future or current participation in a study. A Research ERB-approved signed addendum to the consent form could serve to document this communication. In addition, individuals who have completed a study or who have chosen not to continue their participation should also continue to be informed of any new findings, particularly new toxicology data from animal studies or serious adverse events that could have an effect on a participant's current or future

---

the appropriate oversight and monitoring of the conduct of clinical trials to ensure safety of participants and the validity and integrity of the data for all NIH-supported or conducted clinical trials" (NIH, 1998). Since that time, NIH has provided further guidance about monitoring (NIH, 1998; NIH, 2000a).

[14]21 CFR 312.32 (b)(c).
[15]21 CFR 50.25(b)(5).

health (e.g., primary pulmonary hypertension and cardiac valve damage associated with the use of fenfluramine and phentermine).

In general, trial results are not routinely reported to participants, but rather appear as articles in peer-reviewed journals. However, published articles generally do not appear for many months or even years after a study is completed, and participants would not necessarily have easy access to or knowledge of these reports. Therefore, efforts should be made to utilize other more direct means of informing participants of study results.

Sponsor Communication with Regulatory Agencies, Investigators, Monitors, and Data and Safety Monitoring Boards/Data Monitoring Committees

The regulations for FDA-regulated products during IND development studies detail specific sponsor reporting requirements to the agency.[16] These include periodic progress and annual IND and Investigational Device Exemption (IDE) reports of safety data and protocol amendments. Sponsors are also required to inform investigators about "new observations discovered by or reported to the sponsor on the drug, particularly with respect to adverse effects and safe use."[17] These observations may require that participants be "reinformed" and that a new consent form containing the updated information be discussed and signed. Sponsors are also responsible for selecting monitors to oversee the progress of an investigation and report to the sponsor their findings regarding investigator compliance with the protocol, reporting of adverse events, and the proper consent of subjects. Currently, this information is shared only with the sponsor and the investigator, but the material could provide valuable information to a local or central Research ERB regarding study conduct.[18] Thus, sharing these reports with boards could improve their ability to protect research participants.

As discussed, DSMB/DMCs typically are established to provide a mechanism for looking at unblinded safety and efficacy data on an interim basis (while the study is ongoing) and determining whether it is appropriate to continue the study, a determination that is often driven by risk-benefit considerations. Currently, typically little or no communication occurs between DSMB/DMCs and IRBs because they are generally constituted under different premises (sponsor versus institution).

There is a similar lack of communication to IRBs regarding findings com-

---

[16] 21 CFR 312.

[17] 21 CFR 312.55 (b).

[18] Currently, only 21 CFR 812.40 compels research sponsors of IDEs to notify reviewing IRBs, as well as FDA, of significant new information about an investigation.

piled for sponsors and regulatory agencies. Such findings would include monitoring reports submitted to sponsors about investigator compliance, closed session reports by the DSMB/DMC, or observations issued to an investigator in a form FDA 483 or a Letter of Determination issued by OHRP.

Monitoring reports that are currently performed for the sponsor are not routinely shared with the IRB. Yet, monitoring visits performed on behalf of the sponsor are usually the only real-time oversight activities that are conducted at the site, and they would be extremely useful for ethics review purposes. Violations in ethical conduct and/or noncompliance with regulations would require immediate action and remedy by the investigator.

A likely result of direct DSMB/DMC-Research ERB communication could be increased participant protection as a function of increased and timelier attention to risk-benefit analysis under unblinded conditions. However, it should be noted that the DSMB/DMC is a "protected body" that is able to look at unblinded data at a point at which no one else can. Premature disclosure of data and findings can in fact invalidate an entire study, and diligent care should be taken to ensure that this is avoided.

DATA SECURITY: PROTECTING CONFIDENTIALITY

All research with identifiable research participants involves issues related to the protection of confidentiality and privacy. Just as the protection program should monitor studies to ensure that risks are minimized and participant safety is assured, it also should take precautions to protect the privacy and confidentiality of participants during and after the study. (The Committee on National Statistics/Board on Behavioral, Cognitive, and Sensory Sciences and Education panel makes a number of recommendations regarding confidentiality in Appendix B.) In some cases, invasion of privacy or breeches of confidentiality might be the only research-related risks for participants (NBAC, 2001b). Current regulations regarding privacy require that IRBs only approve a study if "adequate" provisions are made to protect privacy and maintain confidentiality. Recent legislation, specifically the Health Insurance Portability and Accountability Act of 1996 (HIPAA),[19] includes some provisions for protecting privacy in the research context, but is limited in its reach. Recent activities in the realm of privacy protection in the research context are described below.

Privacy and Confidentiality Provisions

New regulations provide increased protection for medical records being sought for research purposes in circumstances in which it may not be

---

[19]45 CFR 160,164.

feasible to obtain authorization from patients. Under HIPAA,[20] access to medical records that was once taken for granted will be more difficult to obtain. Research organizations and Research ERBs need to review their policies regarding exempt review in light of these regulations because they will affect organizational practices concerning the waiver of the requirement for informed consent and the need for ethics review. The regulations codify privacy standards throughout the United States and will have an effect on medical and behavioral research (see Chapter 7).

Food and Drug Administration Special Requirements for Management of Electronic Data in Clinical Trials

In March 1997, FDA issued a Final Rule addressing requirements for using electronic records and signatures.[21] The regulation applies to a broad array of records and activities in the clinical trial setting used to support FDA product review and approval. The new ruling applies to all FDA-required records, including those generated during a clinical trial.

It is the sponsor's responsibility to ensure that a computerized system design complies with federal regulations and is validated by qualified information technology personnel. In addition, the sponsor should provide appropriate training and tools to research personnel at the clinical site involved with the collection, correction, and transmission of data electronically. If an investigator at an institution is sponsoring research subject to 21 CFR 11 and utilizing computer systems under the jurisdiction of the research organization, then the research organization should assure that systems design, validation, and training comply with these regulations.

SUMMARY

The collection and assessment of information about participant safety and data integrity while a trial is ongoing is an essential component of any protection program. Thus, a DSMP is essential for research that has the potential for more than minimal risk. The intensity of monitoring beyond the DSMP should also be scaled to a study's particular level of risk; this focusing of resources will help ensure that more HRPPP attention can be directed to studies that pose the greatest risks to participant safety.

Research organizations should explore their own monitoring activities and guidelines at the institutional level. To facilitate this examination, OHRP should provide guidance and educational opportunities. In addition,

---

[20] 45 CFR 164.508(b)(3)(i).
[21] 21 CFR 11.

federal agencies should harmonize their guidelines about safety monitoring at various risk levels and share information with the research community and the public regarding the results of federalwide monitoring. High-risk NIH studies (intramural or extramural) should be monitored with the same scrutiny as FDA-regulated trials, and for certain high-risk studies, DSMB/DMCs are essential. NIH should therefore take the lead in developing and funding more DSMB/DMCs. Federal agencies also need to standardize their adverse event definitions and reporting requirements so that these reports can be more effectively used by Research ERBs to ensure participant safety.

To protect research participants as fully as possible, it is essential that the relevant program mechanisms communicate with one another effectively. To this end, the DSMB/DMC should advise the Research ERB regarding whether new information affects participant safety and, as appropriate, this information should in turn be communicated to participants.

6

Improving Human Research Participant Protection Program Performance and Clarifying Roles

Throughout this report, the committee has emphasized that protection of human research participants is most effective when delivered in the context of a "system." This system is complex and multifaceted and sometimes operates through elements or modules that cross organizational boundaries—and includes a number of distinct and definable processes.

This chapter continues the committee's theme that program responsibilities include much more than the ethical review of protocols. Previous chapters have stressed the need to promote the incorporation of ethical principles in the design and conduct of studies, ensure that independent scientific review occurs—as well as considerations of financial conflicts of interest—and that mechanisms are in place for continuing review and monitoring of protocols, particularly those that pose more than minimal risk.

This chapter further argues for the need to "purify" the role of the Research Ethics Review Board[1] (Research ERB) and the informed consent process by differentiating participation protection from other institutional matters. Also included are descriptions of various conflict of interest issues

---

[1]Recommendation 3.1 calls for "Institutional Review Boards" (IRBs) to be named and referred to within research organizations by a title reflective of their focus on the ethics underlying participant protection activities. The committee has adopted the term "Research Ethics Review Board" (Research ERB) for this purpose. Therefore, Research ERB refers herein to the committee's idealized protection program, and IRB to descriptions of the current system.

162

and recommendations regarding the need to compensate participants for research-related injury, a topic that has been discussed at the national level for decades but never adequately addressed in practice. This chapter also highlights the need for continuous quality improvement (CQI), a critical means for ensuring that the various Human Research Participant Protection Program (HRPPP) functions are performing at optimal levels, and the potential of accreditation programs.

CONTINUOUS QUALITY IMPROVEMENT

Quality improvement (QI) in the context of health care involves individuals working together to improve systems and processes with the intent of securing the best possible outcomes. A catch phrase used in the quality field is, "If you always do what you always did, you will always get what you always got." The premise, of course, is that standing pat is not a viable strategy when better performance is demanded. "Zero defects" may be a reasonable description of public expectations of protection programs, but it is far from a reality in current practice, in perception or in fact. Formal, systematic QI methods are widely used in the health care system and are at the heart of health care accreditation. One of the promises of accrediting protection programs previously highlighted by this committee is the much greater visibility of and attention to QI in participant protection efforts. Programs seeking accreditation will have to learn and implement this management approach.

However, even in the absence of accreditation preparation, programs can and should work on CQI of their program. Elements of CQI include the following:

- identifying standards for the program,
- benchmarking performance against that of leading programs,
- searching for best practices to accomplish program functions and processes,
- adapting identified best practices to the individual institution's or sponsor's situation,
- performing self-assessments to determine the degree to which these processes are being successfully implemented,
- using continuous improvement techniques to further refine the best practices, and
- disseminating these refinements to aid other programs in the research community through journal articles and other channels.

Best practice in this context should not connote a belief that no further performance gains are possible—or expected. This term is used in QI to indicate a proven approach to carrying out a work process efficiently and effectively. The word "proven" is important; most definitions of best practices anticipate that the process improvement has stated objectives, has been evaluated, and that sufficiently robust measurements exist to establish that the organization accomplishes the prescribed objectives. Hence, rather than an ultimate end, a best practice merely becomes the next target for additional process improvement, analyses, and refinement.

An illustration of a nascent QI intervention development process can be found in the area of informed consent, in which advanced protection programs have utilized "consent monitors" in studies involving significant risk and/or participants with impaired decision-making capacity and have assessed the monitors' impact on the informed consent process (Silber, 2001). Such innovation is desirable in any program and can produce significant breakthroughs in QI processes.

The value of data to support both problem definition at the national level and quality assessment and QI at the program level cannot be too strongly emphasized. Data provide the program with the means to discharge its responsibilities for the participant protection system and enable decision makers to make programmatic decisions and allocate resources. Data on outcomes are especially important in assessing system performance. Yet the committee has been struck by the paucity of even the most basic information.

Information Tracking at the Federal Level

Recommendation 6.1: The Department of Health and Human Services should commission studies to gather baseline data on the current system of protections for participants in the research that it oversees and to assess whether the system is improving over time.

In recognition of the continuing need for information collection on the national human research protection system, the committee repeats this recommendation from its earlier report, *Preserving Public Trust: Accreditation and Human Research Participant Protection Programs* (IOM, 2001a, p.90). Clearly, this represents a formidable undertaking, yet it is one that as a society we should carry out if we are to understand and make appropriate changes in the current system (see also Recommendation 9 in Appendix B). The committee provides some suggestions about the kinds of data that are needed (Box 6.1), but recognizes that not all of these data can be collected at once and that some may be better suited to special studies than to ongoing reporting and collection mechanisms. In many cases, conducting scientific surveys involving representative samples rather than a full census will serve the development of policy as well and more cost effectively.

Box 6.1
Potential Data Inputs to Develop Federal Baseline Information on a Protection System

- A taxonomy of research institutions: The number of institutions conducting human research and the number and different types of studies (e.g., clinical trials, surveys, student projects, and behavioral studies) reviewed and approved/disapproved by Institutional Review Boards (IRBs).
- A taxonomy of review boards: The number of existing IRBs and the fraction of them that are primarily devoted to studies of particular types.
- A taxonomy of studies with humans: The number and distribution of investigations with humans under way by type of study—for example, clinical trials of various stages, health services research, epidemiological and statistical investigations, cross-sectional and longitudinal surveys, and behavioral and social science experiments.
- The number of participants involved in research and, among them, how many are involved in research involving more than minimal risk according to whether the study holds a prospect of direct benefit to the participant; the number of participants enrolled in studies under IRB review, and an estimate of the number enrolled in studies not under IRB review or any other form of review.
- The fraction of studies with more than minimal risk that have formal safety monitoring boards and how (and how well) those boards operate.
- The type and number of inquiries, investigations, and sanctions by the Food and Drug Administration (FDA) and the Office for Human Research Protections (OHRP).
- A taxonomy of research harms and injuries, including physical, psychological, dignitary, and social domains.
- The type and number of serious and unanticipated adverse events attributable to research, and the type and number of research injuries attributable to research and/or to failures of participant protection.

An initial step to the collection of data is to establish a prospective plan and to begin thinking about data needs, their sources, and their priority for action. Some conceptual and categorical clarification will be necessary in order to identify these data needs. For example, a study of research injury or harm cannot proceed without the prior development of a taxonomy that encompasses the spectrum of types of injury and harm and the contexts in which they occur. Research injury or harm is not limited to physical injury, and it does not always occur at the level of the individual. Research injury may include harm to dignity, psychological harm, or harm at the social level, such as the stereotyping or labeling of a group or community.

The studies and the data collection that would take place under this recommendation have several uses. They will provide essential data on which to base policy decisions in the future. They will also point to ways in which the protection system can be improved and may help prioritize strategies for improving the system by pointing to strengths and weaknesses in the current national approach. Finally, the availability of these data could reassure the public and policy makers about those aspects of the current system that are functioning well and more clearly define those that are not.

In addition to sponsoring studies about the system as a whole, federal agencies facilitate performance improvement in other ways. For instance, the National Institutes of Health (NIH) intramural program participated as a test site in the pilot phase of the accreditation efforts. Agencies and other organizations interested in promoting accreditation and/or QI can support and promote such efforts by, for example, disseminating best practices, QI data metrics, and databases and by providing other general tools.

Notably, both the OHRP Division of Assurance and Quality Improvement and the Department of Veterans Administration (VA) Office of Research Compliance and Assurance (ORCA) have developed self-assessment tools[2] that should enable programs to establish useful baseline measures against which they can assess their progress (Mather, 2002; OHRP, 2002a,b; ORCA, 2002; Roswell, 2002). These activities move in the right direction, because they highlight how oversight offices with responsibilities in compliance as well as education can facilitate improvement rather than focus solely on punitive measures. Based initially on a quality assurance (QA) self-assessment tool, OHRP is encouraging programs to work with it to identify areas for improvement in what ultimately will be a multiphased approach.

QA is an approach that compares current practice to defined standards of good quality (in the human research area, it would be rooted in compliance with basic regulatory requirements) and includes self-assessment, which provides a structured (and generally nonpunitive) way to determine the degree of compliance and areas of significant shortfall. QI goes beyond QA's focus on identifying and correcting errors (Box 6.2); QI is a methodology and set of statistical and qualitative analysis tools that programs use to ascertain the most common underlying causes of shortfalls in, for example, Research ERB work processes and procedures, and develop improvements that would eliminate them. OHRP indicates that it will phase in a QI assessment tool and subsequently a CQI process at the institutional level (OHRP, 2002b).

An important aspect of the OHRP program is the intent to protect information submitted for QA/QI purposes from the compliance investigation function of OHRP, in recognition of the reality that institutions would not want to submit an honest self-assessment if it were to result in penalties

[2]The OHRP tool is available online at ohrp.osophs.dhhs.gov/humansubjects/qip/qatooli.htm. The ORCA tool is available online at www.va.gov/orca/docs/Human_Subjects_Checklist.doc.

Box 6.2
Quality Assurance Versus Quality Improvement

QA and QI are complementary, yet distinct strategies. QA asks the question, "Did we do the things that should be done?" and redresses problems as they are identified. QI asks the question, "What causes us not to do the things that should be done?" and seeks to modify the cause.

An illustration of QA and QI in participant protection might be found in continuing review of protocols. For example, a QA self-assessment might show that the Research ERB is late in completing continuing reviews on 20 percent of studies that, under regulation, should have ceased enrolling patients once the approval period expired. Having identified these errors, it would be necessary for the Research ERB to notify the investigators of this and to take steps to bring the institution and the studies into compliance. In contrast, a QI approach would be to prevent this from occurring.

QI would collect data about the processes used by the Research ERB and analyze more frequent and less frequent causes of the failure to learn why these deadlines were missed. Hypothetically, the QI study might determine that there is no system to trigger reminders, that the investigators fail to respond to notices, or that the Research ERB sometimes loses its quorum and cannot complete scheduled reviews. The most frequent causes would be subject to a review and refinement of the Research ERB's work processes to prevent future occurrences—e.g., education of investigators or a longer lead-time in a reminder system. Subsequently, a QI study would remeasure the same variables to see if improvement occurred and to identify remaining causes of failure.

This illustration is a simple one, involving a *process* measure used in research reviews, but, of course, QI studies should also be undertaken to posit and measure participant protection *outcomes*.

---

for noncompliance.[3] Unlike OHRP, ORCA does not have regulatory authority, and thus is currently better able to emphasize proactive, culture-building efforts within its oversight activities (as this committee has encour-

---

[3]The information provided to OHRP in these documents can be requested under the Freedom of Information Act, but there is an exemption that allows an institution not to release any information that could potentially reveal noncompliance. Regarding communication with the compliance office of OHRP, the Division of Assurances and Quality Improvement "will not ordinarily communicate its observations during the QI activity to the OHRP Division of Compliance Oversight. In the unlikely event that serious systemic noncompliance or a serious problem(s) that had resulted in or may pose a threat to the safety and well-being of research subjects is discovered during a QI consultation, institutional officials will be appropriately notified and will be expected to take immediate action to remedy the situation, including filing an appropriate corrective action plan with OHRP. In such a case, OHRP will work intensively with the institution to develop and implement a corrective action plan in a timely and collegial manner" (OHRP, 2002b).

aged OHRP to do previously within this report).[4] It is also important to note that although it is Research ERB processes that are the main focus of the current OHRP and ORCA self-assessment tools, the responsibility for assessing and improving program quality rests with the research organization, as the Research ERB is only one element of the protection program.

Information Tracking and Quality Improvement Within the HRPPP

Efforts to initiate QI measures in the research community have been stymied by the lack of empirical data regarding the performance of HRPPPs, measurable outcomes or other criteria for the ongoing evaluation of protection programs, and the scant formal knowledge of the approaches and methods by which effectiveness of protection programs has been improved. This is particularly surprising in clinical research programs, because CQI has been a prominent feature of health care QI for two decades (Berwick, 1990; Hughes, 1988; Juran and Godfrey, 1999). There is an extensive literature available in both scientific and professional journals about CQI in health care generally, addressing both the results of CQI efforts as well as methods, approaches, statistical metrics, and other aspects of the CQI process itself.[5] Yet, with the exception perhaps of studies involving ways to conduct informed consent, there is a notable lack of published CQI literature on the elements of human research participant protection, much of which paradoxically takes place in the same settings in which CQI evolved and currently flourishes. The CQI field can accelerate QI if programs and their protection functions are made the focus of sound scientific research. In this way, experts in many disciplines—health services researchers, social and behavioral scientists, ethics researchers, and quality measurement experts—can contribute to building a new empirical knowledge base.

Recommendation 6.2: Research sponsors should initiate research programs and funding support for innovative research that would develop

---

[4]ORCA does maintain a "reactive mode" of compliance oversight through retrospective inquiries in instances of alleged non-compliance or impropriety. However, the prospective oversight model is heavily emphasized within their initiatives (Mather, 2002).

[5]Initially, clinical quality studies attempted to apply the techniques of industrial quality improvement, variously known as Total Quality Management, Shewhart Plan-Do-Study-Act method, etc. (Deming, 2000). Subsequently, modifications were devised for its use in health care settings to reflect the different systems and work processes. It should also be noted that no one would overstate the impact of these efforts on health care quality, for many problems continue, and rest, in system problems not susceptible to CQI efforts. See the IOM report, *Crossing the Quality Chasm: A New Health System for the 21st Century* (IOM, 2001b).

criteria for evaluating program performance and enhancing the practice of quality improvement.

The development and validation of criteria for evaluating effectiveness is one type of research that is needed, as few efforts have been made to define appropriate, quantifiable outcomes of participant protection. For the most part, performance assessment has been based largely on how accurately protection *processes* have been conducted—adequacy of record keeping, adequacy of disclosures and warnings in consent forms, for example. There is a need to connect this process information in a scientific and measurable way to develop evaluation criteria that accurately reflect program performance. For example, criteria should be developed for assessing participant understanding and for measuring and reassessing it on a continuing basis. One key aspect relevant to these criteria would be measures of understanding of the differences between research and treatment. Once data systems are in place for monitoring safety, it will also be necessary to develop protocols for assessing whether injuries or other negative outcomes were avoidable.

Similarly, research into innovative or more effective ways to conduct HRPPPs is vital to address the need to devise suitable end points for measuring effectiveness. Another important research area is QI methodologies devised and/or adapted for use in the unique health settings of protection programs, as there is little experience to draw upon that is explicit to participant protection efforts.

Dedicated research funding would help move this objective forward. Federal agencies should provide support, given the public policy importance of this effort. The committee lauds the NIH effort to provide short-term interim support for institutional activities to strengthen participant protection efforts at institutions that receive significant NIH support for clinical research and the reopening of the program announcement on ethics (NIH, 2002b,c).

This research area would also be a fertile field for philanthropic organizations with an interest in enhancing the contribution of science to people's lives. Moreover, industry sponsors have a need, an opportunity, and a responsibility to provide investigators and programs with information about processes central to their research and should support independent researchers in the study of human protection, in particular, in clinical trials. The use of a very small fraction of the resources now committed to clinical trials would vastly improve what is known about human protection.

Quality Assurance Database Needs

Many programs lack routine or automated systems for tracking key information regarding the studies under their purview. Information track-

**Box 6.3
Examples of What a Quality Assurance Database
Might Contain**

- Resources allocated to the protection program and its elements (e.g., budget, FTEs, space)
- The number of ongoing protocols
- The target sample size for each protocol and the number of participants actually enrolled
- The type of studies being conducted (e.g., clinical trial, observational study, survey, randomized)
- Number and types of adverse events and protocol modifications adopted
- Sentinel events (more broadly construed than deaths)
- The duration of studies
- Target populations
- Dates of Research ERB submission, approval, and continuing review for each study
- Consultations sought by the Research ERB
- Dates of Data and Safety Monitoring Board/ Data Monitoring Committee (DSMB/DMC) actions, as relevant
- Principal investigators and collaborators
- Research staff profile and delegated responsibilities
- Training documentation

ing systems are integral to the protection of research participants because they feed into QI and QA efforts, are likely to be required for some accreditation purposes, and are a means for measuring compliance. Mechanisms should be in place at critical junctures in the research process to ensure that the safety and interests of individual participants are maintained throughout the course of a project and that the data generated are valid.

Collecting research review data is a complex task that should be integrated into the practices of the program. Databases could be used to track, for example, protocol activity at each site, research personnel involved in study conduct, and appropriate credentialing and training per institution requirements (Box 6.3). There are often unforeseen uses for the types of information gathered in the conduct of human research, and a central database, with appropriate archiving and security measures to ensure confidentiality, assures that this information is available for self-assessment, policy development, research purposes, and QA support. Although QA is *not* QI, it provides programs with data about the conduct of human research, and it provides investigators an opportunity to learn through external evaluation. Data collection and analysis are a necessary precondition for both QA and QI.

STATUS OF ACCREDITATION

In its first report, *Preserving Public Trust*, this committee recommended the careful implementation of pilot projects for nongovernmental accreditation programs for HRPPPs and the research organizations responsible for them (IOM, 2001a). This recommendation was based on the potential for a constructive, performance-based accreditation system to facilitate within protection programs an emphasis on outcome measures as well as to provide a proactive, responsive mechanism that was able to incorporate feedback from accreditation stakeholders in order to meet evolving program needs. Further, participation in accreditation programs is a form of QA, as efforts to prepare to meet accreditation standards should ordinarily have beneficial effects, and at a minimum, will help ensure that programs will conduct self-assessments, presumably noting and addressing deficient areas.

Accreditation has considerable potential to systematize and accelerate QI processes. Site visits by accreditation programs determine if activities meet the standards set by the accreditation process and whether the organization has documented that it meets them. In addition, however, they require the organization to demonstrate that it has undertaken individualized local efforts to improve its activities. For example, the National Committee for Quality Assurance (NCQA) accreditation program, recommended in *Preserving Public Trust* as a suitable pilot program for the Department of Veterans Affairs (VA) medical centers, identified numerous areas in which it will review program QI activities. The expectation is that programs routinely collect QI data, systematically perform QI studies and analyses, and act to implement them. Examples explicitly identifying QI requirements in the NCQA standards include the following:

- databases and information systems that provide QI data;
- compliance in drug/device studies, correction of deficiencies;
- adequacy and effectiveness of Research ERB processes; and
- appropriate investigator conduct of informed consent process (NCQA, 2001).

Accreditation site visits provide a mechanism for identifying performance deficiencies, as well as for finding and commending strengths and excellent program performance. Accreditation organizations, such as the Association for the Accreditation of Human Research Protection Programs, Inc. (AAHRPP) and NCQA, as well as federal agencies participating in and promoting accreditation, can expedite the wider adoption of best practices by identifying them and, with the permission of the particular program, extending their reach through broader dissemination.[6]

---

[6]Included within the AAHRPP website is a section devoted to the dissemination of Best Practices identified in the course of accreditation evaluations (www.aahrpp.org/best_practices.htm).

Amendments to improve and strengthen accreditation standards are also sometimes derived from these site visits. For example, descriptions of standards in accreditation guidance, responses to inquiries, Web site documents, and manuals produced and disseminated by federal and other research sponsors have the potential to raise the bar for future human protection program expectations and accomplishments.

Subsequent to the committee's initial report, both the NCQA and AAHRPP accreditation programs have continued to work toward implementation. Each has developed its own set of standards and has conducted pilot site visits to begin refining them.

National Committee on Quality Assurance

NCQA is in the second year of a five-year contract with VA to develop and implement an accreditation program, which will apply to more than 120 VA medical centers that conduct research involving human participants. On November 15, 2001, NCQA released its final *VA Human Research Protection Accreditation Program Accreditation Standards*,[7] to remain in effect until July 1, 2004 (NCQA, 2001). However, in response to problems identified during the initial series of site visits, revised standards currently are under development[8] (Otto, 2002a). NCQA indicates that it will review and revise the standards annually in the future (Briefer French, 2002). As drafted in November 2001, however, the standards continue to fall short of sufficiently ensuring meaningful participant protection at various levels of program decision making and policy making.

During 2001, NCQA conducted pilot tests and subsequently more extensive field tests at VA hospitals to prepare to conduct active accreditation visits. Accreditation site visits began in September 2001, with visits to additional VA medical centers planned to take place at approximately weekly intervals. One anecdotal impression concerning the initial evaluations offered to the committee was a curious lack of awareness of CQI on the part of research institutions (Briefer French, 2002). Formal QI efforts—which are at the heart of health care delivery and hospital accreditation—seem more or less unknown and little practiced in research programs within the same settings. If this is so, it is a gap that accreditation preparation should close through the provision of training programs, the dissemination of research reports, and the provision of greater specificity in standards, guidelines, and site visit measurement tools.

---

[7]The NCQA standards are available online at http://www.ncqa.org/Programs/QSG/VAHRPAP/vahrpapfinstds.pdf.

[8]As this report went to press, the revised standards were available for comment at http://www.ncqa.org/Programs/QSG/VAHRPAP/vahrpapdraftstds.htm until October 4, 2002.

NCQA announced the results of its first 12 accreditation assessments in early April 2002. Within this group, nine VA medical centers received conditional accreditation and three failed to pass the evaluation[9] (Otto, 2002b). The most common deficiencies identified included the lack of local policies and procedures regarding IRB structure and operations, inadequate procedures relating to the informed consent process and consent forms, and problems in the documentation of the initial protocol review evaluations IRBs are required to make (Roswell, 2002).

In response to feedback from VA centers that participated in the first round of the accreditation process, NCQA suspended its accreditation visits to institutions in April 2002. This pause was requested in order to assess and respond to those areas already identified through the accreditation process as requiring refinement or further development (Otto, 2002a). The committee notes that it is this ability to identify problems and take responsive action that makes the nongovernmental accreditation model advantageous.

Association for the Accreditation of Human Research Protection Programs

AAHRPP is a nonprofit organization established in 2001 that seeks to accredit organizations engaged in human research. AAHRPP's declared intent is to provide accreditation of organizations involved in biomedical as well as social sciences, humanities, and other nonmedical types of research, such as business and engineering. AAHRPP states that its accreditation process "is voluntary, peer-driven and educationally focused, and aims to foster 'a culture of conscience and responsibility' within institutions seeking its services" (2002b). The accreditation process involves rigorous self-assessment, followed by a site visit from AAHRPP accreditors who are experts in practicing, teaching, and promoting human research protections.

AAHRPP released interim standards for public comment on October 15, 2001. The group was responsive to concerns expressed in this committee's initial report[10] about the need for broader utility within the standards, inclusion of more specific standards regarding participants and sponsors, and attention to CQI. One of nine "principles" enunciated by AAHRPP (Box 6.4) is that *"Standards should promote the development and implementation of outcome measures that can provide a basis for demonstrating quality improvement over time"* (AAHRPP, 2002c). The

---

[9]As this report went to press, each of the three centers denied accreditation had appealed the NCQA ruling, as had one of the nine to receive conditional accreditation status.

[10]In *Preserving Public Trust*, the committee reviewed standards provided by Public Responsibility in Medicine and Research; those standards served as the basis for AAHRPP's standards.

BOX 6.4
Association for the Accreditation of Human Research Protection Programs: Principles for Accreditation of Human Research Protection Programs

1. Regulatory compliance is a minimal expectation for a Human Research Protection Program.

2. Protecting the rights and welfare of human research participants must be a research organization's first priority. Beyond assessing compliance with applicable regulations, accreditation standards should promote a research environment where ethical, productive investigation is valued.

3. Accreditation must approach the Human Research Protection Program from a broad organizational perspective, moving beyond a narrow focus upon Institutional Review Board (IRB) operations to examine whether policies and procedures of the organization as a whole result in a coherent, effective scheme for the protection of human research participants.

4. The accreditation process should be flexible and responsive to changes in federal and state regulation of research. The accreditation process must also accommodate continuing evolution of the standards in response to growing experience in their application across the multiple disciplines and settings in which research involving human participants takes place.

5. Accreditation should primarily be an educational process involving collegial discussion and the provision of constructive feedback. The accreditation process must identify areas in which a Human Research Protection Program does not yet meet established standards, and it should afford inspected organizations the opportunity to discuss potential program improvements.

6. Standards should be performance-based, assessed through an evaluation scheme that is sufficiently detailed to support the accreditation process, yet capable of effective and efficient implementation. Program evaluation should result in a grade of pass or fail for each standard, but should also include commendations or recommendations for meeting standards, as appropriate.

7. Standards should be applicable to Human Research Protection Programs across the full range of settings (e.g., university-based biomedical, behavioral and social science research, independent review boards, government agencies, and others). Standards should address any special concerns (e.g., the use of vulnerable populations or heightened risk to privacy and confidentiality) that may arise in each setting.

8. The accreditation process should provide a clear, understandable pathway to accreditation, along with equally clear pathways for appeal and the remediation of identified shortcomings.

9. Standards should promote the development and implementation of outcome measures that can provide a basis for demonstrating quality improvement over time.

SOURCE: AAHRPP Accreditation Principles (AAHRPP, 2002b).

group began pilot site visits at the end of 2001 and finalized its standards[11] and procedures based on public comment and the results of pilot site visits in the spring of 2002, at which point it also began accepting applications for accreditation (AAHRPP, 2002a; Softcheck, 2002; Speers, 2002a). Accreditation evaluations of applicant institutions are expected to begin in the fall of 2002.[12]

Under AAHRPP's program, an institution will receive Full Provisional Status or Qualified Accreditation, or Accreditation Withheld, based on a self-evaluation process and a subsequent site visit. The program will operate on a fee-for-service basis, with fees depending on several variables, including the number of research protocols and Research ERBs at an institution (AAHRPP, 2002d). The accreditation will be valid for three years.

Future Opportunities in Accreditation

The committee is encouraged by the efforts of these two organizations and notes that the fact that difficulties were encountered during the initial roll-out of accreditation programs is not unexpected. As the committee stated in *Preserving Public Trust*, "accreditation will not be successful until it is widely accepted as a mark of excellence" (IOM, 2001a, p.86), and this will require consistent and iterative feedback between the various parties involved. AAHRPP indicates that its accreditation standards are intended to apply to universities, hospitals, and pharmaceutical companies among others. NCQA, while currently applying its accreditation standards and procedures to VA medical centers under its contract, indicates that it is developing a business plan for accreditation of other sites and research sponsors as well (Briefer French, 2002). These two programs are to be commended for their progress, but the committee stresses that accreditation remains a nascent process that will require substantial time and development before a meaningful assessment of its added value can be made (see Recommendation 6.4).

> Recommendation 6.3: Human Research Participant Protection Program accreditation programs should include a standard directed at establishing and identifying accountability for specific protection functions.

---

[11]AAHRPP's accreditation standards are available online at www.aahrpp.org/standards.htm.

[12]Personal communication, Marjorie Speers, Executive Director, AAHRPP, August 19, 2002.

Current efforts to establish accreditation systems are just under way, and the proposed standards remain relatively new and untested. The process for the accreditation of programs is still being configured, and the organizations thus far identified to carry it out are taking on an unprecedented task. The committee therefore offers further suggestions for areas that can still benefit from action by NCQA and AAHRPP:

- Continue to move toward valid performance measures in lieu of static "documentation" reviews.
- Identify strategies and dissemination opportunities to share best practices and measured outcomes with the research community.
- Contribute, by making it explicit in the standards, to clarifying and systematizing accountability for all functions of programs within the various settings and systems in which they can and do operate.
- Consider accreditation not only of the research organization, but also of organizations established to carry out only one of the functions of a program, such as protocol review (e.g., independent Research ERBs).

As stated in this committee's first report, independent, nongovernmental accreditation programs, operating under a voluntary mechanism, are likely to be more responsive to the changing demands and needs of protection programs than other existing models (IOM, 2001a). Emerging accreditation programs are, however, still best viewed as pilot projects that should be evaluated in light of field experience. Any accreditation system should be constructed as an evolving tool, and it cannot be expected to immediately correct deficiencies in the collective protection system. As a component of a long-term strategy to improve the quality of research oversight, however, these nongovernmental accreditation processes show promise. It remains unclear, however, how the research universe will be sorted between the two organizations and what ramifications any distinctions between programs might bring. It is encouraging to note that efforts are underway to develop a mechanism that will allow Research ERBs that serve VA facilities and are elements of an academic protection program that has been accredited by AAHRPP to be exempted from NCQA inspection (Otto, 2002a; Speers, 2002b).

Furthermore, the advent of these programs should not prevent the development of other strategies and options for the accreditation of participant protection programs. It may be efficient, for example, to incorporate protection program standards into other existing accreditation systems. For instance, most research organizations involved in health research are already involved in other accreditation reviews, such as medical school or university accreditation. Relevant accreditation bodies can usefully look at their overall accreditation program to ascertain if HRPPP functions might reasonably be added to the multiple domains already covered in the institution's self-assessment process and accreditation site visits.

Recommendation 6.4: Voluntary accreditation should continue to be pilot tested as an approach to strengthening human research participant protections. The Department of Health and Human Services should arrange for a substantive review and evaluation of the accreditation process after five years, to be conducted under the purview of an independent entity.

Recommendation 11 in the committee's earlier report called for Congress and the Department of Health and Human Services (DHHS) to initiate studies evaluating accreditation (IOM, 2001a). The committee suggests that accreditation is a major system change and that it may take as long as five years to establish the value of this significant investment on the part of research organizations, accrediting bodies, and others involved in the national protection system. Moreover, an evaluation of such significance would benefit from being conducted in a scrupulously independent fashion by a credible party. DHHS should make arrangements to secure this independent review, bearing in mind that identifying the appropriate measures and assuring the availability of baseline information should be accomplished well in advance of the actual evaluation. Accreditation of HRPPPs may indeed be a powerful tool for accelerating and maintaining improvement in the provision of research protections to participants; however, the research community, accreditation programs, and government regulators should proceed prudently with the implementation and analysis of this strategy's utility.

ROLE DIFFERENTIATION WITHIN THE HRPPP

As described in Chapter 3, Research ERBs should be reshaped to perform the role that they were originally intended to serve—ensuring participant protection through the careful ethical review of protocols. Although they are the cornerstone of a system in which other entities also have participant protection obligations, Research ERBs should not be expected to assume all of the responsibilities of a protection program, and they should be properly constituted to carry out their duties (Recommendation 3.5). The traditional IRB has too often become the "fall guy" for the institution and the review function, and consequently, it has become a catchall for various responsibilities of the research organization. In the committee's refocused paradigm, the Research ERB should not be responsible for institutional risk management, for ensuring that the informed consent process protects the institution from harm, or for ensuring institutional compliance with all research rules and regulations. These responsibilities should be clearly assigned to other units within the program.

Risk Management

Recent, widely publicized problems involving research injury have led to legal complaints and lawsuits,[13] causing a number of sponsors and organizations conducting research to consider the extent of their liability (Blumenstyk, 2002; Dembner, 2002; Washburn, 2001). However, there is no research that is devoid of risk, and science could not advance without volunteers' understanding and acceptance of the risks a study is expected to present. A wide range of risks is covered under the Common Rule's[14] current threshold of "more than minimal risk." Hence, parent organizations of research programs may prudently bring risk management activities into their agreement to conduct research. As laudatory as this may be, however, the focus of risk management is to protect the organization from harm, and it would be unfortunate, from the broader societal perspective, if this became a barrier to capturing the public good of research findings or if it led to the implementation of formal efforts to curtail legal risks in lieu of genuine efforts to protect participants or to carry out ethical research.

Moreover, because it is distinct from participant protection, risk management should be a separate and discrete function from those that reside within the protection program. It is inappropriate to expect members of review boards to conduct their primary duties while also attempting to represent the institution's need to identify and manage risk. It may be possible to link risk management activities to the deliberations in the scientific review process that precede full Research ERB review—recognizing that a careful review of methodologies and associated human exposures may help identify the true level of institutional risk involved. However, risk management operates through different mechanisms with different objectives than a protection program and cannot be assigned within a protection program.

Organizational Compliance

When encountering risk issues, Research ERBs in particular and protection programs more generally should also consider the parent organiza-

---

[13]Examples of these lawsuits include *Gelsinger v. University of Pennsylvania*; *Wright v. Fred Hutchinson Cancer Research Center, et al.*; *Berman v. Fred Hutchinson Cancer Research Center, et al.*; *Pamela H. Lett and Jim Lett v. the Ohio State University, et al.*
[14]45 CRR 46, Subpart A.

tion's corporate compliance office and program as a useful adjunct to an effective protection program. Health care institutions, for example, increasingly rely on a corporate compliance office. As contrasted with those responsible for risk management, compliance officers are more likely to focus on institutional conformity with legal requirements than on institutional protection per se. In that sense, compliance is similar to the QA functions described earlier.

Hospitals and other health care providers are probably most familiar with corporate compliance programs as they relate to the enforcement of the Medicare and Medicaid fraud and abuse laws (Box 6.5). Some of the functions of an HRPPP may be similar to those already being addressed by compliance programs. For example, assuring conformity with federal and institutional conflict of interest requirements might be one function performed by the compliance office. Generally assuring compliance with the Common Rule or FDA requirements might be yet another. Compliance offices would also be appropriate venues for reviewing compliance with the Health Insurance and Portability Accountability Act of 1996 (HIPAA) privacy requirements. In particular, they could review whether data had been properly de-identified or whether use and disclosure of data had been properly authorized in conformity with regulatory criteria.

There are several arguments for involving the compliance office in human participant protection:

- It has direct access to the leadership of the institution and thus can call the attention of leadership to research compliance problems;
- it carries on a standard-setting and education function within the institution that could incorporate research concerns;
- it could establish a hotline for participants, as well as provide protection for whistleblowers;
- in many institutions, the compliance office will be relatively well resourced, and can thus take pressure off Research ERBs and protection programs; and
- it should already be identified within the institution with the authority of the law and thus has the advantage of having its concerns treated as priorities.

In fact, even in institutions in which the compliance office is solely concerned with fraud and abuse enforcement, the office should attend to research issues because of potential liability under the federal False Claims Act.[15] Cases claiming research fraud have already been brought against

---

[15]31 U.S.C. 3729-3733.

Box 6.5
Compliance Offices

The DHHS Office of Inspector General (OIG) has published a series of guid-ances covering hospitals, physician's practices, and a variety of other Medicare providers (see www.oig.hhs.gov/fraud/complianceguidance.html for more informa-tion). Compliance with the guidance is not mandatory, except for Medicare+Choice organizations. The OIG recommends implementation of compliance plans, howev-er, and many health care institutions have followed this advice.

Although the OIG guidances are directed at compliance with the fraud and abuse laws, they are based on the Federal Sentencing Guidelines that apply to sentencing of corporate criminals. The basic idea behind corporate compliance is that an organization that effectively attempts to comply with the law should receive a mitigated sentence if it is later found guilty of in fact violating the law. Under the Federal Sentencing Guidelines, criminal fines can be reduced up to 94 percent under certain circumstances where an effective compliance program was in place.

The Sentencing Guidelines apply to all federal criminal laws, and thus compli-ance programs should address compliance with all federal laws, not simply the fraud and abuse laws.

An effective corporate compliance program has seven elements, defined in the Sentencing Guidelines and reaffirmed in the OIG's compliance guidances:

1)   The development and distribution of written standards of conduct, as well as policies and procedures that promote the entity's commitment to compliance,
2)   The designation of a chief compliance officer and other appropriate bodies responsible for compliance and reporting directly to the Chief Executive Officer and governing board,
3)   Due care in delegating substantial discretionary authority,
4)   Effective communication to employees at all levels, including the development and implementation of effective education and training programs,
5)   Taking reasonable steps to achieve compliance, including
     a)   The use of audits or other techniques to monitor compliance and
     b)   The maintenance of a process such as a hotline to receive complaints anonymously, and the adoption of systems to protect whistleblowers,
6)   Consistent enforcement of compliance standards, including disciplinary stan-dards, and
7)   Taking, upon detection of a violation, reasonable steps to respond and to pre-vent further similar offenses (Jost and Davies, 2002).

In fact, even in institutions in which the compliance office is solely concerned with fraud and abuse enforcement, the office should attend to research issues. Several cases have already been brought against health care institutions by qui tam relators claiming various types of research fraud. See *United States* v. *Christ*, 2000 WL 432781 (S.D. Ohio 2000); *United States* v. *Hektoen Institute for Medical Research*, 35 F.Supp.2d 1078 (N.D. Ill. 1999); *Moor-Jankowski* v. *Board of Trust-ees*, 1998 WL 474084 (S.D.N.Y. 1999); *Milam* v. *Regents*, 912 F.Supp. 868 (D. Md. 1995). Although these cases have generally ruled against the qui tam relator, when considered together with other cases supporting false claim act liability for noncompliance with regulatory requirements, they support the notion that health care institutions face potential liability for knowing noncompliance with federal re-search requirements.

health care institutions. Although unsuccessful to date, these suits, when considered together with other cases supporting False Claim Act liability for regulatory noncompliance, suggest the potential liability risk of being aware of noncompliance with federal research requirements (Box 6.5).

Some institutions have found both the need and the resources to add compliance functions within the protection program mechanisms. Kaiser Permanente, for example, recently approved the establishment of two new headquarter positions: a research compliance training leader to support investigator and Research ERB training and a research compliance QA leader to focus on FDA-regulated clinical trials and human participant protection. Both positions will support and work with Kaiser Permanente's eight region-based research programs and Research ERBs, with each region contributing a portion of the cost.[16]

Separating the Consent Process from Institutional Legal Matters

One expression of how sponsor and institutional interests have become entangled in the effort to conduct the Research ERB's participant protection mission is the current informed consent document.[17] In clinical trials, these documents can run to 8, 12, or even 20 single-spaced pages. It strains credulity to suppose that this amount of text supports the ethical purpose of such documents, which is to appropriately inform a potential participant's decision to enroll in a study. Rather, these documents increasingly are driven by legal concerns, administrative needs, and many other interests beyond the three principles elucidated in the *Belmont Report*—respect for persons, beneficence, and justice (National Commission, 1979). The committee strongly believes that in the informed consent process and in its documentation, efforts should be made to separate and highlight the participant protection needs from the legal and liability requirements of the institution (Recommendation 3.4). This can be accomplished by substituting an informed consent *process* for the current document-driven approach (see Chapter 4). It also requires innovation and simplification in the delivery and communication of relevant information to participants. Non-protectionist issues increasingly have crept into the consent form and the trend seems to be worsening.

For example, revisions to the HIPAA final rule allow an authorization

---

[16]Personal communication, Robert Crane, Senior Vice President, Kaiser Permanente, February 1, 2002.

[17]Recommendation 3.4 calls for these forms to be referred to as "consent forms" to more accurately reflect their actual function.

for use and disclosure of protected health information to be included in a research consent form[18] (Davidson, 2002). The committee would instead encourage programs to separate this disclosure documentation from the research consent process.

MANAGING CONFLICTS OF INTEREST

In 2001, the U.S. General Accounting Office (GAO) conducted a survey of five institutions undertaking human research and found that institutional policies regarding financial conflicts of interest had variable thresholds for disclosure, timetables for disclosure, requirements for IRB involvement, and procedures for disclosure (GAO, 2001). Guidelines about what constitutes acceptable and unacceptable levels of conflict and policies for managing them are in various stages of development among public and private organizations (Boxes 6.6. and 6.7).

> **Recommendation 6.5: Research organizations are responsible for the in-depth review of potential individual conflicts of interest for investigators, primary research staff, and Research Ethics Review Board (Research ERB) members. Such reviews should be carried out by a conflict of interest committee or designated oversight body that is shielded from institutional pressures or influence. Relevant findings should be transmitted to the Research ERB to inform the review process of proposed studies.**

Research organizations have the ultimate responsibility for assuring that conflicts of interest are assessed and managed, and the organization where the research is conducted or under whose aegis the research is conducted (in the case of private practice investigators) should establish an independent, chartered, auditable conflict of interest body charged with determining the degree and extent of financial conflict of interest in specific research proposals. Many organizations already have a conflict of interest process and/or committee in place as a result of federal requirements (NHRPAC, 2001), but as noted in Chapter 3, it is imperative that explicit mechanisms be in place for this body to feed information about financial conflicts of interest into the Research ERB's comprehensive ethical review of protocols. An organization might wish to have a liaison from the conflict of interest committee to the Research ERB. The qualifications of members of the conflict of interest committee should be articulated in an organization's policies and procedures, which should also ensure that the operations of the conflict of interest body are not subject to organizational pressures.

Public and private research organizations should continue to build on the concordant principles emerging from federal and professional organiza-

---

[18]45 CFR 164.508(b)(3)(i).

Box 6.6
Professional Societies' Policies on Conflicts of Interest

One of the first attempts by professional organizations to address conflicts of interest in research was the 1990 report from the Association of American Medical Colleges (AAMC), in which conflicts of interest were defined as "situations in which financial or other personal considerations may compromise, or have the appearance of compromising, an investigator's professional judgment in conducting or reporting research" (1990).

More recently, AAMC has offered detailed policy guidelines on individual financial conflicts of interest in research involving human participants (2001). AAMC declares that institutions should create and implement policies regarding financial conflicts of interest that should follow federal regulations and should contain a number of specific elements, including definitions; a description of the processes to report, assess, and manage conflicts of interest; the criteria for assessing conflicts; the sanctions for violations; and the processes for appeal.

The Association of American Universities (AAU) also released a report on conflicts of interest in 2001. That report, which addresses institutional as well as individual conflicts, classifies institutional conflicts into two categories: "potential conflicts involving university equity holdings or royalty arrangements and research programs; and potential conflicts involving university officials who make decisions with institution-wide implications, which can include department heads and leaders of laboratories" (2001, p.10). (AAMC released its Task Force on Financial Conflicts of Interest Report dealing with institutional conflicts of interest as this report went to press.) AAU emphasizes the need for effective policies to deal with conflicts of interest in research involving human participants and asserts that management of such conflicts is often more important than the conflicts themselves. AAU also offers a checklist of questions for institutional leaders regarding the management of individual conflicts of interest.

In 2000, the American Society of Gene Therapy (ASGT) adopted a policy on financial conflict of interest that states that "all investigators and team members directly responsible for patient selection, the informed consent process and/or clinical management in a trial must not have equity, stock options or comparable arrangements in companies sponsoring the trial. The ASGT requests its members to abstain from or to discontinue any arrangement that is not consonant with this policy" (ASGT, 2000).

The Association of Clinical Research Professionals' Code of Ethics exhorts members to "avoid conflicts of interest in [their] own affairs and make full disclosure in advance of undertaking any matter that may be perceived as a conflict of interest" (ACRP, 2001).

Other professional societies also have policies on their members' conflicts of interest and how to properly deal with them.

Box 6.7
Federal Policies and Guidance on Conflicts of Interest

In 1995, the Public Health Service (PHS) and the National Science Foundation (NSF) adopted federal regulations for financial conflicts of interest, setting $10,000 or more than 5 percent ownership in any single entity as the threshold for disclosure of financial arrangements [42 CFR 50 subpart F; 60 *Fed. Reg.* 132, 35809 (July 11, 1995)]. FDA released its own financial disclosure regulations in 1998 that required investigators to report, among other things, payments of $25,000 beyond the cost of research and equity interests valued at more than $50,000 in sponsor companies (21 CFR 54, 312, 314, 320, 330, 601, 807, 812, 814, 860). FDA review of such conflicts is retrospective, whereas the PHS/NSF regulations require disclosure by the time a grant application is submitted. An important point, however, is that the federal regulations were intended to encourage objectivity in research practice—not to protect human research participants per se.

DHHS has begun to address conflicts of interest in research involving human participants, releasing a draft interim guidance on financial relationships in clinical research in 2001 (2001a). Based on a public conference held in August 2000, the guidance includes considerations for institutions, investigators, and IRB members and staff. It also offers suggestions for informed consent considerations. The guidance has not been finalized as of publication of this report.

There is broad agreement among research organizations and policy makers that clear policies and procedures about financial conflicts of interest are needed and that these should apply to all research with human participants regardless of the funding source. Although organizations whose research is funded by PHS or NSF or regulated by FDA are mandated to have such policies and procedures, GAO found inconsistency among policies at five research organizations and notes that the policies are not accessible to staff (GAO, 2001).

The National Human Research Protections Advisory Committee (NHRPAC) and the National Bioethics Advisory Commission (NBAC) also have addressed the topic in their recommendations to federal entities (NBAC, 2001b; NHRPAC, 2001). NHRPAC, commenting on the draft guidance of DHHS, advises DHHS to use the PHS threshold for the disclosure of conflicts and suggests procedures for assessing and managing conflicts of interest. It also addresses the need for disclosure, education, and compliance.

NBAC notes that "IRB review alone is not sufficient to manage financial conflicts" and suggests that institutions should increase their regulation of investigators' financial conflicts (2001b, p.59). NBAC also proposes that noninstitutional IRB members can help to mitigate conflicts of interest and that conflicts should be disclosed to participants.

tions for dealing with individual and organizational financial conflicts of interest, regardless of the funding source and in addition to federal guidelines or guidance. These include but are not limited to the need for conflict of interest oversight bodies that are separate from Research ERBs, increased attention to institutional financial conflicts, and meaningful disclosure of conflicts to participants.

Institutional Conflicts of Interest

Recommendation 6.6: Research organizations should establish an external mechanism for the review of potential institutional conflicts of interest regarding research protocols. Findings from this body should be communicated to the Research Ethics Review Board for its consideration in the review of individual protocols.

Although research organizations often implement mechanisms to identify and manage financial conflict of interest at the individual level, they frequently neglect the same issues at the institutional level. The possibility that institutional conflicts of interest may undermine the validity of a research study, cause harm to individual research participants, and ultimately erode public trust in the research enterprise has not been explored sufficiently.

As academic institutions have increasingly entered into financial and collaborative research arrangements with private industry, as encouraged by the Bayh-Dole Act of 1980,[19] institutional conflicts of interest have become a topic of growing concern and increasing public scrutiny (AAU, 2001; DHHS, 2001a; Emanuel and Steiner, 1995; Gillis, 2002; Moses and Martin, 2001).

Currently, no federal regulations or final guidance address institutional financial or nonfinancial conflicts of interest, although the DHHS draft interim guidance does address institutional conflicts of interest, as does proposed federal legislation.[20] Federal agencies and appropriate interest groups should continue to develop guidelines for evaluating, and if appropriate, managing institutional conflicts of interest with the same rigor that is on-going to the pursuit of professional norms and standards regarding individual financial conflicts of interest.

DHHS draft interim guidance states the following:

---

[19]The Patent and Trademark Law Amendments Act of 1980. P. L. No. 96-517 (1980).

[20]A Bill to Amend the Public Health Service Act with Respect to the Protection of Human Subjects in Research. H.R. 4697. 107th Congress, 2nd Sess. (2002).

When institutions consider entering into such business arrangements, they should consider establishing an independent advisory and oversight committee (institutional conflict of interest committee), if one does not already exist, to determine when their financial arrangements pose a conflict of interest, and if so, how those conflicts should be managed (DHHS, 2001a, p.3).

The committee believes that the conflict of interest committee charged to review institutional interests should be an external oversight or advisory committee if it is to ensure appropriately independent evaluation of conflicts and make recommendations to the Research ERB. Institutions should disclose relevant conflicts of interest to this body, which would then determine how to manage them or whether the institution should be prohibited from carrying out the research in which the conflict exists.

If the external conflict of interest committee or the Research ERB, in consultation with the conflict of interest body, determined that the research could proceed, it could require that the institution divest questionable holdings; conduct the research in question only as part of a multicenter trial; or identify an independent entity to monitor participant recruitment, the informed consent process, participant enrollment, data monitoring, and other aspects of the trial that could be adversely affected (or appear to be adversely affected) by the conflict. Outside experts also might be contracted to perform data analysis and interpretation. If the conflict involves an institutional official, the Research ERB could require that the official be excluded from decisions about the research or that the institution or official sell equity holdings or royalty interests if the research is to go forward at that institution.

Nonfinancial Conflicts of Interest

Although nonfinancial conflicts of interest have existed for a long time, they have attracted little formal attention or analysis. These nonfinancial conflicts of interest are, by their nature, more common in academic settings and largely intrinsic to the research profession itself. Examples include a researcher's desire to attain academic advancement or tenure or to receive professional prestige or win scientific prizes, the need to obtain grants, etc. (Levinsky, 2002). Every successful investigator has some degree of self-interest in the research, and without the desire to increase knowledge or find new ways to prevent or treat disease, advances in health and medicine would not be possible. Although the focus in the press and in public and private organizations has been on financial conflicts, which are quantifiable, nonfinancial interests are more common and potentially more damaging to participants and to the integrity of the research itself. Self-interest becomes unethical in human research when it clashes with the protection of research participants. Awareness should be raised at every level within research organizations that conduct human participant research regarding the nature of excessive self-interest and its harmful effects and to promote institutional cultures that do not tolerate runaway ambition (Levinsky, 2002). The evolving accreditation process should incorporate attention to nonfinancial conflicts in its assessments of human research protection programs, and the groups pursuing conflict of interest policies should work to develop guidelines that are as rigorous as those directed at individual financial conflicts.

At the institutional level, structural relationships could threaten the independent activities of individuals or committee operations. For example, junior faculty members serving on Research ERBs may be reluctant to raise concerns about protocols submitted by senior colleagues; this hesitancy may be particularly strong when reviewing a department chair's project. Similarly, Research ERBs may feel pressure to support institutional perspectives or organizational interests in specific situations (see Chapter 3). Research organizations should take deliberate steps to avoid the potential impact of such scenarios on decisions that affect the protection of research participants.

Disclosure of Conflicts of Interest to Research Participants

Although many private and public organizations agree that information about potential conflicts of interest should be disclosed to participants, agreement on the level of detail and how the conflict should be effectively communicated has not been reached. Concern exists that detailed disclosures in a consent form could be overwhelming and not understandable to most participants. Nevertheless, in order to make informed decisions, participants have a right to know if the investigator, staff, or institution has a potential conflict of interest in the experiment and what that conflict is. Research ERBs should make the final determination about how information about these conflicts is presented to participants.

The consent form might include detailed information about a financial interest and its management (whether it is determined to be a conflict of interest or not). The participant should be advised that more information about the conflict and its management is available upon request. However, simple disclosure is not a substitute for in-depth conflict of interest review and subsequent Research ERB review or for the obligation to adhere to other aspects of ethical research.

COMPENSATION FOR RESEARCH-RELATED INJURY

Research cannot be entirely free of risk. Some research participants may incur a research-related injury even if the study is carried out without negligence and in full conformity with the protocol. Research participants injured as a result of a product defect or malfeasance or incompetence in the design and execution of the study can resort to the tort system for compensation, but those injured through no fault of their own or of anyone else have no legal recourse.

It is the committee's impression that many research organizations conducting clinical trials agree to provide short-term medical care (during the course of the study) for research-related injuries (IOM, 1994a). The same is true of the medical centers of VA,[21] NIH, and the Department of Defense (DoD, 2002; NIH CC, 2000). However, it is also the committee's impression that few research organizations cover other relevant costs or compensation for lost earnings (IOM, 1994a; Levine, 1986). (The University of Washington, which covers long-term medical costs, is one of the exceptions; see below.) The committee is unaware of any organization that agrees to provide compensation for pain and suffering.

Compensation for research injury is not required by the Declaration of Helsinki or by the European Convention on Human Rights and Biomedicine (the Ovieto Convention) (Council of Europe Publishing, 1997; World Medical Association, 2000). However, the Council for International Organizations of Medical Sciences (CIOMS) does require that participants are equitably compensated for any physical, research-related injury, and the issue is much discussed, both in the United States and elsewhere (CIOMS, 1993). Indeed, a number of countries have already made such provisions (Box 6.8).

Because the contributions of science benefit society as a whole, it seems indisputable that society is obligated to assure that the few who are harmed in government-sponsored scientific research are appropriately compensated for study-related injuries. As the Department of Health, Education, and Welfare (DHEW) Taskforce, which focused solely on federally funded research, noted in 1977, "Because society is both the beneficiary and the sponsor of research, compensatory justice may come into play for the redress of injuries suffered by persons in connection with biomedical or behavioral research conducted, supported, or regulated by the Federal Government" (1977, p.VI-4). The costs of the loss should not fall on the research participant.

The same argument applies to privately funded research, perhaps to an even greater extent, as the economic survival of a company depends largely

---

[21]38 CFR 17.85.

Box 6.8
International Experience in Compensation for
Research-Related Injury

The **CIOMS** Guideline 13 states, "Research subjects who suffer physical injury as a result of their participation are entitled to such financial or other assistance as would compensate them equitably for any temporary or permanent impairment or disability. In the case of death, their dependants are entitled to material compensation. The right to compensation may not be waived" (CIOMS, 1993). (The subtext of the Guideline states, however, that those "who suffer expected and foreseen adverse reactions from investigational therapies or other procedures performed to diagnose or prevent disease" are not owed compensation.)

The **International Conference on Harmonization** (ICH) Guidelines for Good Clinical Practice defers to national law, with respect to compensation for injury, stating:

"5.8.2 The sponsor's policies and procedures should address the costs of treatment of trial subjects in the event of trial-related injuries in accordance with the applicable regulatory requirement(s).

5.8.3 When trial subjects receive compensation, the method and manner of compensation should comply with applicable regulatory requirement(s)" (ICH, 1996).

The laws of other nations vary, but most make some provision for compensation:

Germany has long required research sponsors to provide insurance to cover injuries to research subjects in pharmaceutical and medicinal product trials. The German scheme provides for no-fault compensation for research subjects from this insurance fund. The insurance covers economic loss, but not pain and suffering. The research subject must, however, show that the research resulted in an injury to the subject's body or health, or death, and that no other person was liable in tort or contract for the injury. Also, injuries must occur within three years of the conclusion of the research. Finally, liability is limited, e.g., to 30 million DM for trials including more than 3,000 persons, 50 million DM per year.

New Zealand also provides for no-fault compensation for those injured through clinical trials involving mental or physical health or disease under its general accident compensation scheme.

In **France**, the research sponsor must carry liability insurance. If a research subject suffers injury, the sponsor will be liable on a no-fault basis for nontherapeutic research. If the subject is injured through research involving treatment, fault on the part of the research sponsor is presumed, but the sponsor may prove that neither the sponsor, the research institution, nor the researcher was at fault and thus escape liability.

Spanish law makes the sponsor of a trial, the principal researchers, and the medical director of the hospital in which research is carried out jointly liable for any injury suffered by a research subject not otherwise covered by insurance during a clinical trial. The law also establishes a presumption that injuries to the health of a subject suffered within a year of the trial were caused by the trial.

Finally, although **British** law does not require compensation for research participants, absent fault, the guidelines of the Association of the British Pharmaceutical Industry do provide that sponsors should enter into contracts with nonpatient research subjects. Sponsors agree to compensate for "any significant deteriora-

(continued)

Box 6.8   Continued

tion in health or well-being caused" by participation in a study, "calculated by reference to the amount of damages commonly awarded for similar injuries by an English court if liability is admitted." Compensation is to be offered without proof of
negligence. When patient volunteers are involved, compensation need only be
paid when it is established, on the balance of probabilities, that the injury was
caused by the research intervention, and then only for serious injury of an enduring
and disabling character (including exacerbation of an existing condition) and not
for temporary pain or discomfort or less serious or curable complaints. Although
sponsors are counseled to pay compensation in close cases where proof of causation might be difficult, they are also excused from payment in cases in which the
treated disease was very serious and the disclosed risk of treatment high. The
contract is to provide arbitration for cases for which agreement cannot be reached.

The British National Health Service (NHS) itself does not accept responsibility
for compensation for injury to research subjects, although NHS staff is liable for
negligence in carrying out clinical trials. NHS is also supposed to enter into indem-
nity agreements with sponsors of clinical trials carried out within NHS institutions to
protect NHS from liability. NHS guidelines do, however, provide that in exceptional
circumstances NHS can provide ex gratia payments of up to £50,000 for non-
negligent injury. The Royal Commission on Civil Liability and Compensation for
Personal Injury recommended in 1978 some form of no-fault compensation for
research participants, but no law providing generally for this has yet been adopted.

SOURCE: Deutsch and Taupitz, 2000; Kennedy and Grubb, 2000; Taupitz, 2001.

---

on the availability of participants to test new therapies, drugs, and other
products. Because the participants are ultimately contributing to the profits
of the company, any costs that result from the research should be the
responsibility of the sponsor. Furthermore, whether a study is privately or
publicly sponsored, the results are intended to eventually benefit all of
society.

In the absence of a compensation system, lawsuits alleging research-
related injury are increasing (Blumenstyk, 2002; Dembner, 2002;
Washburn, 2001). The claims to date relate to inadequacy of consent,
departure from the protocol, or other negligent activities. Inevitably, these
cases invite the courts to expand the legal grounds of recovery, and in an
uncertain legal environment cases can be inconsistently resolved.[22] A no-

---

[22]This occurred in the case of vaccine injuries prior to enactment of the National Childhood Vaccine Injury Act of 1986 (P.L. 99-660). For more information about the parallel
problems in the vaccine injury situation, see the IOM report *Vaccine Supply and Innovation*
(IOM, 1985).

fault system could reduce pressure on the judicial system and allow injured parties speedier resolution of claims. The Tuskegee Syphilis Ad Hoc Advisory Panel has noted that "No matter how careful investigators may be, unavoidable injury to a few is the price society must pay for the privilege of engaging in research which ultimately benefits the many. Remitting injured subjects to the uncertainties of the law court is not a solution" (1973, p.23).

However, when the participant alleges that the injury was caused by a possibly defective product or possible negligence in the design and conduct of the study, the tort system is likely to remain the appropriate channel for redress, serving as a back up to the no-fault compensation agreement for cases in which elements of liability can be proved. (Were a no-fault compensation system in effect, risk management needs and concerns might be lessened to some degree, making it easier to achieve simplified consent forms as suggested in Recommendation 3.4.)

It has been argued that a participant relinquishes his or her right to compensation when giving informed consent, but in the committee's view, a right to compensation for research-related injury should not be subject to waiver. The DHEW Task Force declared in its report that "The fact that a person has volunteered does not eliminate that person's right to be compensated in the event of injury, whether or not the injury was foreseeable.... Even if a subject perfectly understands a research procedure and agrees to participate in that procedure, the subject's consent does not, in and of itself, include, explicitly or implicitly, a waiver of compensation" (1977, p.VI-5-6).

Recommendation 6.7: The Department of Health and Human Services should assemble data on the incidence of research injuries and conduct economic analyses of their costs to help establish the potential magnitude of claims that would arise under a no-fault compensation system for such injuries.

The main impediment to the implementation of a compensation program for research-related injuries in the United States is that, despite decades of discussion and studies by a number of federal commissions, there remains little quantitative information regarding the number and severity of potentially compensable injuries and about the costs of implementing compensation programs (ACHRE, 1995; DHEW, 1977; NBAC, 2001a,b; President's Commission, 1982a). The 1977 DHEW Task Force report estimated that of the 132,615 research subjects participating in the research reported in its survey, 3.7 percent of them suffered injuries. Of those injured, 79.2 percent of them had trivial injuries, 19.6 percent were temporarily disabled, 3 percent were permanently disabled, and 9 percent died

(1977). Although this information is the most comprehensive available, it has a number of serious limitations[23] and is severely outdated.

The University of Washington is one of the few organizations, to this committee's knowledge, that offers long-term compensation for research injuries.[24] When the system was first established in the 1970s, few formal claims for compensation were processed, but officials at the university attributed this to a lack of knowledge about the program among participants (President's Commission, 1982a). In 1998, University of Washington officials estimated that the School of Medicine enrolled about 100,000 people per year in clinical studies with potential for adverse effects and that the compensation program for those injured paid $2,300 to $5,000 total annually (Marwick, 1998). At the University of Washington, the investigator is responsible for reporting whether an adverse effect was the result of research, at which point the plan goes into effect. The school pays for medical care and related expenses, such as travel.

The DHEW report and the more recent University of Washington examples appear to provide the most relevant information about the number and cost of injuries, but, obviously, this information is both sketchy and inconsistent. However, based on the media attention given to adverse research events in recent years,[25] the increased attention given by regulatory agencies to institutional noncompliance and financial conflicts of interest, and the growing pressures on the research system, the potential for diminished public trust in the research community is real (Marwick, 2002).

To ensure credibility, it is critical to have data about the number, severity, and costs of research injuries, and it is not acceptable for society to continue to leave unaddressed a fundamental ethical obligation for the simple want of basic information. Some pertinent information could be abstracted from FDA and research institutions' adverse event reports or experiences at institutions such as the University of Washington that already offer self-funded no-fault compensation. Similarly, such analysis can make use of the international experience (Box 6.8).

---

[23]In its telephone interviews, the Task Force relied on data provided by investigators using their own judgment; the interviewers suggested nontherapeutic research if the determination of the type of research was vague; the Task Force had to make assumptions about the length of participation by subjects; and the definition of therapeutic injury did not include the word "unanticipated." Also, in 1977, the Common Rule was not in effect, and the research landscape was very different from that found today.

[24]For more information see depts.washington.edu/hsd/INFO/MANUAL/99-VII.htm#VII-g.

[25]Some recent articles on the topic include Blumenstyk, 2002; DeYoung and Nelson, 2000a,b; Flaherty, et al., 2000; Flaherty and Struck, 2000; LaFraniere, et al., 2000; Lemonick and Goldstein, 2002; Nelson, 2000; Shaywitz and Ausiello, 2001; Stephens, 2000; Stolberg, 2002; Wilson and Heath, 2001a,b,c,d,e,f,g.

One of the key questions that will require more sophisticated research is the portion of participant illness and injury attributable to the research itself versus the underlying condition of the participant, and the ease with which such determinations can be made. These determinations pertain to the basic issue that must be addressed in any no-fault system—that of causation. Was the injury attributable to the research, or was it a manifestation of the participant's underlying condition? If this cannot be easily resolved when claims are presented, the costs of resolving the dispute may escalate the costs of the compensation system itself. Making such determinations will require supplemental studies, and the committee recommends that these studies be commissioned as soon as possible in order to guide public policy decisions and accreditation standard development in this area.

Recommendation 6.8: Organizations conducting research should compensate any research participant who is injured as a direct result of participating in research, without regard to fault. Compensation should include at least the costs of medical care and rehabilitation, and accrediting bodies should include such compensation as a requirement of accreditation.

In light of the ongoing need to recognize and address the needs of those who have been harmed[26] as a result of research, the committee believes that a fair compensation system should be established as soon as possible. Accordingly, the committee endorses the conclusion reached by NBAC that "a comprehensive system of oversight of human research should include a mechanism to compensate participants for medical and rehabilitative costs from research injuries" (2001b, p.123). Furthermore, this committee believes that, in principle, adequate compensation to those harmed as a result of research should be more generous than that recommended by NBAC and should include full recovery for economic loss, including work-related disability, and in appropriate cases, for lost earnings of a deceased participant. However, in light of the existing uncertainties concerning the number and severity of research-related injuries, the committee recognizes that this objective is attainable only in stages and therefore suggests a two-step approach.

The first step, which should be taken as soon as possible, would implement a compensation program along the lines recommended by NBAC as a requirement for HRPPP accreditation. Accredited research organizations would be expected to identify, characterize, and report research-related injuries and to cover costs of medical care and rehabilitation that are attributable to research-related injury. Meanwhile, voluntary efforts would be

---

[26]As discussed previously in this chapter, research harms are not limited to the physical domain, but also include harm to dignity, harm at the social level, and psychological harm.

simultaneously undertaken by NIH and private sponsors to establish demonstration programs that would also cover lost income due to temporary or permanent disability or death under various plans for valuation and payment. After three to five years of experience and data collection, the entire compensation effort would be evaluated, including an assessment of whether the fee scale(s) used in the demonstration programs are perceived as fair and easy to administer by those who are affected by it. The assessment should provide a basis for informed judgments about the best approach to take, including the best model for measuring work-related disability.

Under the approach envisioned by the committee, the responsibility for compensation would fall initially on the institution or organization actually accountable for conducting the research, and its terms would be specified in the documentation accompanying the participant's agreement to participate. Presumably, most research organizations will attempt to insure themselves against such losses, and a market for such insurance may eventually emerge, especially after the necessary data have been compiled. In the context of pharmaceutical research, the allocation of responsibility for compensation between the sponsoring company and the research organization will presumably be determined by contract. This strategy embraces the basic approach of the Association of the British Pharmaceutical Industry (see Box 6.8).

Alternatively, the government could establish a federal compensation program, which could be included as a direct cost within grants, a surcharge on medical bills, or money from general revenues (Annas, et al., 1977). The National Childhood Vaccine Compensation Injury Act of 1986 (P.L. 99-660) addressed similar concerns regarding those injured by vaccines by establishing a federal program to compensate those who were injured as a result of their contribution to public health. The act was prompted by concerns that lawsuits would diminish vaccine manufacturing, and thus limit access to vaccines, endangering public health. On moral grounds, both those who receive vaccines and research participants are contributing to society and deserve compensation if they are hurt while doing so.

PERSONAL LIABILITY OF RESEARCH ERB MEMBERS

As noted, litigation over research injury appears to be increasing (Blumenstyk, 2002; Washburn, 2001). Research organizations with effective protection programs, including effective Research ERBs, should be better protected from legal losses than those that employ less robust efforts. It is the hallmark of both QI and risk management to invest in good practice ("right the first time") rather than later having to make costly responses to problems that could have been prevented.

Some recent legal filings have sought to name as defendants, among others, members of Research ERBs (*Gelsinger v. University of Pennsylvania*; *Robertson, et al. v. McGee, et al.*). Although no such lawsuits have yet prevailed, they may exert a chilling effect on both the willingness of individuals to become board members and on the independence of their decision making. Indemnification, which appears to be a common practice among larger research universities,[27] remains important in the present litigation climate. Given the desirability of recruiting and appointing external members to review boards, it is especially important to insulate them from personal liability concerns. Organizations should indemnify both internal and external board members to prevent them from being unduly influenced by the personal risks of potential litigation, a protection that should be extended to individuals of other boards, such as DSMB/DMCs, Scientific Review Boards, and ethics and research expert consultants used by Research ERBs and other review bodies.

SUMMARY

An effective protection program should have QA and QI measures in place in order to continuously assess its strengths and weaknesses and to redress those weaknesses. DHHS should facilitate the activities of those studying the effectiveness of the collective system by gathering baseline data about the current system in order to assess improvements. Research sponsors should take on a similar responsibility by funding original research that would enhance the practice of QI.

There is also a need for data about the prevalence, nature, and costs of research-related injuries. Organizations conducting research with human participants should compensate any participant who is injured as a direct result of participation in the research; this compensation should include that for direct medical care, rehabilitative costs, and after appropriate study, lost work time. Accrediting bodies should include this requirement within their accreditation standards.

Accreditation by design is intended to encourage organizations to strive for a high standard of performance. Current accreditation efforts in the field of research involving human participants are nascent and merit review after a sufficient period of pilot testing (likely five years or so). Because of the significance of the task, DHHS should arrange for such a review through a credible, independent entity. Accreditation organizations should also fos-

---

[27]Lydia Villa Komaroff, personal communication, April 22, 2002.

ter accountability within programs by adding a standard to explicitly establish and identify who is accountable for specific protection functions.

Because the Research ERB is responsible solely for the protection of research participants, it should not be held accountable for matters of institutional interest such as risk-management and the resolution of conflicts of interest. Therefore, these issues should be referred to the research organization's management for resolution or delegation.

7

Improving an Evolving National Human Research Participant Protection System

The preceding chapters have outlined various steps that can be taken to improve the protection of research participants throughout the research process. Chapter 6 described how protection programs could improve quality and clarify roles within a program to enhance performance. This chapter focuses on the relationship of individual Human Research Participant Protection Programs (HRPPPs) to a larger protection system—one that includes sponsors, regulatory agencies, journal publishers, and policy makers. The intent of this discussion is not to be comprehensive—other groups have assessed the overall system of protections in recent years (ACHRE, 1995; NBAC, 2001b; OIG 1998a,b,c,d,e, 2000a,b,c)—but rather to highlight issues that should be recognized and addressed to improve the functioning of the protection system as a whole.

In particular, this final chapter discusses the need for independent advice to be provided from the public to the federal policy makers responsible for oversight of the protection system. It also discusses the requirement for a publicly accessible clinical trials registry for those interested in considering participation. Several emerging and evolving areas of policy directly related to human research are then considered, including discussions regarding how the developing debate over patient privacy might affect protection programs in future years, the role of scientific publishers in responsibly communicating research results, and considerations relevant to research to counter bioterrorism.

THE NEED FOR BETTER ADVICE AND GUIDANCE
AT THE FEDERAL LEVEL

Complexity, opacity, and contradiction abound in interpretations of the rules and regulations that apply to human research; these confound clear communication between agencies and institutions. Federal regulations are complex and subject to broad interpretation. Although the language of the Common Rule[1] deserves a careful and comprehensive reassessment for clarity and relevancy, revising it would be time consuming and difficult, because each signatory agency must agree to the changes. Eventually, Congress will need to take the necessary steps to broaden and strengthen the federal oversight system and to modify the Common Rule where needed. In the interim, however, several steps can be taken to promote its uniform interpretation and clarify its intent.

The committee applauds the emphasis of the Office for Human Research Protections (OHRP) on "protection without over-reaction" and the increased emphasis on providing education and engaging in discussion. However, agencies such as OHRP and the Food and Drug Administration (FDA) should do more to clarify the existing regulations and to provide illustrative guidance to institutions. This could occur through a number of approaches: agencies (and perhaps the accreditation bodies) could place this information on the Web, conduct workshops, visit institutions to provide education, begin the process of developing best practices through case studies (see Recommendation 3.8), and compile and disseminate examples of acceptable and unacceptable scenarios.

Clear guidance from the funding agencies and recognition that the situations that face research organizations are more alike than different would help dissipate the self-protective, over-reactive climate found in many research organizations today. Because it is not uncommon for multiple points of contact to occur between agencies and research organizations, it is even more important that readily accessible information is available to research organizations and that their staff members make frequent use of it. A body such as the Federal Demonstration Partnership[2] could assess the effectiveness of the communication and interaction between the relevant oversight and funding agencies and the academic research organizations.

---

[1]45 CFR 46, Subpart A.

[2]The Federal Demonstration Partnership was convened by the Government-University-Industry Research Roundtable to provide a forum where universities, research institutions, and federal representatives come together to assess university-government research collaborations. See www.fdp3.org.

Independent Advice

Recommendation 7.1: Congress should authorize and appropriate funding for a standing independent, multidisciplinary, nonpartisan expert Committee on Human Research Participant Protections whose membership would include the perspective of the research participant.

Before the creation of OHRP in June 2000, the Office for Protection from Research Risks (OPRR) existed within the National Institutes of Health (NIH). Concerns were raised in a document commissioned by the then-Department of Health and Human Services (DHHS) Assistant Secretary for Health regarding the propriety of OPRR's location within NIH, with the majority of NIH-funded research subject to OPRR oversight (OPRR Review Panel, 1999). A determination was made to rename OPRR and move it to DHHS' Office of Public Health and Science (OPHS) in order to eliminate any concerns regarding the appearance of potential impropriety or conflict of interest.

It also was decided that OHRP should receive independent advice from the communities it serves. Thus, DHHS created the National Human Research Protections Advisory Committee (NHRPAC) to provide expert advice and recommendations to the Secretary of DHHS, the Director of OHRP, and other departmental officials on a broad range of issues and topics pertaining to or associated with the protection of human research subjects.[3] NHRPAC's charter reads in part as follows:

> The Committee will provide advice on the development and management of collaborations and communications between HHS and its operating and staff divisions and other pertinent elements of the federal government; the biomedical, academic, and research communities; non-governmental entities; and other organizations as necessary to further the interests of the human subjects protection enterprise. The Committee will provide counsel on opportunities to improve public awareness of the function and importance of human subjects protection activities (DHHS, 2001b).

In order for NHRPAC to achieve these goals, it is crucial that it be sufficiently independent of the regulatory agency that it advises. NHRPAC currently is administered by OHRP, with a budget controlled by the OHRP Director. However, for NHRPAC to receive candid and constructive input from researchers, research organizations, and participants and to provide

---

[3]As this report went to press, it was reported that DHHS had disbanded NHRPAC (Weiss, 2002; Otto, 2002c). This underscores the need for Congressional direction in the establishment of a nonpartisan, independent advisory committee focused on the policy issues relevant to ensuring the protection of research participants, as discussed in this chapter.

advice to other "pertinent elements of the federal government" as well as nongovernment entities, its position within the DHHS bureaucracy should be modified. In its capacity as an advisory committee, NHRPAC should be established as an independent entity within OPHS under the aegis of the DHHS Assistant Secretary of Health. To ensure the public's trust, it should have its own budget and be impartial and free from the appearance or existence of impropriety or undue influence. Any perception on behalf of the public or other federal agencies that NHRPAC is not an independent entity free to identify and examine concerns regarding the protection of research participants could cast doubt on its credibility.

Assuring the ability of NHRPAC to provide independent advice to the federal government is a necessary first step to strengthening the voice of public stakeholders in the development and evolution of human research policy. To most effectively ensure that OHRP and the entire protection system receive independent advice, Congress should establish a nonpartisan, multidisciplinary, independent body of experts that could operate with total independence and provide balanced representation of the perspectives of participants, scholars in a range of scientific disciplines and bioethics, and IRB experts. The Institute for Laboratory Animal Research (ILAR) provides an example of a successful model for providing such advice. ILAR is a standing committee in the National Research Council at the National Academies that provides independent, expert advice and guidance on the care and use of laboratory and other animals in research. It also provides guidance on relevant accreditation standards.[4] A similar independent body could be useful to the ongoing development of protections for research participants.

The potential for conflicts in the current configuration of OHRP and NHRPAC justifies this proposal of an alternative model, which would provide ongoing advice and guidance on the scientific (clinical and social/behavioral), technological, and ethical issues related to participant protection, including quality improvement, accreditation standards, conflict of interest, resource needs, and system performance changes over time at the federal oversight and organizational levels.

THE NEED FOR PUBLIC INFORMATION REGARDING ONGOING CLINICAL RESEARCH

According to central tenets of ethical research, the community of individuals that stands to benefit or be harmed by research should 1) have an

---

[4]The *Guide for the Care and Use of Laboratory Animals* (NRC, 1996) is produced and updated by ILAR and is heavily utilized by the Association for Assessment and Accreditation of Laboratory Animal Care in its accreditation program.

opportunity to comment on the research design and operation; 2) have an opportunity to participate in the research; 3) reasonably expect that the research will not involve unnecessary duplication; and 4) have access to study findings.

It is difficult to justify denying the public knowledge about existing research, particularly if it is publicly funded. Even in the context of classified research sponsored or funded by the government, the protection of Research Ethics Review Board[5] (Research ERB) review should be provided (ACHRE, 1995). Secrecy often has led to abuses of human rights. The pharmaceutical and other industries cite the need for protection of proprietary interests, and in a capitalist economy this claim is generally respected (DHHS, 1999). The potential for profit, however, should never overshadow the rights of individuals and the public to have access to information, particularly in the high-risk area of clinical trials. Therefore, systems for providing access to information about clinical research that are responsive to both industry and public needs should be developed.

Recommendation 7.2: The Department of Health and Human Services should facilitate the establishment of a central registry for all clinical trials. Protection programs should provide the basic information for submission to the registry.

Section 113 of the FDA Modernization Act of 1997[6] requires that Phase 2, 3, and 4 clinical trials conducted under an Investigational New Drug application (IND) be included in a publicly available registry for access by patients, researchers, and health care providers, if that drug or biologic product is intended to treat a serious or life-threatening disease. The provision stipulates that the information in the databank must include a brief description of the clinical trial, the purpose of the investigational treatment, patient eligibility criteria, locations of clinical trial sites, and either central or site-specific contacts for the trial. The law also requires that the language of the databank entries be readily understandable by the public.

In 2000, the National Library of Medicine (NLM) established a clinical

---

[5]Recommendation 3.1 calls for "Institutional Review Boards" (IRBs) to be named and referred to within research organizations by a title reflective of their focus on the ethics underlying participant protection activities. The committee has adopted the term "Research Ethics Review Board" (Research ERB) for this purpose. Therefore, Research ERB refers herein to the committee's idealized protection program, and IRB to descriptions of the current system.

[6]P.L. 105-115, 1997.

trials registry,[7] which originally included principally NIH-sponsored trials, but has expanded to include data from other registries[8] and serves as the FDA-required site for submissions about clinical trials subject to Section 113's registry requirement. The database also includes a Protocol Registration System, a Web-based data processing program for sponsors to register the relevant FDA-regulated studies. The first version of the system, publicly available in February 2000, contains more than 4,000 records, most of which are trials sponsored by NIH.

The NLM system design and implementation have been guided by several principles. First, all stages of system development focused on the needs of the primary target audience—patients and other members of the public. Second, broad agreement was obtained on a common set of data elements for submission. Third, the system was designed in a modular and extensible way, and search methods that take extensive advantage of the NLM's Unified Medical Language System were developed (McCray and Ide, 2000).

The NLM registry is an important first step toward providing high-quality clinical trial information to the public. However, no truly centralized system exists for disseminating information about clinical trials of drugs or other interventions, making it difficult for consumers and health care providers to identify ongoing studies in which consumers could participate. In the absence of a centralized mechanism, hundreds of registries or accessible databases of ongoing studies have been created in the last several years, and their numbers are growing (Anderson et al., forthcoming).[9] Many of these registries are established by medical centers hoping to recruit patients. Others are funded by publishing companies with strong links to drug companies (e.g., CenterWatch Trial Listings, published by Thomson Publishing Company) or by the government (e.g., the NLM registry). Although many are high quality, in the absence of common oversight, there is always a risk that inaccurate or misleading data could lead to inappropriate participant recruitment or enrollment in trials (Crocco, 2002).

Despite the vast contribution these registries have made to inform those who are interested in trials, their content, quality, and information vary widely. For example, although an interested party may learn that a trial is available for a given condition, the drug name, study location, and phase of

---

[7]www.clinicaltrials.gov.

[8]These registries include the AIDS Clinical Trials Information System, the Physician's Data Query, and the Rare Diseases and National Institute of Aging Databases.

[9]A sampling of online registries, some of which are tailored to specific criteria, include www.clinicaltrials.gov; www.centerwatch.com/patient/trials.html; www.trialscentral.org/; www.controlled-trials.com/; www.wiley.co.uk/wileychi/genmed/clinical/DATABASE/db/genesearch.cgi; www.actis.org/intltrials.html; www.update-software.com/National/.

testing may not be provided. Often, the patient interested in participating in a listed study may be required to self-identify to the research entity before learning more about the design details. Eric Manheimer has shown that a patient with prostate or colon cancer who wishes to participate in a drug trial would have to spend many hours searching dozens of online registries to compile a list of potentially appropriate Phase 3 trials for either condition and would still not have a complete list (forthcoming).

In addition to having access to information, consumers should expect that any research in which they are asked to participate could lead to the generation of new knowledge or knowledge required to confirm inconclusive or insufficient information from other sources. Yet with no central listing of all research projects undertaken, either completed or ongoing, studies may be unnecessarily duplicated. Antman, Lau, and colleagues provide several examples of randomized clinical trials that were conducted long after knowledge about a treatment's efficacy should have been accepted (1992).[10] Treatment recommendations in textbooks and review articles have also reflected a failure to keep track of initiated and completed research, in some cases leading to decades elapsing between the production of reliable efficacy evidence and recommendations for general use (ibid.).

Further, as the United States moves increasingly toward an evidence-based health care system, access to trial findings is vital. Results of far too many trials will never be known, because perhaps half of all initiated studies are never published, and selective publication occurs of studies based on the strength or direction of findings (Egger and Smith, 1998). Because it is nearly impossible to identify unpublished studies (Hetherington, 1989), any summary or systematic review of existing research is therefore most likely to rely on published research. If a disproportionate number of trials showing an effective intervention are published, then research reviews could result in overestimated effectiveness of interventions, which could lead to inappropriate patient care policies. In addition, patients who consent to participate in a clinical trial do so believing they are contributing to the advancement of scientific knowledge. If the trial's results are never disseminated, the investigator-participant trust is broken, creating an ethical breach.

For these as well as other reasons, observers have called for decades for a comprehensive registry of all initiated studies (Chalmers, 1977). More recently, the Institute of Medicine (IOM) Committee on Medicare Payment for Participation in Clinical Trials has made the same recommendation (2000a).

In 2002, the DHHS Office of Inspector General (OIG) released a report

---

[10]For example, this is what happened in the case of thrombolytic drugs for secondary prevention of myocardial infarction. Tens of thousands of patients were unnecessarily randomized believing they were contributing to new knowledge.

that assessed the role of clinical trial Web sites in fostering understanding about informed consent and the role of Research ERBs in overseeing the information on these sites (OIG, 2002). The study found that clinical trial Web sites are emerging as an important recruitment strategy and show promise as a means of increasing knowledge about informed consent. However, these sites sometimes provide inaccurate information about the clinical trial process, exclude key information in trial listings, and fail to disclose policies that address the use of personal information that is collected by the site. Based on these findings, the OIG recommended that FDA and OHRP jointly provide guidance to Research ERBs regarding their responsibility for reviewing Web sites, facilitate the adoption and use of voluntary standards for clinical trial Web sites, and encourage clinical trial Web sites to undergo periodic review by independent bodies.

Although the OIG report encourages the adoption of voluntary standards across sites to improve the quality and consistency of registry entries, the inaccessibility of information caused by the need to search multiple databanks is not addressed. One possible mechanism for facilitating central registration would be through a federal system using Research ERBs. This model would not require investigators to submit additional registration materials to multiple Web sites. Instead, basic material submitted to the Research ERB would serve as the backbone of the registry.[11] If all human research studies are reviewed and approved by a Research ERB, as recommended by this committee (Recommendation 2.1), this strategy would allow comprehensive registration of initiated clinical trials.

The committee recognizes the challenges involved in designing, initiating and maintaining such an endeavor, as well as the resources that would be required, but believes that clinical trials are of such public concern and benefit that the effort should be pursued. The creation of a comprehensive clinical trials database that is soundly structured for public use would ensure that information about all clinical trials undertaken would be available to contribute to generalizable knowledge regardless of whether their results are viewed as positive or negative by investigators, sponsors, or publishers.

---

[11]Basic material submitted for approved protocols might include disease target, a general description of the intervention, trial site locations, and contact information to learn more about the study. One option would be to adopt at a minimum the same inputs required for compliance with Section 113 of the FDA Modernization Act (P.L. 105-115, 1997). It should be noted that the basic information submitted to the registry would not need to include trial results.

COMMUNICATING RESEARCH RESULTS: A ROLE FOR PUBLISHERS

Scientific journals and other outlets for disseminating research results serve as an integral part of the protection system (Altman, 2002), as has been evident since 1966, when Henry Beecher published an article presenting 22 examples of "unethical or questionably ethical studies" that had appeared in mainstream medical journals (Beecher, 1966). As the major distribution channel of research results and as an important contributor to the professional advancement of scientists (through publication of their work), scientific journals are obligated to publish research that meets high ethical standards and offers unique contributions to the field (i.e., research that does not constitute an unnecessary or unjustified replication of previous work) and for which the authors have attested to their compliance with regulatory and ethical standards (e.g., Research ERB review, disclosure of relevant conflicts of interest). Several journals have already taken positive steps in this regard (see Box 7.1), and there has been recent improvement in the percentage of published papers citing compliance with IRB and informed consent procedures in major medical journals (Yank and Rennie, 2002). The committee encourages other publications to pursue similar standards.

THE IMPACT OF THE HEALTH INSURANCE PORTABILITY AND ACCOUNTABILITY ACT OF 1996 REQUIREMENTS AND PRIVACY ISSUES ON HRPPPS

The regulatory landscape regarding patient privacy has continued to evolve in recent years. Clearly, among the most important issues that should be faced when conducting research involving human participants are protecting the privacy of information and assuring confidentiality. Thus, programs should keep abreast of the relevant policy developments. Private information is defined in the Common Rule to include

> ...information about behavior that occurs in a context in which an individual can reasonably expect that no observation or recording is taking place, and information which has been provided for specific purposes by an individual and which the individual can reasonably expect will not be made public (for example, a medical record).[12]

Confidentiality becomes an issue when information disclosed by an individual (such as a research participant) to a particular person or persons for a specific purpose is further disclosed to other individuals or institutions for other purposes without the participant's authorization (IOM, 2000c).

---

[12]45 CFR 46.102(f).

Box 7.1
Sample Journal Policies Regarding Research
Participant Protections

International Committee of Medical Journal Editors (ICMJE)
Protection of Patients' Rights to Privacy

Patients have a right to privacy that should not be infringed without informed consent. Identifying information should not be published in written descriptions, photographs, and pedigrees unless the information is essential for scientific purposes and the patient (or parent or guardian) gives written informed consent for publication. Informed consent for this purpose requires that the patient be shown the manuscript to be published.

Identifying details should be omitted if they are not essential, but patient data should never be altered or falsified in an attempt to attain anonymity. Complete anonymity is difficult to achieve, and informed consent should be obtained if there is any doubt. For example, masking the eye region in photographs of patients is inadequate protection of anonymity.

The requirement for informed consent should be included in the journal's instructions for authors. When informed consent has been obtained it should be indicated in the published article.

Ethics

When reporting experiments on human subjects, indicate whether the procedures followed were in accordance with the ethical standards of the responsible committee on human experimentation (institutional or regional) and with the Helsinki Declaration of 1975, as revised in 1983. Do not use patients' names, initials, or hospital numbers, especially in illustrative material. When reporting experiments on animals, indicate whether the institution's or a national research council's guide for, or any national law on the care and use of laboratory animals was followed.
SOURCE: www.icmje.org/index.html#top.
NOTE: Hundreds of journals have agreed to the ICJME requirements, including *Journal of the American Medical Association, New England Journal of Medicine, British Medical Journal, Lancet, American Journal of Medicine.* A full list of the journals is available at www.icmje.org/jrnlist.html.

British Medical Journal
Patient confidentiality and consent to publication

If there is any chance that a patient may be identified from a case report, illustration, or paper we ask for the written consent of the patient for publication. Patients are almost always willing to give such consent.
Black bands across the eyes are wholly ineffective in disguising the patient, and changing details of patients to try to disguise them is bad scientific practice.
SOURCE: bmj.com/advice/.

Journal of the American Medical Association (JAMA)
Ethical Requirements. For experimental investigations of human or animal subjects, state in the Methods section of the manuscript that an appropriate institutional review board approved the project. For those investigators who do not have

(continued)

Box 7.1 Continued

formal ethics review committees (institutional or regional), the principles outlined in the Declaration of Helsinki should be followed. For investigations of human subjects, state in the Methods section the manner in which informed consent was obtained from the subjects.

Patient Descriptions, Photographs, and Pedigrees. Include a signed statement of informed consent to publish (in print and online) patient descriptions, photographs, and pedigrees from all persons (parents or legal guardians for minors) who can be identified in such written descriptions, photographs, or pedigrees. Such persons should be shown the manuscript before its submission.

SOURCE: www.jama.ama-assn.org/info/auinst.html#a3.

Lancet

Patients' consent and permission to publish—Studies on patients or volunteers require ethics committee approval and informed consent, which should be documented in your paper. Where there is an unavoidable risk of breach of privacy—e.g., in a clinical photograph or in case details—the patient's written consent, or that of the next of kin, to publish must be obtained and enclosed with your submission. Consent must be obtained for all Case reports and Clinical pictures. A consent form is available at image.thelancet.com/consent/consentform.pdf.

SOURCE: www.thelancet.com/authorinfo.

Privacy and confidentiality are vital issues throughout all stages of research design and implementation. Research projects should be designed to intrude on the privacy of research participants no more than is necessary, and the confidentiality of information obtained during a research project should be protected throughout the project as well as after it is completed.

Although privacy and confidentiality issues are involved in all forms of research involving human participants, they are particularly important with respect to health services and social science research, because in these forms of research (as compared to clinical research), privacy and confidentiality threats are often the primary risks to human participants. Two years ago, IOM completed a project considering privacy and confidentiality issues in health services research (IOM, 2000c). The report of the Committee on National Statistics/Board on Behavioral, Cognitive, and Sensory Sciences and Education panel advising this committee also identified confidentiality as a major issue in social and behavioral science research and offered five recommendations related to confidentiality (Appendix B, recommendations 1-5).

Recent regulations promulgated pursuant to the Health Insurance Portability and Accountability Act of 1996 (HIPAA) expand considerably the regulatory obligations of health plans and providers that conduct research involving human participants.[13] This rule (referred to in this report as the "Privacy Rule") will go into final effect in April 2003.[14]

The Privacy Rule applies to individually identifiable health information held by a health plan, a health care clearinghouse, or a health care provider that transmits any health care information electronically.[15] It does not, therefore, apply to social science research conducted outside of health care institutions, and it may not even apply to clinical research that is not conducted by health care providers.[16] The definition of research found in the Privacy Rule is intentionally identical to that found in the Common Rule: "Research means a systematic investigation, including research development, testing, and evaluation, designed to develop or contribute to generalizable knowledge."[17]

The Privacy Rule supplements and does not replace the Common Rule for regulating research. Federally funded research must, therefore, comply with both. Privately funded research conducted within health plans or by providers must comply with the Privacy Rule, even though it is not covered by the Common Rule. Researchers must also comply with state laws that are more stringent than the Privacy Rule; these state laws are specifically protected from preemption under the Rule.[18]

The Privacy Rule permits information to be used or disclosed for research only under the following conditions: First, if information used in research is not individually identifiable, it is not protected health information and is not subject to the Rule.[19] The revised Rule also provides for "Limited Data Sets," from which sixteen specific identifiers have been deleted, for research purposes if the covered entity obtains from the data user a data use agreement that limits use of the data and prevents further disclosure.[20] Second, if use or disclosure of protected health information is authorized by the research participant, it may be used or disclosed to the extent of that authorization.[21] Third, protected health information may be

---

[13]The DHHS Standards for Privacy of Individually Identifiable Health Information; Final Rule, 65 *Fed. Reg.* 82461, et seq., adopted on December 28, 2000. See also, explaining the Rule, technical guidance regarding research found at www.hhs.gov/ocr/hipaa/research.html. Amendments to the Rule were published on August 14, 2002 (DHHS, 2002).

[14]Small health plans have a year longer to comply with HIPAA, which also includes special transition provisions for ongoing research (45 CFR 164.532).

[15]45 CFR 160.102(a), 164.501.

[16]Health care provider is defined by cross reference to the Medicare statute, but also includes "any other person or organization who furnishes, bills, or is paid for health care in the normal course of business" (45 CFR 160.103).

[17]45 CFR 164.501.

[18]45 CFR 160.203.

[19]Standards for de-identified data are found at 45 CFR 164.514.

[20]45 CFR 164.514(e).

[21]45 CFR 164.508.

used or disclosed for research without authorization for certain purposes explicitly authorized by the Rule, including research conducted on decedents and review of patient information for preparing research protocols.[22] Fourth, protected health information may be used or disclosed for research without authorization if authorization is waived by an Institutional Review Board (IRB) or a privacy board (see below), as permitted by the Rule.[23]

The HIPAA Privacy Rule imposes a new task on Research ERBs— granting waivers to permit the use and disclosure of identifiable health care information without authorization by the research participants from whom the information was generated. The Rule also permits authorization waivers to be granted by new entities, called "privacy boards," which include members of varying backgrounds who are competent to review privacy issues, have at least one nonaffiliated member, and do not allow members to review research with which they have conflicts of interest.[24] It appears that privacy boards have been created to review research that is not subject to Research ERB approval, such as nonfederally funded research, and Research ERBs will normally review privacy issues for research otherwise subject to their jurisdiction.

Research ERBs and privacy boards can alter or waive authorization if specific criteria are met (see Box 7.2). Research ERBs must follow Common Rule procedures in determining authorization for waivers and alterations.[25] Privacy boards must review authorization waivers or alterations at meetings during which a majority of the board, including an unaffiliated member, is present and approves the waiver by a majority vote. However, the chair or one or more members of the board may authorize a waiver in an expedited review procedure when the research involves no more than a minimal risk to privacy.[26] The waiver must be signed by the chair or other member designated by the chair of the privacy board or IRB.[27]

The preface to the original Privacy Rule notes that waivers will rarely apply in clinical trials, since the researcher normally will have contact with the participant and could request authorization. The primary use of the waiver process will therefore be in health services research, in which large numbers of records are reviewed retrospectively.

Although Research ERBs have a legitimate role in deciding whether research using identifiable information should be permitted without participant authorization, the practical application of the waiver criteria is likely

---

[22]45 CFR 164.612(i)(1)(ii) & (iii).
[23]45 CFR 164.512(i)(1)(i).
[24]45 CFR 164.512(i)(B).
[25]45 CFR 164.512(i)(2)(iv)(A).
[26]45 CFR 164.512(i)(2)(iv)(B) & (C).
[27]45 CFR 164.512(i)(2)(v).

**Box 7.2
Health Insurance Portability and Accountability
Act of 1996 (HIPAA) Waiver Criteria
(under modifications to the HIPAA Privacy Rule)**

1. The use of disclosure of the information involves no more than minimal risk, based on the presence of at least:
    a. an adequate plan to protect identifiers from improper use or disclosure;
    b. an adequate plan to destroy identifiers as soon as possible consistent with the research unless there is a health or research reason to retain them, or retention is otherwise required by law (the preface specifically recognizes that FDA or International Organization for Standardization requirements may prohibit the destruction of identifiers) (65 *Fed. Reg.* at 81698); and
    c. there are adequate written assurances that protected information will not be reused or disclosed except as required by law, for research oversight, or for other research for which the use or disclosure of protected health information would be authorized by the Rule.
2. The research could not practicably be conducted without the alteration or waiver.
3. The research could not be practicably conducted without access to and use of the protected health information [45 CFR 164.512(i)(2)(ii)].

---

to be problematic. In particular, it is not clear whether the Privacy Rule uses the term "minimal risk" in a manner consistent with the way the term is used in the Common Rule, though the preface to the revised final Rule asserts this intention.[28] The fact that expedited review is permitted by privacy boards under the Privacy Rule when minimal risk is involved suggests that the two Rules are not using the term consistently.

It is also important that other obligations under the Privacy Rule not be indiscriminately transferred to Research ERBs. Someone within a health care plan or a provider that conducts research involving de-identified data (or limited data sets) must be responsible under the Privacy Rule for determining if data have been properly de-identified in conformity with the Rule's complex requirements. Someone also must be responsible for assuring that authorizations to use or disclose information for research contain the elements specified by the Privacy Rule. The Rule does not specify, however, that these functions must be performed by a Research ERB. Given the limited resources of Research ERBs in most settings and the committee's goal of refocusing their attention on the ethics of research, it would be inappropriate to assign these compliance responsibilities to a Research ERB (see Chapter 6).

---

[28]*67 Fed. Reg.* at 53230.

Although it is not this committee's task to comment in detail on the Privacy Rule, it agrees that the Rule's basic organizing principle is sensible. In particular, identifiable information concerning research participants should not be used or disclosed without either informed authorization from the participant or pursuant to a judgment from a Research ERB or equivalent body that 1) identifiable information is necessary for a particular research project, 2) it is impracticable to obtain consent from all participants, and 3) privacy risks are minimal. The committee's concern, expressed in Chapter 6, that the Research ERB should not be burdened with responsibilities tangential to its focus on ethics would suggest that policing compliance with the Privacy Rule might be better handled elsewhere in the organization, such as in a compliance office.

RESEARCH EFFORTS TO COUNTER TERRORISM

The terrorist attacks of 2001 have had a profound impact on American society, prompting an increased emphasis on the need to conduct research to counter terrorism. Although such research will focus on myriad security and related issues, issues involving humans—including drug, vaccine, and prophylactic trials—deserve particular attention in the context of this report.

The United States previously has conducted investigations into protective and therapeutic methods to combat the effects of various threat agents. However, based on the President's proposed budget for FY 2003, NIH plans to designate $1.48 billion to bioterrorism-related research and infrastructure—an increase of $1.47 billion from FY 2002 (NIH, 2002a). Of that amount, $977 million would fund bioterrorism research activities.[29] This is a massive increase in funding, and NIH is not the only federal agency that will be conducting such research.

> Recommendation 7.3: Groups addressing bioterrorism response mechanisms and research should pay special attention to the protection of research participants in their studies.

Protection of human participants in research to counter bioterrorism presents special challenges that relate particularly to the understanding of a trial's risks and benefits as described during the informed consent process. A relevant example is that of research on smallpox vaccines. The outpouring of volunteers for trials of different dilutions of available smallpox vaccine for immunogenicity after September 11 likely occurred for several reasons: the belief that the vaccine would provide protection, the knowledge that most of the population has no immunity to smallpox, the atten-

---

[9]These figures are subject to change during the Congressional appropriations process.

tion paid to the disastrous effects that would result from the release of smallpox in a bioterrorist attack, and, significantly, a lack of understanding of the true risks and experimental nature of the trials (Argetsinger, 2001; Connolly and Goldstein, 2001).

On the other hand, experience with the anthrax situation in October 2001 indicated reluctance to participate in the use of antibiotics by those exposed to anthrax, even though the antibiotics likely helped prevent further illness (Brookmeyer and Blades, 2002; Double Exposure, 2001). Because the duration of treatment to prevent pulmonary anthrax was unknown, those being treated were participants in an informal investigation of a different use of approved drugs. The already difficult process of obtaining fully informed consent for an effort that could be considered somewhere between a study and an application of a therapeutic measure not yet approved by FDA was further complicated by the fact that people had few options.

The anthrax vaccine had been approved in the 1970s and used prophylactically in the military and by laboratory workers and veterinarians. However, before the anthrax incidents of 2001, it had not been used post exposure, and thus, it was treated as an IND under FDA regulations, which meant that informed consent documents had to be signed. Press reports citing concerns of "experts" about experiments similar to the Tuskegee syphilis studies and confusing recommendations made by public health officials resulted in public misunderstanding of the status of anthrax vaccines for therapeutic use and loss of public trust in official pronouncements. Of the 10,000 people who had the option of taking the vaccine post exposure, only 130 chose to do so; another 1,168 took only the antibiotics as part of the study administered by the Centers for Disease Control and Prevention (Stolberg, 2002). Again, obtaining truly informed consent was difficult.

A further concern regarding research in these circumstances is that current products have generally been developed and approved for a healthy, young population and may have unknown effects when used in the population at large. The defensive research on prophylactic or therapeutic products against agents such as anthrax in the past was targeted mainly to those in the armed forces. Vulnerable groups, such as pregnant women, children, the elderly, the chronically ill, or the immune-compromised, were not included. If new prophylactic and therapeutic products are to be developed for use in the general population, additional research will be needed regarding the effects of these products in all populations.

With the increased emphasis on bioterrorism research, all parties involved should understand that the basic ethical principles underlying the involvement of human participants apply, no matter how urgently needed the research may be. Studies involving bioterrorism, some of which will be classified, will be carried out within a climate of public fear (Spieler, 2002), and in times of crisis, potential participants may be more prone to minimize known and stated risks, especially considering the desire to protect one's self and family, and this could override the informed aspect of consent. Additionally, in times of uncertainty and fear, the full range of civil liberties sometimes is not respected or enforced in order to enhance security, and the government's support of individual autonomy can decrease if resources are scarce and the need for data is great. Thus, the coercion of individuals to participate in trials that would support national needs could be tolerated under extreme conditions (ACHRE, 1995; Moreno, 2000).

In May 2002, FDA amended its New Drug and Biological Product regulations so that certain human drugs and biologics that are intended to reduce or prevent serious or life-threatening conditions may be approved for marketing with research evidence of effectiveness from appropriate animal studies, if human efficacy studies are not ethical or feasible (FDA, 2002b). This so-called Animal Rule—part of FDA's effort to help improve the nation's ability to respond to emergencies, including terrorist events—will apply when adequate and well-controlled clinical studies in humans cannot be ethically conducted because the studies would involve administering a potentially lethal or permanently disabling toxic substance or organism to healthy human volunteers. The new rule has postmarketing and labeling restrictions, however, and it does not apply if the product could be approved on the basis of any other standard under FDA's jurisdiction.

Although human participants are used for safety trials before approval, this modification of regulations is appropriate given the need to develop products to counter bioterrorism. Because questions will inevitably arise the first time these drugs and vaccines are used in practice, HRPPPs should be particularly vigilant in such situations.

Classified Research

The Advisory Committee on Human Radiation Experiments (ACHRE), formed by former President William Clinton to investigate past classified radiation experiments involving humans, has addressed the special concerns of classified research, and its efforts should serve as a guide to conducting ethical classified research (ACHRE, 1995). In its expansive report, ACHRE made a number of recommendations regarding the ethical aspects of classified research. Most relevant to this discussion is the recommendation that the informed consent requirement in classified research should not be waived and that an independent panel of nongovernmental experts should approve classified research (see Box 7.3). Under proposed legislation, these recommendations would be enforceable by law.[30]

---

[30]A Bill to Amend the Public Health Service Act with Respect to the Protection of Human Subjects in Research. H.R. 4697. 107th Congress, 2nd Sess. (2002).

Box 7.3
Advisory Committee on Human Radiation Experiments
Recommendations for Balancing National Security Interests
and the Rights of the Public

Recommendation 15:
15a: The Advisory Committee recommends to the Human Radiation Interagency
Working Group the adoption of a federal policy requiring the informed consent of
all human subjects of classified research and that this requirement not be subject
to exemption or waiver. In all cases, potential subjects should be informed of the
identity of the sponsoring federal agency and that the project involves classified
information.
15b: The Advisory Committee recommends to the Human Radiation Interagency
Working Group the adoption of a federal policy requiring that classified research
involving human subjects be permitted only after the review and approval of an
independent panel of appropriate nongovernmental experts and citizen representatives, all with the necessary security clearances. This panel should be charged
with determining (1) that the proposed experiment has scientific merit; (2) that risks
to subjects are acceptable and that the balance of risk and potential benefit is
appropriate; (3) that the disclosure to prospective subjects is sufficiently informa-
tional and that the consent solicited from subjects is sufficiently voluntary; and (4)
whether potential subjects must have security clearances in order to be sufficiently
informed to make a valid consent decision, and if so, how this can be achieved
without compromising the privacy and voluntariness of potential subjects. Complete documentation of the panel's deliberations and of the informed consent documents and process should be maintained permanently. These records should be
made public as soon as the national security concern justifying secrecy no longer
applies (ACHRE, 1995, p.828).

In 1997, President Clinton issued a memorandum that required all
agencies subject to the Common Rule to promulgate final rules regarding
the protection of human participants in classified research. The same memorandum also prohibited agencies from conducting such research until those
changes were incorporated into the Common Rule (Clinton, 1997). Although the changes have been accepted by 13 of the departments and
agencies subject to the Common Rule, the Central Intelligence Agency and
the Department of Defense are among those that have not signed off on the
alterations (Spieler, 2002).

The power to classify research has generally been reserved for security
agencies, but in December 2001, President Bush extended the power to
classify information as secret to the Secretary of DHHS (Mitchell, 2001).
The documents that could be classified include those related to bioterrorism
and preparedness of response. Thus, recent comment that federal regula-

tions governing classified human research should be implemented as soon as possible is very timely (Spieler, 2002).

Federal agencies such as DHHS and groups including The National Academies, the Center for Strategic and International Studies, and the RAND Corporation have and will continue to address the various aspects of bioterrorism threats. As outlined in this section, research in these circumstances, and classified research in general, involves special considerations if it is to be carried out ethically. National pressure to prepare for possible attacks involving biological or chemical agents is significant, and those exploring and recommending responses to bioterrorism should consider the protection of research participants in classified and terrorism-related research to be of the highest priority.

SUMMARY

When the original system for the protection of human participants in research was created, the typical study was conducted at a single research institution by a single investigator or a small team of investigators. There might have been one IRB, formed from volunteers at the research site to ensure an independent review of proposed research. Today, however, some research involves scores or even hundreds of centers and tens of thousands of participants, with multiple investigators, review boards, and institutions possibly involved. In addition, with the dramatic increase in privately funded research, a separate system of independent IRBs has been created. The recommendations made in this report aim to improve the system of protections as a whole, as it has not adequately adapted to the vast growth in the scale and complexity of research.

Trust in the human research enterprise demands that the system responsible for protection be credible and accountable. To be credible, the system requires ongoing independent advice, with input from a population that is as diverse as possible. Regulatory agencies, such as OHRP, would benefit from ongoing review of and advice regarding the policies, practices, and needs of the national protection system. To be accountable, information about new and ongoing clinical trials should be available in a centralized, user-friendly, and accessible database. After research is completed, results should be published in a manner that makes the value of the research and its compliance with ethical norms clear.

Emerging social issues will continue to influence the nature and direction of research involving humans. The potential for growth in research directed at countering terrorism or that is classified for national security requires extraordinary vigilance to ensure that public and social goals do not inappropriately and unfairly trample human rights and protections in research. Finally, the issue of privacy will continue to be debated in American society, especially in medicine and the health care system. Because protection programs are mandated to protect the rights and welfare of research participants, it is essential that they keep abreast of developments in the changing landscape of privacy regulations as they relate to health care and research.

References

AAHRPP (Association for the Accreditation of Human Research Protection Programs). 2002a. *Final Standards*. [Online]. Available: http://www.aahrpp.org/images/standards.PDF [accessed February 28, 2002].

AAHRPP. 2002b. *Accreditation Principles*. [Online]. Available: http://www.aahrpp.org/accreditation_principles.htm [accessed February 28, 2002].

AAHRPP. 2002c. *Accreditation Step-by-Step*. [Online]. Available: http://www.aahrpp.org/steps.htm [accessed May 7, 2002].

AAHRPP. 2002d. *Fees*. [Online]. Available: http://www.aahrpp.org/fees.htm [accessed February 28, 2002].

AAMC (Association of American Medical Colleges). 1990. *Guidelines for Dealing With Faculty Conflicts of Commitment and Conflicts of Interest in Research*. [Online]. Available: http://www.aamc.org/research/dbr/coi.htm [accessed May 23, 2001].

AAMC. 2001. *Protecting Subjects, Preserving Trust, Promoting Progress—Policy and Guidelines for the Oversight of Individual Financial Interests in Human Subjects Research*. Washington, DC: AAMC.

AAU (Association of American Universities) Task Force on Research Accountability. 2001. *Report on Individual and Institutional Financial Conflict of Interest*. Washington, DC: AAU.

AAUP (American Association of University Professors). 2001. Protecting Human Beings: Institutional Review Boards and Social Science Research. *Academe* 87(3):55–67.

ACHRE (Advisory Committee on Human Radiation Experiments). 1995. *Final Report: Advisory Committee on Human Radiation Experiments*. Washington, DC: Government Printing Office.

ACRP (Association of Clinical Research Professionals). 2001. *Code of Ethics*. [Online]. Available: http://www.acrpnet.org/ethics/index.html [accessed December 28, 2001].

Agre P, Kurtz RC, Krauss BJ. 1994. A Randomized Trial Using Videotape to Present Consent Information for Colonoscopy. *Gastrointestinal Endoscopy* 40(3):271–276.

Alberti KG. 2000. Multicentre research ethics committees: Has the cure been worse than the disease? No, but idiosyncracies and obstructions to good research must be removed. *British Medical Journal* 320(7243):1157–1158.

Altman D. 2002. Poor-Quality Medical Research: What Can Journals Do? *JAMA* 287(21):2869–2871.

Amdur RJ. 2000. Improving the Protection of Human Research Subjects. *Academic Medicine* 75(7):718–720.

Andejeski et al. 2002. Quantitative impact of including consumers in the scientific review of breast cancer research proposals. *Journal of Women's Health and Gender-Based Medicine* 11(4):351–360.

Anderson D, Costa I, Dickersin K. Forthcoming. Building Trials Central, an online register of clinical trials registers. *Controlled Clinical Trials*.

Angell M. 2000. Presentation at the August 15-16, 2000, Conference on Human Subject Protection and Financial Conflicts of Interest, National Institutes of Health, Bethesda, MD.

Annas GJ. 1991. Ethics Committees: From Ethical Comfort to Ethical Cover. *Hastings Center Report* 21(3):18–21.

Annas GJ and Grodin M. 1992. *The Nazi Doctors and the Nuremberg Code: Human Rights in Human Experimentation*. Oxford: Oxford University Press.

Annas, et al. 1977. Compensation for Harm: An Additional Protection for Human Subjects. In: *Informed Consent: The Subject's Dilemma*. Cambridge, MA: Ballinger Publishing Company. Pp. 257–277.

Antman EM, et al. 1992. A Comparison of Results of Meta-analyses of Randomized Control Trials and Recommendations of Clinical Experts: Treatments for Myocardial Infarction. *JAMA* 268(2):240–247.

Appelbaum PS, Roth LH, Lidz C. 1982. The therapeutic misconception: Informed consent in psychiatric research. *International Journal of Law and Psychiatry* 5(3-4):319–329.

Argetsinger A. 2001, October 27. Smallpox Vaccine Studies Swamped with Volunteers. *The Washington Post*. p. B1.

ASGT (American Society of Gene Therapy). 2000. *Policy of the American Society of Gene Therapy on Financial Conflict of Interest in Clinical Research*. [Online]. Available: http://www.asgt.org/policy/index.html [accessed December 28, 2001].

Atkinson HG. 2000. Decision-making dialogue. *Health News* 6(2):4–5.

Barnbaum D. 2002. Making More Sense of "Minimal Risk." *IRB: Ethics and Human Research* 24(3):10–13.

Bastian H. 1994. *The Power of Sharing Knowledge: Consumer Participation in the Cochrane Collaboration*. [Online]. Available: http://www.cochraneconsumer.com/p_Involve.asp [accessed August 14, 2002].

Batt S. 1994. *Patient No More: The Politics of Breast Cancer*. Canada: Gynergy Books.

Bazell R. 1998. *HER-2: The Making of Herception, a Revolutionary Treatment for Breast Cancer*. New York City: Random House.

Beecher HK. 1966. Ethics and Clinical Research. *New England Journal of Medicine* 274(24): 1354–1360.

Bell J, et al. 1998. *Prepared for the Office of Extramural Research, NIH. Evaluation of NIH Implementation of Section 491 of the Public Health Service Act, Mandating a Program of Protection for Research Subjects*. Alexandria, VA: James Bell and Associates.

Benson PR, et al. 1988. Information Disclosure, Subject Understanding, and Informed Consent in Psychiatric Research. *Law and Human Behavior* 12(4):455–475.

Berwick DM. 1990. Peer review and quality management: Are they compatible. *Quality Review Bulletin* 16(7):246–251.

Blumenstyk G. 2002, January 11. Crusader for the Rights of Research Volunteers. *The Chronicle of Higher Education*. p. A34.

Blumenthal D. 2001. *Financial Conflict of Interest in Academic Medicine: How Much and Who?* Presentation at the October 16, 2001, annual meeting of the Institute of Medicine, Washington, DC.

Bodenheimer T. 2001. *Industry, Academia, Investigator: Managing the Relationships: What is the impact on science?* Presentation at the October 16, 2001, annual meeting of the Institute of Medicine, Washington, DC.

Bohaychuck W, et al. 1998. Ethics Committee and IRB Audit Results. *Good Clinical Practice.* November 1998:46–55.

Briefer French J. 2002. Presentation at the March 26, 2002, meeting of the IOM Committee on Assessing the System for Protecting Human Research Participants, Washington, DC.

Briguglio J, et al. 1995. Development of a Model Angiography Informed Consent Form Based on a Multiinstitutional Survey of Current Forms. *Journal of Vascular and Interventional Radiology* 6(6):971–978.

Brookmeyer R and Blades N. 2002. Prevention of Inhalational Anthrax in U.S. Outbreak. *Science* 295:1861.

CAC (Citizen Advocacy Center). 1994. *Public Representation on Health Care Regulatory, Governing, and Oversight Bodies: Strategies for Success: Proceedings of a Workshop Convened by The Citizen Advocacy Center. Preface, Executive Summary, Introduction, and Keynote.* Washington, DC: The Citizen Advocacy Center.

CAC. 2002. *About CAC.* [Online]. Available: http://www.cacenter.org/about.htm [accessed August 28, 2002].

Centerwatch. 2001. *Background Information on Clinical Research.* [Online]. Available: http://www.centerwatch.com/patient/backgrnd.html [accessed July 25, 2002].

Chalmers TC. 1977. Randomize the first patient. *New England Journal of Medicine* 296:107.

Cho MK, et al. 2000. Policies on Faculty Conflicts of Interest at U.S. Universities. *JAMA* 284(17):2203–2208.

Cho M, Billings P. 1997. Conflict of Interest and Institutional Review Boards. *Journal of Investigative Medicine* 45(4):154–159.

Churchill LR, et al. 1998. Genetic Research as Therapy: Implications of "Gene Therapy" for Informed Consent. *Journal of Law and Medical Ethics* 26:38–47.

CIOMS (Council for International Organizations of Medical Sciences). 1993. *International Ethical Guidelines for Biomedical Research Involving Human Subjects.* Geneva: CIOMS.

CIOMS. 1982. Bankowski Z and Howard Jones N, eds. *Human Experimentation and Medical Ethics.* Geneva: CIOMS.

Clinton WJ. 1997. Strengthened Protections for Human Subjects of Classified Research. *Federal Register* 62(92):26369–26372.

Cohen J. 1994. Clinical Trial Monitoring: Hit or Miss? *Science* 264:1536.

Cohen P. 2001. Statement at the November 2, 2001, meeting of the IOM Committee on Assessing the System for Protecting Human Research Participants, Washington, DC.

Connolly C, Goldstein A. 2001, December 20. Anthrax Vaccine Plan Sows Confusion: DC Advises Workers Against Treatment. *The Washington Post.* p. A1.

Cooke RA and Tannenbaum AS. 1978. A Survey of Institutional Review Boards and Research Involving Human Subjects. In: National Commission for the Protection of Human Subjects of Biomedical and Behavioral Research. *Appendix to Report and Recommendations: Institutional Review Boards.* Washington, DC: Department of Health, Education, and Welfare.

Coulter A. 1999. Shared Decision-Making: A Summary and Future Issues. In: Maslin A. *Breast Cancer: Sharing the Decisions.* Oxford: Oxford University Press. Pp. 99–108.

Council of Europe Publishing, ed. 1997. *Convention on Human Rights and Biomedicine (Oviedo, 4.IV.1997).* Europe: Council of Europe Publishing.

Council on Ethical and Judicial Affairs, AMA (American Medical Association). 2000. *Code of Medical Ethics: Current Opinions.* Chicago, IL: AMA.

Cowdry, R. 2001. Presentation at the November 2, 2001, meeting of the IOM Committee on Assessing the System for Protecting Human Research Participants, Washington, DC.

CPMP Working Party on Efficacy of Medicinal Products. 1995. Biostatistical Methodology in Clinical Trials in Applications for Marketing Authorizations for Medicinal Products. Note for Guidance III/3630/92-EN. *Statistics in Medicine* 14:1659–1682.

Crocco A, Villasis-Keever M, Jadad A. 2002. Analysis of Cases of Harm Associated with Use of Health Information on the Internet. *JAMA* 287(21):2869–2871.

Daugherty C, et al. 1995. Perceptions of cancer patients and their physicians involved in phase I trials. *Journal of Clinical Oncology* 13(5):1062–1072.

Davidoff F, DeAngelis CD, Drazen JM, et al. 2001. Sponsorship, Authorship, and Accountability. *JAMA* 286(10):1232–1234.

Davidson, D. 2002. *Statement on HHS' Proposed Changes to the Medical Privacy Rules.* [Online]. Available: http://www.aha.org/info/releasedisplay.asp?passreleaseid=402 [accessed May 6, 2002].

Davis DA, et al. 1995. Changing physician performance. A systematic review of the effect of continuing medical education strategies. *JAMA* 274(9):700–705.

Davis DA and Taylor-Vaisey AL. 1997. Translating guidelines into practice: A systematic review of theoretical concepts, practical experience, and research evidence in the adoption of clinical practice guidelines. *Canadian Medical Association Journal* 157(4):408–416.

Day SJ, Altman DG. 2000. Blinding in clinical trials and other studies. *British Medical Journal* 321:504.

Dembner A. 2002, August 12. Lawsuits Target Medical Research. *The Boston Globe.* p. A1.

DeMets DL, Pocock SJ, Julian DG. 1999. The agonising negative trend in monitoring of clinical trials. *Lancet* 354(9194):1983–1988.

Deming W. 2000. *The New Economics for Industry, Government, Education.* Cambridge, MA: MIT Press.

DeRenzo EG. 2000. Coercion in the Recruitment and Retention of Human Research Subjects, Pharmaceutical Industry Payments to Physician Investigators, and the Moral Courage of the IRB. *IRB* 22(2):1–5.

Deutsch E and Taupitz J. 2000. *Freedom and Control of Biomedical Research.* Berlin: Springer.

DeYoung K, Nelson D. 2000a, December 21. Firms Find Costa Rica "Special" Place for Trials. *The Washington Post.* p. A19.

DeYoung K, Nelson D. 2000b, December 21. Latin America is Ripe for Trials, and Fraud. *The Washington Post.* p. A01.

DHEW (Department of Health, Education, and Welfare) Secretary's Task Force on the Compensation of Injured Research Subjects. 1977. *Report of the Task Force.* Report No. OS-77-003. Bethesda, MD: DHEW.

DHHS (Department of Health and Human Services). 1999. *A Device Clinical Trials Data Bank—Public Health Need and Impact on Industry. A Report to Congress by the Secretary of Health and Human Services.* [Online]. Available: http://www.fda.gov/cdrh/modact/113b.html [accessed June 19, 2002].

DHHS. 2000a. Final PHS Policy for Instruction in the Responsible Conduct of Research. *Federal Register* 65(236):76647.

DHHS. 2000b. Office of Public Health and Science, and the National Institutes of Health, Office of the Director; Statement of Organization, Functions, and Delegations of Authority. *Federal Register* 65(114):37136–37137.

DHHS. 2001a. *Draft Interim Guidance: Financial Relationships in Clinical Research: Issues for Institutions, Clinical Investigators, and IRBs to Consider When Dealing With Issues of Financial Interests and Human Subject Protection.* [Online]. Available: http://ohrp.osophs.dhhs.gov/nhrpac/mtg12-00/finguid.htm [accessed December 28, 2002].

DHHS. 2001b. *National Human Research Protections Advisory Committee Charter.* [Online]. Available: http://ohrp.osophs.dhhs.gov/nhrpac/charter.htm [accessed May 13, 2002].

DHHS. 2002. 45 CFR 160 and 164: Office of the Secretary; Standards for Privacy of Individually Identifiable Health Information. *Federal Register* 67(157):53182–53273.

Dickersin KD, et al. 2001. Development and implementation of a science training course for breast cancer activists: Project LEAD (leadership, education and advocacy development). *Health Expectations* 4(4):213–220.

DoD (Department of Defense). 2002. Department of Defense Directive Number 3216.2: Protection of Human Subjects and Adherence to Ethical Standards in DoD-Supported Research.

Double Exposure. 2001, December 19. *The Washington Post.* p. A38.

Dresser R. 2001. *When Science Offers Salvation: Patient Advocacy and Research Ethics.* New York: Oxford University Press.

Dretchen K. 2001. *The Relationship of IBCs to IRBs and IACUCs: Their Respective Purview, Roles, and Responsibilities.* Presentation at the December 7, 2001, meeting, IBCs in a Changing Research Landscape: A Policy Conference, Bethesda, MD.

Duke University. 2002, January 9. Press Release. *Study Aims to Improve Protection of Research Participants.*

ECRI (formerly Emergency Care Research Institute). 2002. *Should I Enter A Clinical Trial. A Patient Reference Guide for Adults With Serious or Life-Threatening Illness.* Washington, DC: American Association of Health Plans.

Egger M and Smith GD. 1998. Bias in location and selection of studies. *British Medical Journal* 316(7124):61-66.

Emanuel EJ and Steiner D. 1995. Institutional Conflict of Interest. *New England Journal of Medicine* 332(4):262–268.

Epstein S. 1996. *Impure Science: AIDS, Activism, and the Politics of Knowledge.* USA: University of California Press.

Erb T and Sugarman J. 2000. Ethical Issues on Informed Consent and Recruitment for Clinical Trials. *Anesthesiology* 92(6):1851–1852.

Erickson S. 2001. Written comments to the IOM Committee on Assessing the System for Protecting Human Research Participants.

Faden RR, Beauchamp TL. 1986. *A History and Theory of Informed Consent.* New York: Oxford University Press.

FDA (Food and Drug Administration). 1996. Protection of Human Subjects; Informed Consent. *Federal Register* 61(192): 51497–51531.

FDA. 1998. *Guideline for the Monitoring of Clinical Investigations.* [Online]. Available: http://www.fda.gov/ora/compliance_ref/bimo/clinguid.html [accessed February 13, 2002].

FDA. 2001a. Draft Guidance for Clinical Trial Sponsors: On the Establishment and Operation of Clinical Trial Data Monitoring Committees. *Federal Register* 66(224):58151–58153.

FDA. 2001b. International Conference on Harmonisation; E10 Choice of Control Group in Clinical Trials. *Federal Register* 66(93):24390–24391.

FDA. 2001c. *Food and Drug Administration Compliance Program Guidance Manual: Bioresearch Monitoring: Sponsors, Contract Research Organizations, and Monitors.* [Online]. Available: http://www.fda.gov/ora/compliance_ref/bimo/7348_810/48-810.pdf [accessed June 12, 2002].

FDA. 2002a. Institutional Review Boards: Requiring Sponsors and Investigators to Inform IRBs of Any Prior IRB Reviews. *Federal Register* 67(44):10115–10116.

FDA. 2002b. New Drug and Biological Drug Products; Evidence Needed to Demonstrate Effectiveness of New Drugs When Human Efficacy Studies Are Not Ethical or Feasible. *Federal Register* 67(105): 37988–37998.

Feussner JR. 2001, March 14. *Memorandum: Submission of Research Proposals.*

Flaherty MP, Nelson D, Stephens J. 2000, December 18. The Body Hunters: Overwhelming the Watchdogs. *The Washington Post.* p. A01.

Flaherty MP and Struck D. 2000, December 22. Life by luck of the draw. *The Washington Post.* p. A01.

Francis L. 1996. IRBs and Conflict of Interest. In: Spece RG, Shimm DS, Buchanan AE, eds. *Conflicts of Interest in Clinical Practice and Research.* New York: Oxford University Press. Pp. 418–436.

Freedman B. 1987. Equipoise and the Ethics of Clinical Research. *New England Journal of Medicine* 317(3):141–5.

Freedman B, Weijer C, Glass K. 1996. Placebo orthodoxy in clinical research. In: Empirical and methodological myths. *Journal of Law, Medicine, and Ethics* 24(3):243–251.

Fureman I, et al. 1997. Evaluation of a Video-Supplement to Informed Consent: Injection Drug Users and Preventive HIV Vaccine Efficacy Trials. *AIDS Education and Prevention* 9(4):330–341.

Gallin JI, ed. 2002. *Principles and Practice of Clinical Research.* San Diego: Academic Press.

Ganter J. 2002. Are Subjects Really Informed? *Applied Clinical Trials* January 2002:121.

GAO (General Accounting Office). 1996. *Scientific Research: Continued Vigilance Critical to Protecting Human Subjects.* Report No. GAO/HEHS-96-72. Washington, DC: GAO.

GAO. 2000. *VA Research: Protections for Human Subjects Need to Be Strengthened.* Report No. GAO/HEHS-00-155. Washington, DC: GAO.

GAO. 2001. *Biomedical Research: HHS Direction Needed to Address Financial Conflicts of Interest.* Report No. GAO 02-89. Washington, DC: GAO.

Gelsinger P. 2000. Jesse's Intent. *Guinea Pig Zero* 8:7–17.

Getz K, Borfitz D. 2002. *Informed Consent: The Consumer's Guide to the Risks and Benefits of Volunteering for Clinical Trials.* Boston, MA: Centerwatch.

Gifford AL, et al. 2002. Participation in Research and Access to Experimental Treatments by HIV-Infected Patients. *New England Journal of Medicine* 346(18):1373–1382.

Gillis J. 2002, June 30. A Hospital's Conflict of Interest: Patients Weren't Told of Stake in Cancer Drug. *The Washington Post.* p. A01.

Glass K and Lemmens T. 1999. Conflict of Interest and Commercialization of Biomedical Research: What is the Role of Research Ethics Review? In: Caulfield and William-Jones, eds. *The Commercialization of Genetic Research.* New York: Kluwer Academic/Plenum Publishers. Pp. 79–99.

Goldman C. 2000. *Paying for University Research Facilities and Administration.* Washington, DC: RAND.

Gonsalvez G. 2001. Statement at the November 2, 2001, meeting of the IOM Committee on Assessing the System for Protecting Human Research Participants, Washington, DC.

Grossman SA, Piantadosi S, Covahey C. 1994. Are Informed Consent Forms That Describe Clinical Oncology Research Readable by Most Patients and their Families? *Journal of Clinical Oncology* 12(10):2211–2215.

Harris Interactive. 2002. There Are Many Reasons Why People Are Reluctant to Participate in Clinical Trials. *Health Care News* 2(7):1–4.

Hayes GJ, Hayes SC, Dykstra T. 1995. A Survey of University Institutional Review Boards: Characteristics, Policies, and Procedures. *IRB* 17(3):1–6.

Heart Special Project Committee. 1967. Heart Special Project Committee: Organization, Review, and Administration of Cooperative Studies (Greenberg Report to the National Advisory Council). *Controlled Clinical Trials* 9:137–148.

Hetherington J, et al. 1989. Retrospective and prospective identification of unpublished controlled trials. Lessons from a survey of controlled trials. *Pediatrics* 84:374–380.

Hinestrosa C. 2001. *What Is Project Lead?* Presentation at the November 2, 2001, meeting of the IOM Committee on Assessing the System for Protecting Human Research Participants, Washington, DC.

Hochhauser M. 1997. Some Overlooked Aspects of Consent Form Readability. *IRB* 19(5):5–9.

Hogg C, Williamson C. 2001. Whose interests do lay people represent? Towards an understanding of the role of lay people as members of committees. *Health Expectations* 4:2–9.

Holm S. 2001. The Danish Research Ethics Committee System—Overview and Critical Assessment. In: NBAC. *Ethical and Policy Issues in Research Involving Human Participants. Volume II*. Bethesda, MD: NBAC. Pp. F-1–F-25.

Hughes EFX. 1988. *Perspectives on Quality in American Health Care*. Washington, DC: McGraw-Hill Book Company.

ICH (International Conference on Harmonisation of Technical Requirements for Registration of Pharamaceuticals for Human Use). 1996. *ICH Harmonised Tripartite Guideline: Guideline for Good Clinical Practice (E6)*. [Online]. Available: http://www.ich.org/pdfICH/e6.pdf [accessed September 5, 2002].

IOM (Institute of Medicine). 1985. *Vaccine Supply and Innovation*. Washington, DC: National Academy Press.

IOM. 1994. *Women and Health Research: Ethical and Legal Issues of Including Women in Clinical Studies*. Washington, DC: National Academy Press.

IOM. 1999. *The Unequal Burden of Cancer: An Assessment of NIH Research and Programs for Ethnic Minorities and the Medically Underserved*. Washington, DC: National Academy Press.

IOM. 2000a. *Extending Medicare Reimbursement in Clinical Trials*. Washington, DC: National Academy Press.

IOM. 2000b. *To Err Is Human*. Washington, DC: National Academy Press.

IOM. 2000c. *Protecting Data Privacy in Health Services Research*. Washington, DC: National Academy Press.

IOM. 2001a. *Preserving Public Trust: Accreditation and Human Research Participant Protection Programs*. Washington, DC: National Academy Press.

IOM. 2001b. *Crossing the Quality Chasm: A New Health System for the 21st Century*. Washington, DC: National Academy Press.

IOM. 2002. *Unequal Treatment: Confronting Racial and Ethnic Disparities in Healthcare*. Washington, DC: National Academy Press.

IOM and NRC (National Research Council). 2002. *Integrity in Scientific Research: Creating an Environment that Promotes Responsible Conduct*. Washington, DC: National Academy Press.

Jacobs WC. 2001. Statement at the November 2, 2001, meeting of the IOM Committee on Assessing the System for Protecting Human Research Participants, Washington, DC.

Jost TS and Davies S. 2002. *Medicare and Medicaid Fraud and Abuse*. 2002-2003 edition. Minnesota: Westgroup.

Juran JM and Godfrey AB, eds. 1999. *Juran's Quality Handbook*. New York: McGraw-Hill Professional Publishing.

Kahn J, et al. 1998. Changing Claims About Justice in Research. In: Kahn JP, et al. *Beyond Consent: Seeking Justice in Research*. New York: Oxford University Press. Pp. 1–10.

Kass NE and Sugarman J. 1996. Are Research Subjects Adequately Protected? A Review and Discussion of Studies Conducted by the Advisory Committee on Human Radiation Experiments. *Kennedy Institute of Ethics Journal* 6(3):271–282.

Katz J. 1993. Human Experimentation and Human Rights. *Saint Louis University Law Journal* 38(1):7–54.

Kelsey FO. 1991. The Bioresearch Monitoring Program. *Food Drug Cosmetic Law Journal* 46:59–63.

Kennedy I and Grubb A. 2000. *Medical Law*. London: Butterworths.

King NMP. 1995. Experimental Treatment. *Hastings Center Report* July/August 1995:6–15.

Kirchstein R. 2000. Presentation at the August 15-16, 2000, Conference on Human Subject Protection and Financial Conflicts of Interest, National Institutes of Health, Bethesda, MD.

Koski G. 2000. Letter to OHRP Staff. [Online]. Available: http://ohrp.osophs.dhhs.gov/references/ohrpcomp.pdf [accessed April 30, 2002].

LaFraniere S, Flaherty MP, Stephens J. 2000, December 19. The Dilemma: Submit or Suffer. *The Washington Post*. p. A01.

Lehrman S. 2000a. The Gelsinger Story. *GeneLetter*. [Online]. Available: http://www.geneletter.com/05-01-00/features.gelsinger1.html [accessed February 20, 2001].

Lehrman S. 2000b. The Gelsinger Story: Aftermath. *GeneLetter*. [Online]. Available: http://www.geneletter.com/06-01-00/features.gelsinger2.html [accessed February 20, 2001].

Lemmens T and Freedman B. 2000. Ethics Review for Sale? Conflict of Interest and Commercial Research Review Boards. *Milbank Quarterly* 78(4):547–584.

Lemmens T and Thompson A. 2001. Noninstitutional Commercial Review Boards in North America: A Critical Appraisal and Comparison with IRBs. *IRB* 23(2):1–12.

Lemonick MD and Goldstein A. 2002. At Your Own Risk. *Time Magazine* 159(16):46–56.

Levine C. 1998. Placebos and HIV: Lessons Learned. *Hastings Center Report* 28(6):43–48.

Levine RJ. 1986. *Ethics and Regulation of Clinical Research*. New Haven, CT: Yale University Press.

Levine RJ. 2001a. Institutional Review Boards: A Crisis in Confidence. *Annals of Internal Medicine* 134(2):161–163.

Levine RJ. 2001b. *Human Subjects Protection System: A crisis in confidence*. Presentation at the August 21, 2001, meeting of the IOM Committee on Assessing the System for Protecting Human Research Participants, Washington, DC.

Levinsky NG. 2002. Nonfinancial Conflicts of Interest in Research. *New England Journal of Medicine* 347(10):759–761.

Lidz CW, et al. 1983. Barriers to Informed Consent. *Annals of Internal Medicine* 99(4):539–543.

Lilford R and Jackson J. 1995. Equipoise and the ethics of randomization. *Journal of the Royal Society of Medicine* 88(10):552–559.

Lo B, Wolf LE, Berkeley A. 2000. Conflict-of-interest policies for investigators in clinical trials. *New England Journal of Medicine* 343(22):1616–20.

Love SM. 1995. *Dr. Susan Love's Breast Book*. 2nd edition. Reading, MA: Perseus Books.

MacQueen KM, et al. 2001. What is Community? An Evidence-Based Definition for Participatory Public Health. *American Journal of Public Health* 91(12):1929–1938.

Manheimer E, Anderson D, Dickersin K. Forthcoming. Identifying ongoing trials online: The need for a comprehensible, comprehensive register. *Controlled Clinical Trials*.

Marwick C. 1998. Compensation for Injured Research Subjects. *JAMA* 279(23):1854.

Marwick C. 2002. Failure to inform public is undermining confidence in clinical trials. *BMJ* 325:356.

Mastroianni A, Kahn J. 2001. Swinging on the Pendulum: Shifting Views of Justice in Human Subjects Research. *Hastings Center Report* 31(3):21–28.

Mather JH, Chief Officer, Office of Research Compliance and Assurance, Department of Veterans Affairs. 2002. *Statement on Oversight of Research and Other Issues*. Statement at the May 16, 2002, hearing of the Subcommittee on Oversight and Investigations and Subcommittee on Health, Committee on Veterans Affairs, U.S. House of Representatives.

McCray AT, Ide NC. 2000. Design and Implementation of a National Clinical Trials Registry. *Journal of the American Medical Informatics Association* 7(3):313–323.

McNeilly PJ and Carome M. 2001, July 19. *Letter to Edward D. Miller, Chi Van Dang, and Gregory Schaffer Re: Human Subjects Protections Under Multiple Project Assurance (MPA) M-1011.* [Online]. Available: http://ohrp.osophs.dhhs.gov/detrm_letrs/jul01a.pdf [accessed June 19, 2002].

Meinert C, Tonascia S. 1986. *Clinical Trials: Design, Conduct, and Analysis.* New York: Oxford University Press.

Merkatz RB and Summers EI. 1997. Including Women in Clinical Trials: Policy Changes at the Food and Drug Administration. In: Haseltine FP and Jacobson B, eds. *Women's Health Research: A Medical and Policy Primer.* Washington, DC: Health Press International.

Mitchell A. 2001, December 20. Bush Gives Secrecy Power to Public Health Secretary. *The New York Times.* p. B6.

Moreno J, Caplan AL, Wolpe PR. 1998. Updating protections for human subjects involved in research. Project on Informed Consent, Human Research Ethics Group. *JAMA* 280(22): 1951–8.

Moreno J. 2000. *Undue Risk: Secret State Experiments on Humans.* New York: WH Freeman & Co.

Moreno J. 2001. Goodbye to All That: The End of Moderate Protectionism in Human Subjects Research. *Hastings Center Report* 31(3):9–17.

Moses HI and Martin JB. 2001. Academic Relationships with Industry: A New Model for Biomedical Research. *JAMA* 285(7):933–935.

Murray, T. 1997. Genetic Exceptionalism and "Future Diaries": Is Genetic Information Different from Other Medical Information? In: *Genetic Secrets.* Rothstein M, ed. New Haven: Yale University Press. Pp. 60–73.

NAMI (National Alliance for the Mentally Ill). 2001. *NAMI's IRB Training Guide for Consumers and Family Members.* Arlington, VA: NAMI.

NAPBC (National Action Plan on Breast Cancer). 1996. *Executive Summary: Model Consent Form for Biological Tissue Banking Focus Group Report.* [Online]. Available: http://www.4woman.gov/napbc/napbc/model_consent.htm [accessed June 12, 2002].

National Commission for the Protection of Human Subjects of Biomedical and Behavioral Research. 1979. *The Belmont Report: Ethical Principles and Guidelines for the Protection of Human Subjects of Research.* Washington, DC: U.S. Goverment Printing Office.

National Commission for the Protection of Human Subjects of Biomedical and Behavioral Research. 1978. *Report and Recommendations: Institutional Review Boards.* Washington, DC: U.S. Goverment Printing Office.

NBAC (National Bioethics Advisory Commission). 1998. *Research Involving Persons with Mental Disorders That May Affect Decisionmaking Capacity.* Rockville, MD: NBAC.

NBAC. 1999. *Research Involving Human Biological Materials: Ethical Issues and Policy Guidance. Volume 1.* Rockville, MD: NBAC.

NBAC. 2001a. *Ethical and Policy Issues in International Research: Clinical Trials in Developing Countries.* Rockville, MD: NBAC.

NBAC. 2001b. *Ethical and Policy Issues in Research Involving Human Participants, Volume I.* Bethesda, MD: NBAC.

NBAC. 2001c. Federal Agency Survey on Policies and Procedures for the Protection of Human Subjects in Research. In: NBAC. *Ethical and Policy Issues in Research Involving Human Participants. Volume II: Commissioned Papers and Staff Analysis.* Bethesda, MD: NBAC. Pp. J-1–J-33

NCI (National Cancer Institute, NIH). 1998. *Taking Part in Clinical Trials: What Cancer Patients Need to Know.* NIH Publication No. 97-4250.

NCQA (National Committee for Quality Assurance). 2001. *VA Human Research Protection Accreditation Program Accreditation Standards.* Washington, DC: NCQA.

Nelson D. 2000, December 18. Drug's Approval Reveals Cracks in the System. *The Washington Post.* p. A16.

NHRPAC. 2001. *NHRPAC Recommendations on HHS's Draft Interim Guidance on Financial Relationships in Clinical Research.* [Online]. Available: http://ohrp.osophs.dhhs.gov/nhrpac/documents/aug01a.pdf [accessed April 4, 2002].

NIH (National Institutes of Health). 1996. Waiver of Informed Consent Requirements in Certain Emergency Research. *Federal Register* 61(192):51531–51533.

NIH. 1998. *NIH Policy for Data and Safety Monitoring.* [Online]. Available: http://grants.nih.gov/grants/guide/notice-files/not98-084.html [accessed June 18, 2002].

NIH. 2000a. *Further Guidance on a Data and Safety Monitoring for Phase I and Phase II Trials.* [Online]. Available: http://grants.nih.gov/grants/guide/notice-files/NOT-OD-00-038.html [accessed January 23, 2002].

NIH. 2000b. *Required Education in the Protection of Human Research Participants.* OD-00-039. [Online]. Available: http://grants2.nih.gov/grants/guide/notice-files/NOT-OD-00-039.html [accessed June 13, 2002].

NIH. 2001. *NIH Training Opportunities: K30 Clinical Research Curriculum Award.* [Online]. Available: http://grants1.nih.gov/training/k30.htm [accessed June 13, 2002].

NIH. 2002a. *Press Release for the FY 2003 President's Budget.* [Online]. Available: http://www.nih.gov/news/budgetfy2003/2003NIHpresbudget.htm [accessed February 27, 2002].

NIH. 2002b. *Human Subjects Research Enhancements Program.* OD-02-003. [Online]. Available: http://grants1.nih.gov/grants/guide/rfa-files/RFA-OD-02-003.html [accessed June 13, 2002].

NIH. 2002c. *Research on Ethical Issues in Human Studies.* PA-02-103. [Online]. Available: http://grants2.nih.gov/grants/guide/pa-files/PA-02-103.html [accessed June 13, 2002].

NIH CC (NIH Clinical Center). 2000. *Protomechanics: A Guide to Preparing and Conducting a Clinical Research Study* (Figure 7). [Online]. Available: http://www.cc.nih.gov/ccc/protomechanics/ [accessed July 23, 2002].

NIH COPR (NIH Council of Public Representatives). 2001. *Human Research Protections in Clinical Trials: A Public Perspective.* [Online]. Available: http://public-council.nih.gov/COPRReportOctober2001.asp [accessed November 6, 2001].

NIH CSR (NIH Center for Scientific Review). 2001. *Review Procedures for Scientific Review Group Meetings.* [Online]. Available: http://www.csr.nih.gov/guidelines/proc.htm [accessed May 2, 2002].

NIH CSR. 2002. New Instructions for Evaluating Grant Applications Involving Human Subjects. *Peer Review Notes.* January 2002:6-8.

NRC (National Research Council). 1996. *Guide for the Care and Use of Laboratory Animals.* Washington, DC: National Academy Press.

NRC. 2001. Presentations at the June 28, 2001, meeting of the Panel on Institutional Review Boards, Surveys, and Social Science Research, Washington, DC.

NSF (National Science Foundation). 2001. *NSF Grant Proposal Guide.* [Online]. Available: http://www.nsf.gov/pubs/2002/nsf022/nsf022.pdf [accessed April 11, 2002].

Nuremberg Code. 1949. In: *Trials of War Criminals Before the Nuremberg Military Tribunals Under Control Council Law No. 10.* Vol. 2, Nuremberg, October 1946–April 1949. Washington, DC: U.S. Government Printing Office. Pp. 181–182.

OHRP. 2000. *OHRP Compliance Activities: Common Findings and Guidance—Clickable Index.* [Online]. Available: http://ohrp.osophs.dhhs.gov/references/findings.pdf [accessed May 1, 2001].

OHRP. 2001. *OHRP Compliance Data by Institution, by Determination Letters Issues, and by Site-Visited Institution October 1998 to December 2001.* (Unpublished).

OHRP. 2002a. *Quality Assurance/Quality Improvement Self-Assessment Tool.* [Online]. Available: http://ohrp.osophs.dhhs.gov/humansubjects/qip/qatooli.htm [accessed May 13, 2002].

OHRP. 2002b. *Quality Improvement Program.* [Online]. Available: http://ohrp.osophs.dhhs. gov/humansubjects/qip/qipdesc.pdf [accessed May 7, 2002].

OIG (Office of Inspector General, U.S. Department of Health and Human Services). 1998a. *Institutional Review Boards: A Time for Reform.* Report No. OEI-01-97-00193. Washington, DC: DHHS OIG.

OIG. 1998b. *Institutional Review Boards: Promising Approaches.* Report No. OEI-01-97-00191. Washington, DC: DHHS OIG.

OIG. 1998c. *Institutional Review Boards: The Emergence of Independent Boards.* Report No. OEI-01-97-00192. Washington, DC: DHHS OIG.

OIG. 1998d. *Institutional Review Boards: Their Role in Reviewing Approved Research.* Report No. OEI-01-97-00190. Washington, DC: DHHS OIG.

OIG. 1998e. *Low Volume Institutional Review Boards.* Report No. OEI-01-97-00194. Washington, DC: DHHS OIG.

OIG. 2000a. *Protecting Human Research Subjects: Status of Recommendations.* Report No. OEI-01-97-00197. Washington, DC: DHHS.

OIG. 2000b. *Recruiting Human Subjects: Pressures in Industry-Sponsored Clinical Research.* Report No. OEI-01-97-00195. Washington, DC: DHHS OIG.

OIG. 2000c. *Recruiting Human Subjects: Sample Guidelines for Practice.* Report No. OEI-01-97-00196. Washington, DC: DHHS OIG.

OIG. 2002. *Clinical Trial Websites: A Promising Tool to Foster Informed Consent.* Report No. OEI-01-97-00198. Washington, DC: DHHS OIG.

OPRR (Office for Protection from Research Risks). 1993. *Protecting Human Research Subjects: Institutional Review Board Guidebook.* Washington, DC: U.S. Government Printing Office.

OPRR (Office for Protection from Research Risks) Review Panel. 1999. *Report to the Advisory Committee to the Director, NIH From the Office for Protection From Research Risks Review Panel.* Rockville, MD: National Institutes of Health.

ORCA (Office of Research Compliance and Assurance). 2002. *Human Subjects Checklist.* [Online]. Available: http://www.va.gov/orca/docs/Human_Subjects_Checklist.doc [accessed August 19, 2002].

Otto MA. 2002a, August 7. Accreditation: NCQA Halts VA Program Inspections to Revise Accreditation Process, Standards. *BNA Medical Research Law and Policy Report.*

Otto MA. 2002b, June 19. NCQA Inspectors Approve Nine VA Centers But Flunk Three, Halt Recruitment at One. *BNA Medical Research Law and Policy Report.*

Otto MA. 2002c, September 18. NHRPAC Charter Lapses; New Group Planned; Former Advisers Suspect Political Motivations. *BNA Medical Research Law and Policy Report.*

Overbey MM. 2001. Written comments to the IOM Committee on Assessing the System for Protecting Human Research Participants.

Peckman S. 2001. Local Institutional Review Boards. In: NBAC. *Ethical and Policy Issues in Research Involving Human Participants. Volume II.* Bethesda, MD: NBAC. Pp. K-1–K-35.

Pedrazzani L. 2001. Statement at the November 2, 2001, meeting of the IOM Committee on Assessing the System for Protecting Human Research Participants, Washington, DC.

Phelps J. 2000. Presentation at the August 21, 2001, meeting of the IOM Committee on Assessing the System for Protecting Human Research Participants, Washington, DC.

President's Commission for the Study of Ethical Problems in Medicine and Biomedical and Behavioral Research. 1981. *Protecting Human Subjects: The Adequacy and Uniformity of Federal Rules and Their Implementation.* Washington, DC: U.S. Government Printing Office.

President's Commission for the Study of Ethical Problems in Medicine and Biomedical and Behavioral Research. 1982a. *Compensating for Research Injuries: A Report on the Ethical and Legal Implications of Programs to Redress Injuries Caused by Biomedical and Behavioral Research.* Washington, DC: U.S. Government Printing Office.

President's Commission for the Study of Ethical Problems in Medicine and Biomedical and Behavioral Research. 1982b. *Making Health Care Decisions: A Report on the Ethical and Legal Implications of Informed Consent on the Patient-Practitioner Relationship.* Washington, DC: U.S. Government Printing Office.

President's Commission for the Study of Ethical Problems in Medicine and Biomedical and Behavioral Research. 1983. *Implementing Human Research Regulations.* Washington, DC: U.S. Government Printing Office.

Rand Reed K. 2001. Statement at the November 2, 2001, meeting of the IOM Committee on Assessing the System for Protecting Human Research Participants, Washington, DC.

Reason J. 1990. *Human Error.* Cambridge: Cambridge University Press. As quoted in IOM. 2000. *To Err is Human.* Washington, DC: National Academy Press. Pp. 52.

Rettig RA. 2000. The Industrialization of Clinical Research. *Health Affairs* 19(2):129–146.

Roswell RH. Under Secretary for Health, Department of Veterans Affairs. 2002. *Non-profit Research Corporations and Educational Foundations and the Department of Veterans Affairs Human Studies Protection Program.* Statement at the May 16, 2002, hearing of the Subcommittee on Oversight and Investigations and Subcommittee on Health, Committee on Veterans Affairs, U.S. House of Representatives.

Rubin P. 2001. Written comments to the IOM Committee on Assessing the System for Protecting Human Research Participants.

Rudder CE. 2001. Written comments to the IOM Committee on Assessing the System for Protecting Human Research Participants.

Sackett DL. 1983. On Some Prerequisites for a Successful Clinical Trial. In: Shapiro SH and Louis TA, eds. *Clinical Trials: Issues and Approaches.* New York: Marcel Dekker. Pp. 65–79.

Saunders C, et al. 2001. *Foundations of Clinical Research.* Wellesley, MA: Center for Clinical Research Practice.

Schwartz J. 2001. Oversight of Human Subject Research: The Role of States. In: *Ethical and Policy Issues in Research Involving Human Participants, Volume II.* Washington, DC: NBAC. Pp. M-1–M-20.

Shalala D. 2000. Protecting Research Subjects—What Must Be Done. *New England Journal of Medicine* 343(11):808–810.

Shaywitz DA and Ausiello DA. 2001, July 29. The Necessary Risks of Medical Research. *The New York Times.* Week in Review, p. 4.

Shopes L. 2001. Written comments to the IOM Committee on Assessing the System for Protecting Human Research Participants.

Silber T. 2001. Pediatric Research and the Ombudsman. *Pediatric Ethicscope* 12(1&2):1–5.

Softcheck JT. 2002, March 13. NIH offers $28.5 million program to enhance human subjects oversight. *Washington Fax.*

Speers M. 2002a. Presentation at the March 26, 2002, meeting of the IOM Committee on Assessing the System for Protecting Human Research Participants, Washington, DC.

Speers M. 2002b, June 3. Letter to Robert H. Roswell, Under Secretary for Health, Veterans Health Administration.

Spieler R. 2002, March 5. Secret research must adopt Common Rule human subject protections, bioethicists urge. *Washington Fax.*

Spilker B. 1991. Teaching Courses in Clinical Trial Research Methods. *Journal of Clinical Pharmacology* 31:496–508.

Spilker, B. 2001. *An Industry Perspective on Systems for Protecting Human Research Participants.* Statement at the August 21, 2001, meeting of the IOM Committee on Assessing the System for Protecting Human Research Participants, Washington, DC.

Stephens J. 2000, December 17. The Body Hunters: As Drug Testing Spreads, Profits and Lives Hang in the Balance. *The Washington Post.* p. A1.

Stolberg SG. 2001, February 11. Children Test New Medicines Despite Doubts. *The New York Times.* National Desk, p. 1.

Stolberg S. 2002, January 8. A Nation Challenged: Steps Against Anthrax; Civilians Are Reluctant to Join U.S. Test of Anthrax Vaccine. *The New York Times.* p. A13.

Sugarman J. 2001. Presentation at the August 21, 2001, meeting of the IOM Committee on Assessing the System for Protecting Human Research Participants, Washington, DC.

Sugarman J, et al. 1999. Empirical Research on Informed Consent: An Annotated Bibliography. *Hastings Center Report* 29(1):S1–S42.

Swankin D. 2001. Presentation at the November 2, 2001, meeting of the IOM Committee on Assessing the System for Protecting Human Research Participants, Washington, DC.

Taupitz J. 2001. *Haftung und Versicherung in der Forschung am Menschen—Landesbericht Deutschland.* Unpublished.

Temkin O and Temkin L, eds. 1967. *Ancient Medicine: Selected Papers of Ludwig Eidelstein.* Baltimore, MD: Johns Hopkins University Press.

Terry S. 2001. Statement at the November 2, 2001, meeting of the IOM Committee on Assessing the System for Protecting Human Research Participants, Washington, DC.

Thacker E. 2002. Conflicts of interest in institutional-based IRBs versus independent IRBs. *Research Practitioner* 3(1):17–20.

Thomson O'Brien MA, et al. 2002. Continuing education meetings and workshops: Effects on professional practice and health care outcomes (Cochrane Review). In: *The Cochrane Library, Issue 1.* Oxford: Update Software.

Tuskegee Syphilis Study Ad Hoc Advisory Panel. 1973. *Final Report.* Washington, DC: DHEW.

U.S. Congress, Senate, Subcommittee on Public Health, Committee on Health, Education, Labor, and Pensions. 2000. *Gene Therapy: Is There Oversight to Protect for Patient Safety?* 106th Congress. February 2, 2000.

VA (U.S. Department of Veterans Affairs). 2002. *I'm a Veteran: Should I Participate in Research?* (Brochure).

Wagner T. 2001. Unpublished Data. *The Costs of Operating Institutional Review Boards.*

Washburn J. 2001, December 30. Informed Consent. *The Washington Post.* p. W16.

Wayne C. 2001. Statement at the November 2, 2001, meeting of the IOM Committee on Assessing the System for Protecting Human Research Participants, Washington, DC.

Weijer C, et al. 2002. The ethics of placebo-controlled trials. *New England Journal of Medicine* 346:382–383.

Weiss R and Nelson D. 1999, December 8. Methods Faulted in Fatal Gene Therapy. *The Washington Post.* p. A1.

Weiss R. 2002, September 17, 2002. HHS Seeks Science Advice to Match Bush Views. *The Washington Post.* p. A1.

Wilson D and Heath D. 2001a, March 11. Patients never knew the full danger of trials they staked their lives on. *The Seattle Times.* p. A1.

Wilson D and Heath D. 2001b, March 12. He saw the test as a violation of "trusting, desperate human beings". *The Seattle Times.* p. A1.

Wilson D and Heath D. 2001c, March 13. Many patients think that joining testing will help them, but often they're mistaken. *The Seattle Times*. p. A6.

Wilson D and Heath D. 2001d, March 13. With a year or two to live, woman joined test in which she was misled. *The Seattle Times*. p. A1.

Wilson D and Heath D. 2001e, March 14. He helped create the biotech boom and when it went bust, so did he. *The Seattle Times*. p. A1.

Wilson D and Heath D. 2001f, March 14. No wonder they call the place "Mother Hutch". *The Seattle Times*. p. A9.

Wilson D and Heath D. 2001g, March 15. The Hutch zealously guards its secrets. *The Seattle Times*. p. A1.

World Medical Association. 2000. *Declaration of Helsinki: Ethical Principles for Medical Research Involving Human Subjects, Revised*. Ferney-Voltaire, France: World Medical Association.

Wyn Davies H. 2001. *The Role of the Private Sector in Protecting Human Research Subjects: A CRO Perspective*. Presentation at the August 21, 2001, meeting of the IOM Committee on Assessing the System for Protecting Human Research Participants, Washington, DC.

Yamada T. 2001. *The Academic-Industry Interface*. Presentation at the October 16, 2001, annual meeting of the Institute of Medicine, Washington, DC.

Yank V and Rennie D. 2002. Reporting of Informed Consent and Ethics Committee Approval in Clinical Trials. *JAMA* 287(21):2835–2838.

Zieve FJ, McGuire Research Institute. 2002. *Statement on Oversight of Research and Other Issues*. Statement at the May 16, 2002, hearing of the Subcommittee on Oversight and Investigations and Subcommittee on Health, Committee on Veterans Affairs, U.S. House of Representatives.

Appendix A

Data Sources and Methods

I n order to comprehensively assess the system for protecting human research participants, the committee reviewed and considered a variety of data sources and inputs in a concerted effort to collect and evaluate a broad array of information. These sources included a review of relevant literature; presentations before the committee from interested organizations, individuals, and federal agencies; data collected from organizations and people; and materials collected for the committee's first report, *Preserving Public Trust: Accreditation and Human Research Participant Protection Programs*. A summary description of the committee's evidence-gathering methods follows.

THE FIRST PHASE

The committee undertook its task in two phases. The first phase of the committee's work, exploring accreditation of human research participant protection programs (HRPPPs), resulted in the publication of *Preserving Public Trust: Accreditation and Human Research Participant Protection Programs* (IOM, 2001a). In order to gather information for that report, the committee held several open meetings and invited public comment on the draft accreditation standards presented to the committee by Public Responsibility in Medicine and Research (PRIM&R) and the National Committee for Quality Assurance (NCQA). A thorough description of the methods used in the first phase of the committee's task can be found in Appendix A of *Preserving Public Trust*.

PUBLIC MEETINGS AND FEEDBACK

Over the course of the second phase of this study, the committee requested and received written responses and presentations from organizations and individuals concerned with human research participant protections. The first meeting of the committee's second phase of work took place on May 14-15, 2001. Subsequent public meetings were held on August 21-22 and November 1-2, 2001, and March 25-26, 2002. The committee's meetings on January 17-18 and May 20-21, 2002, were held entirely in executive session, and therefore, were closed to the public. The speakers at the various public meetings during phase 2 are listed in Box A.1.

At the May 2001 meeting, presenters addressed the committee's task, the Department of Health and Human Services (DHHS) draft interim guidance on conflicts of interest, and the activities of the National Human Research Protections Advisory Committee. Presenters also provided information regarding NIH insights from proactive compliance site visits, the Food and Drug Administration's (FDA's) bioresearch monitoring data, and common compliance problems observed by the Office for Protection from Research Risks (OPRR)/Office for Human Research Protections (OHRP).

During the August meeting, the presentations covered a variety of topics including the HRPPP system, the role of the pharmaceutical industry and of contract research organizations in protecting human research participants, federal regulations and their legal implications, informed consent processes, international research trials, National Bioethics Advisory Committee recommendations, Institutional Review Board (IRB) administration, and FDA policies and procedures.

The November public meeting was convened to explore the perspectives of human research participants. At that meeting, the committee heard from public members of regional, independent, and academic Institutional Review Boards; representatives of public support organizations, including Project LEAD, Citizen Advocacy Center, and PXE International; and research trial participants.

During the January meeting, the committee focused on report content and recommendation development. In addition, the committee reviewed information compiled at its request by OHRP—*OHRP Compliance Data by Institution, by Determination Letters Issues, and by Site-Visited Institution October 1998 to December 2001.*

In addition to evaluating the report contents and recommendations, the committee gathered information about the ongoing accreditation processes of the Association for the Accreditation of Human Research Protection Programs and the National Committee for Quality Assurance at its March meeting. Representatives from the National Institutes of Health (NIH) and

BOX A.1
Individuals and Organizations Appearing Before the
Committee During Phase 2 Open Sessions

May 14-15, 2001
Michael Carome, DHHS Office for Human Research Protections
Dennis Dixon, NIAID Biostatistics Research Branch
Kate-Louise Gottfried, National Human Research Protections Advisory Committee
Greg Koski, DHHS Office for Human Research Protections
Stuart Nightingale, DHHS Office of the Assistant Secretary for Evaluation and
    Planning
Belinda Seto, NIH Office of Extramural Research
Stan Woollen, FDA Office of Medical Policy

August 21-22, 2001
Helen Wyn Davies, Quintiles, Inc.
Nancy Kass, Johns Hopkins University Bloomberg School of Public Health
David Lepay, FDA Office of the Commissioner
Robert Levine, Yale University School of Medicine
James Phelps, Hyman, Phelps & McNamara
Tom Puglisi, Pricewaterhouse Coopers
Marjorie Speers, National Bioethics Advisory Commission
Bert Spilker, Pharmaceutical Research and Manufacturers of America
Jeremy Sugarman, Duke University Medical Center

November 2, 2001
Pat Barr, IRB Member, community setting
Perry Cohen, Trial Participant
Rex Cowdry, National Alliance for the Mentally Ill
Gregg Gonsalvez, Trial Participant
Carolina Hinestrosa, Project LEAD
William C. Jacobs, IRB member, independent IRB setting
Libby Pedrazzani, Trial Participant
Kathleen Rand Reed, IRB member, academic setting
David Swankin, Citizen Advocacy Center
Sharon Terry, PXE International
Claudia Wayne, Trial Participant

March 26, 2002
Jessica Briefer French, National Committee on Quality Assurance
Greg Koski, DHHS Office for Human Research Protections
Belinda Seto, NIH Office of Extramural Research
Marjorie Speers, Association for the Accreditation of Human Research Protection
    Programs

BOX A.2
Individuals Participating in Conference Calls with
Committee Members

January 10, 2002: IRB Community Perspective
Arthur O. Anderson, U.S. Army Medical Research Institute of Infectious Diseases
Jeffrey A. Cooper, Albany Medical Center
Susan J. Delano, Research Foundation for Mental Hygiene, Inc.
Felix Gyi, Chesapeake Research Review, Inc.
Karen Hansen, Fred Hutchinson Cancer Research Center
Steven Heeringa, University of Michigan
Nancy Hibser-Davis, University of Illinois College of Medicine at Peoria
Kathryn Madden, Oregon Research Institute
Helen McGough, University of Washington
Celia S. Walker, Colorado State University

March 18, 2002: Research Investigator Perspective
William F. Crowley, Massachusetts General Hospital
Steven C. Schachter, Beth Israel Deaconess Medical Center
Susan Weller, University of Texas Medical Branch at Galveston

---

OHRP also updated the committee about activities at their respective organizations.

The final committee meeting in May 2002 focused solely on the report contents and recommendations.

In order to supplement the information gathered during the formal meetings, members of the committee conducted two conference calls to access perspectives from two additional areas of importance to the committee. The first call, held in January 2002, involved members of the IRB community, including IRB administrators and board members. The individual call participants were identified largely in consultation with the Applied Research Ethics National Association in order to gather a group representative of a variety of research organizations and disciplines. The second call, held in March 2002, focused on the investigator perspective. Participating investigators included biomedical and social science researchers who were identified in consultation with relevant professional associations. The participants in both conference calls are listed in Box A.2.

During these meetings and throughout the course of the study, a number of people and organizations shared written materials with the committee. These materials were reviewed and considered with respect to the committee's task and can be examined by the public. The public access files are maintained by the Public Access Records Office, 2101 Constitution Avenue, NAS 171, Washington, DC 20418; tel: (202) 334-3543.

LITERATURE REVIEW

In order to conduct a thorough review, the committee conducted multiple literature searches and read numerous articles, books, policies, and reports concerning the protection of human participants in research. The committee maintained information about the materials in a database that allowed the committee to search for items by keywords or other criteria.

The materials provided to the committee addressed a large variety of topics including information about IRBs; informed consent procedures; federal regulations and compliance problems; the roles of industry, contract research organizations, participants, and other stakeholders in the research enterprise; the problems within the current protection system; the ethics of research involving humans; conflicts of interest; accreditation; regulatory costs; safety monitoring; multisite research; and a number of other topics.

Appendix B

July 1, 2002

Dr. Daniel Federman, *Chair*
Committee on Assessing the System for Protecting
    Human Research Participants
Institute of Medicine
The National Academies
Washington, DC 20418

Dear Dr. Federman:

The current system for protecting human participants in research is widely perceived to be in need of review and improvement (see, e.g., U.S. Department of Health and Human Services, 1998; American Association of University Professors, 2001). Concerns are of two types. One is the potential for serious harm to participants and the need to better protect them from such harm.[1] The other is unnecessary burdens that may result from applying review standards for high-risk research to low-risk studies—burdens on institutional review boards (IRBs), which are the primary bodies for reviewing and monitoring research with human participants; on researchers; and sometimes on participants themselves.[2]

In a climate of heightened scrutiny of IRB procedures, the Institute of Medicine (IOM) established your committee in fall of 2000, with funding from the U.S. Department of Health and Human Services and the Greenwall Foundation. In June 2001 the Committee on National Statistics of the National Research Council, in collaboration with the Board on Behavioral, Cognitive, and Sensory Sciences and Education, established our study panel, the Panel on IRBs, Surveys, and Social Science Research.

---

[1]This concern has been heightened, for example, by the death of Jesse Gelsinger, a participant in an experimental gene therapy study at the University of Pennsylvania. For a summary of pertinent news articles, see http://www.uphs.upenn.edu/ihgt/otcinfo.html.

[2]This concern has been heightened by regulatory actions that temporarily shut down all research, regardless of risk, at two universities, Johns Hopkins University (see Keiger and De Pasquale, 2002) and Duke University (see Stout, 1999).

236

This letter is written to provide input to your committee for use in your final report. It comments on issues of human participant protection in research in the domain of the social, behavioral, and economic sciences (SBES) and outside the domain of biomedical research. In fact, research methods are rarely unique to either domain, although some methods, such as interviews, are more typically used in SBES research than in biomedical research, while the reverse is true for other methods, such as double-blind experiments.[3] Some of the differences between the two domains in research methods and in the frequency and nature of their use create issues of human participant protection for one domain that may receive less emphasis in the other. This letter provides an SBES perspective—on the assumption that your committee by design is more concerned with biomedical research.

In the letter we primarily address field, laboratory, and archival research conducted by such typical SBES methods as mail, telephone, and in-person surveys, structured interviews, participant observation, laboratory research, and other methods that ordinarily pose low risk to participants. By "low risk" we refer to the definition in federal regulations, namely, that a study has a low probability of causing physical, psychological, or economic harm to participants and that the nature of the harm is minimal and no more than is normally encountered in daily life (see the Common Rule, Title 45, *Code of Federal Regulations* (CFR), subpart A, sec 46.102i, revised June 18, 1991).

We focus on low-risk SBES research for two reasons. First, as your committee and our panel deliberated, it became clear that your group's primary focus is on high-risk research, regardless of domain. Second, many of the concerns raised about the protection of human participants in SBES research relate to low-risk research. We do not imply thereby that SBES research is always low risk, nor that biomedical research is always—or even often—high risk. Studies of IRB operations report that high percentages of all types of research—biomedical, social, and psychological—are deemed to be low risk (Gray, Cooke, and Tannenbaum, 1978:1096; Bell, Whiton, and Connelly, 1998:20).

The final report at the conclusion of our work (planned for fall 2002) will discuss in more detail issues of defining risk and other aspects of ethical review of SBES research for a broad audience of IRBs, researchers, and

---

[3]For example, 49 percent and 59 percent of SBES research reviewed by a sample of university IRBs involved interviews or self-administered questionnaires, respectively, compared with 23 percent and 21 percent, respectively, of biomedical research. In contrast, 27 percent, 25 percent, and 21 percent of biomedical research involved invasive procedures, double-blind experiments, and placebo administration, respectively, compared with 3 percent, 3 percent, and 1 percent, respectively, of SBES research (Bell, Whiton, and Connelly, 1998:Fig. 8).

relevant federal agencies. In that report we will address all three basic principles of protection for human research participants, as articulated in the Belmont Report (National Commission for the Protection of Human Subjects of Biomedical and Behavioral Research, 1979). These principles, which apply to all research domains and to low-risk as well as high-risk protocols, include respect for persons (respecting the choices of autonomous individuals and protecting those who are immature or incapacitated); beneficence (minimizing harm and maximizing benefits); and justice (fairness in the selection of research participants with regard to the distribution of the burdens and benefits of research).

This letter provides the panel's initial recommendations on four topics: protection of confidentiality of information obtained from human research participants; requirements for informed consent, particularly for advance written consent; procedures for determination of exempt research and for expedited review of low-risk research; and system-level issues, such as training of researchers and accreditation. The recommendations were developed from an SBES perspective. Some of them may pertain to biomedical research, but we do not make that judgement. Many of the recommendations have benefited from the work of other groups that are active in considering the protection of human participants in SBES research, such as the Behavioral and Social Science Working Group of the National Human Research Protections Advisory Committee[4] and the National Science Foundation's Social, Behavioral, and Economic Subcommittee for Human Subjects.[5]

Several recommendations call for the Office for Human Research Protections (OHRP) in the U.S. Department of Health and Human Services (DHHS) to provide guidance to IRBs, in recognition of the leadership role that OHRP is charged with playing in the federal system. OHRP, which was established in June 2000, has responsibilities that include not only monitoring the operations of IRBs that review DHHS-funded research, but also providing guidance on human research participant protection for the federal and non-federal sectors, developing educational programs, and exercising leadership for human participant protection for the U.S. government in cooperation with other federal agencies (67 *Federal Register*, 10217, March 6, 2002). The director of OHRP serves as the *ex officio* chair of the Human Subjects Research Subcommittee of the White House Office of Science and Technology Policy.[6]

---

[4]See http://www.asanet.org/public/humanresearch.
[5]For information, contact Stuart Plattner, NSF Human Subjects Research Officer, splattne@nsf.gov.
[6]See http://ohrp.osophs.dhhs.gov.

PROTECTING CONFIDENTIALITY

Ensuring that data collected under a pledge of confidentiality are protected from disclosure is a long-accepted requirement of research with human participants. Indeed, for much research using typical SBES methods, the major risk is that of inadvertent disclosure—either during collection, processing, or storage of the original data or through identification of participants in data files that are made available for secondary analysis.

Protecting against a breach of confidentiality is imperative when it could cause substantial harm to a research participant—for example, denial of health insurance or employment because of information supplied about a medical condition. Even if no or only minimal harm is likely, a confidentiality breach could undermine the credibility of researchers and needlessly reduce the willingness of people to participate in research.

Although there can never be a 100 percent guarantee that confidentiality will be maintained, state-of-the-art computer science and statistical methods can reduce to minimal levels the risk of inadvertent identification. OHRP can usefully provide guidance to IRBs by documenting and promulgating good practices for maintaining confidentiality at every stage of the research process and for informing research participants about the scope and limits of confidentiality protection that is offered them.

For some sensitive studies, such as those in which a participant may report illegal behavior, it is particularly important that researchers understand their responsibilities and limits with regard to confidentiality protection and that IRBs review carefully the proposed procedures for preventing disclosure. In some cases, it may be important to obtain a certificate of confidentiality to protect the data from subpoena in legal proceedings.[7]

Another class of studies for which confidentiality protection poses special problems comprises longitudinal panels in which participants are interviewed more than once over a period of time. Researchers must retain identifying information for individual participants to be able to locate them for subsequent interviews; also, panel data are typically richer in subject content than one-time, cross-sectional studies. Both of these features require careful consideration of procedures to minimize the risk of disclosure while not unnecessarily limiting the usefulness of the data for research.

Because the use of new methods of data collection and dissemination, such as the Internet, is increasing the amount of readily available data and the potential for linking data files, continued research and development of methods for confidentiality protection is needed. Also needed is continued

---

[7]Certificates of confidentiality for research on sensitive topics, regardless of funding source, can be obtained from the National Institutes of Health (see http://grants.nih.gov/grants/policy/coc/index.htm).

work on administrative arrangements (e.g., secure enclaves) that permit research access to data for which widespread public dissemination is deemed too risky (see National Research Council, 1993).

> **Recommendation 1: The Office for Human Research Protections and other relevant federal agencies, working with professional associations in the social, behavioral, and economic sciences, should document and promulgate good practices for using state-of-the-art computer science and statistical methods to protect the confidentiality of SBES data that are made available for secondary analysis. OHRP should also provide guidance on good practices for protecting confidentiality at every stage of the research process.**

> **Recommendation 2: When reviewing research protocols, IRBs should pay close attention to the adequacy of proposed plans to safeguard confidentiality in the collection, processing, analysis, dissemination, and storage of SBES data and request improvements as necessary. Because some research exposes participants to risks of harm if even their participation becomes known to others, IRBs should carefully review the adequacy of proposed procedures for preventing such disclosure.**

> **Recommendation 3: Federal funding agencies should sponsor research on procedures and techniques to protect the confidentiality of SBES data that are made available for research use.**

> **Recommendation 4: Public and private data archives that provide data sets on individuals (microdata) to SBES researchers for secondary analysis should keep abreast of disclosure risks and state-of-the-art mechanisms to control disclosures. They should regularly update control mechanisms to protect the data that they house and be able to certify to researchers that the data they provide for secondary use have been rendered acceptably anonymous.**

INFORMED CONSENT

Informed consent is fundamental to the ethical conduct of research with human participants. Current federal regulations include detailed requirements for the kinds of information to be conveyed in the informed consent process and the documentation of consent. The regulations also include provisions for waiving or modifying some or all of these requirements, such as written consent, under specified conditions (45 CFR, sec. 46.116, 117), many of which commonly apply to SBES research.

It appears, however, that some IRBs do not make appropriate use of the flexibility in the regulations. A rigid practice of requiring advance written consent for all research protocols, regardless of method, level of risk, and population studied, can hamper participation and yet not offer more protection to participants than other consent procedures. For example, federal statistical agencies have for decades obtained respondents' cooperation with voluntary mail, telephone, and in-person surveys by procedures other than signed documents obtained in advance. These procedures typically include a prescribed introductory statement by the interviewer about the purpose of the survey and informing the respondent that he or she may break off the interview at any time; they also include, when feasible, an advance letter about the survey. There is no evidence of adverse effects on respondents of such procedures. Indeed, there is evidence that respondents do not view signing a written consent form as protecting their interests.[8]

Other types of research for which written informed consent may not be feasible or appropriate include studies of populations that are not literate or that are unable or unwilling to sign a written consent form but would agree to participate through another consent process. In yet other cases, a signed consent form may be the only identifier of a participant and may thereby present a risk of disclosing his or her participation in a study that would otherwise not exist.

Most, if not all, of the issues surrounding informed consent have been raised by others,[9] and current federal regulations have tried to be sensitive to them. Thus, the Common Rule permits waiver of written consent under certain circumstances (45, CFR, sec. 46.117c). However, in practice, imple-

---

[8]For example, an IRB that reviews surveys conducted by the National Center for Health Statistics (NCHS) a few years ago required advance written consent for participation in the ongoing National Health Interview Survey, although no evidence existed that lack of advance written consent misled participants about the nature of the research in more than 30 years of conducting the survey, and a pilot test estimated that such a requirement would add significant costs to the data collection. From the results of the pilot test, the IRB agreed to a set of procedures, implemented nationwide starting in July 1999, whereby the respondent may sign at the beginning of the interview, after hearing some questions, or at the end of the interview. If the respondent is willing to participate, but does not want to sign, the interviewer may sign the consent form. Based on subsequent research with respondents indicating that they do not see signing a written consent form as offering them protection, NCHS is considering applying for a waiver of that requirement (personal communication, Jennifer Madans, NCHS).

[9]Complex issues, which we do not consider in this letter, surround informed consent procedures in studies of young children and other populations for whom permission must be sought from another party (e.g., a parent or guardian); also, in determining when it is necessary to seek consent from nonparticipating individuals about whom research participants are asked to supply information (e.g., when a survey respondent is asked for information on relatives).

mentation of effective informed consent procedures that accommodate varying situations has been difficult to attain, for complex reasons. One reason involves the organizational setting of most IRBs, which are usually nested within larger institutions faced with pressures to have verifiable evidence for informed consent. Consequently, IRBs may require signed consent forms for all research, even when other consent processes or a waiver of consent would be more appropriate, in order to obtain documentation that is easily archived and retrieved for defending the procedure.

> Recommendation 5: As provided by federal regulations, IRBs should consider a variety of procedures for obtaining informed consent and grant waivers of written consent when to do otherwise would inhibit useful SBES research with no appreciable added protection for the participants.

A related concern about written consent procedures (which may also apply to other forms of consent) is that they may not convey what research participants need to know to make an informed decision to participate in a research study and to understand that their participation is voluntary. Research has documented the difficulties of understanding the benefits, harms, and risks of harm of biomedical research as described in consent forms, which are often highly technical in nature (see, e.g., Davis et al., 1998; Goldstein et al., 1996; Taylor et al., 1998). We imagine that similar problems may affect consent processes in some kinds of SBES research as well. The National Institutes of Health recently announced a program to fund research on ethical issues in human studies, including research on informed consent procedures.[10] We commend this initiative and urge other funding agencies to sponsor studies of informed consent for different types of research and study populations.

> Recommendation 6: Federal funding agencies should sponsor research on procedures for obtaining and documenting informed consent that will facilitate comprehension of research benefits, harms, and risks of harm for different types of SBES research and populations studied.

EXEMPT RESEARCH AND EXPEDITED REVIEW

Federal regulations exempt some types of research involving human participants from IRB review, and some studies, although involving interaction with humans, do not meet the regulatory definition of "human subjects

---

[10]See http://grants1.nih.gov/grants/guide/pa-files/PA-02-103.html.

research" (see 45 CFR, sec. 46.101,102). For studies for which IRB review is appropriate, the regulations provide for expedited review of many types of low-risk studies by the IRB chair or other member(s) to whom the IRB delegates the approval function. (The current list of types of studies that may receive expedited review is in 63 *Federal Register,* 60364, November 9, 1998.) The IRB chair or designee determines whether a particular protocol is exempt or may be reviewed using the expedited procedure.

In response to tragic incidents in biomedical research and increased scrutiny of IRB operations, IRBs appear to be increasingly applying review procedures that are appropriate for high-risk research to studies that are low risk, thereby placing unnecessary burdens on researchers, IRBs, and, sometimes, human participants. A recent survey of IRBs found that one-half or fewer research protocols eligible for exemption are in fact exempted from review and that full IRBs convene to review anywhere from 15 to 83 percent of low-risk protocols that are eligible for expedited review (Bell, Whiton, and Connelly, 1998:Figs. 15, 16). Full board review for such projects imposes delays and adds needlessly to the person-hours required for the review process. For example, Bell, Whiton, and Connelly (1998:Fig. 33) found that 71 percent of expedited reviews are completed in less than 30 days (18% in less than a week), while only 49 percent of full board reviews are completed as expeditiously (and only 5% in less than a week).

Although IRBs are allowed to exceed federal requirements for review of protocols, we believe that the level of review should be commensurate with the level of risk. Given rising workloads for IRBs in terms of numbers and complexity of research protocols (e.g., more multisite projects), it behooves IRBs to concentrate scarce board member and researcher resources on high-risk projects. We believe that added guidance from OHRP could help IRBs make more appropriate choices of level of review for SBES research.

Examples of research that the panel believes should not be considered "human subjects research" include (1) organizational surveys seeking information only about the organization (e.g., number of employees at a business) and not about the individual respondent, and (2) secondary analyses of aggregate (tabular) data when the data are not provided at the individual level of analysis and information about individuals cannot be recovered from the tabulations.

Examples of research that the panel believes are clearly exempt from IRB review under current regulations include secondary analyses of public-use data for individuals (microdata) obtained from suppliers, such as federal statistical agencies and data archives, that regularly follow good practices to minimize the risk of identification of individuals (see recommendations 1 and 4 above). Analyses of microdata from such suppliers as the U.S. Census Bureau, which follows stringent disclosure review and protection procedures, should have blanket exemptions from review.

> **Recommendation 7: OHRP, working with professional associations in the social, behavioral, and economic sciences, should develop clear examples of common social, behavioral, and economic research designs, methods, and procedures that are not to be regarded as "human subjects research" or that are clearly exempt from review. OHRP should include these examples in guidance to IRBs to amplify the existing regulations.**

The current list of types of research that may be reviewed by an expedited procedure (so long as the research is low risk) includes many kinds of specific medical procedures, such as electrocardiograms. It also includes broad categories of SBES research, such as surveys, oral histories, and focus groups. We believe it is important to add *specific* SBES procedures to the list to encourage IRBs to use expedited review procedures for low-risk SBES research.

Examples of specific SBES procedures that could be added to the existing list for using the expedited review procedure are experiments that test responses to noninvasive auditory or visual stimuli of competent adult participants; experiments that study decision-making with competent adult participants; and surveys of competent adults that include standard demographic and socioeconomic questions and other questions (e.g., attitudes) for which there is no reasonable expectation of harm (e.g., from experience with the same or similar questions in other surveys).[11] The importance of providing specific examples is affirmed by evidence that IRBs are most likely to expedite the review of low-risk studies that use *specific* procedures that are currently in the approved list (e.g., studies that obtain nail and hair clippings or dental plaque), in contrast to studies that fall under general categories (e.g., drugs and medical devices) (see Bell, Whiton, and Connelly, 1998:Fig. 16).

> **Recommendation 8: OHRP, working with professional associations in the social, behavioral, and economic sciences, should amplify the existing list of categories of research that may be reviewed using the expedited review procedure. The next revision of this list should include greater specificity of the types of SBES research design and methods that are eligible for expedited review.**

---

[11]Federal regulations require extra protections for children, prisoners, pregnant women, and fetuses.

SYSTEM ISSUES

Data on IRB Operations

Several studies have been conducted over the past few decades on the operation of the IRB system—see, for example, Bell, Whiton, and Connelly (1998); U.S. General Accounting Office (1996); Sieber and Baluyot (1992); Cooke, Tannenbaum, and Gray (1978; see also Gray, Cooke, and Tannenbaum, 1978). It is difficult to compare the results of the different studies, and some are quite limited in sampling frame and sample size.

In order to have a richer set of data on IRB operations and to track the strengths and weaknesses of the IRB system over time, we believe there is a need for a continuing survey of IRBs, with a longitudinal component. Our recommendation pertains specifically to the need for a continuing survey of IRB characteristics and procedures with respect to SBES research. In our final report, we plan to analyze further the data from existing studies of IRBs and to provide details on the requirements for a useful data system.

> **Recommendation 9: OHRP and other relevant agencies, working with professional associations in the social, behavioral, and economic sciences, should develop an ongoing survey of IRB composition and practices, as an informational resource that can help assess strengths and weaknesses of the system for protecting human participants in SBES research. The design should permit analysis of review practices for SBES research by type of IRB (all fields, SBES fields only), representation of SBES expertise on IRBs, and related issues.**

Accreditation

One of the major tasks of the IOM committee is to recommend standards for accrediting human research protection programs. The committee's initial recommendations included that "[t]he first step is implementation of pilot programs to test standards, establish accreditation processes, and build confidence in accrediting organizations" (Institute of Medicine, 2001:53). We support the plan to evaluate accreditation standards through the use of pilot tests. We also agree with the committee that the accreditation process should accommodate organizations involved in research beyond the traditional academic health centers and Veterans Administration and with models other than clinical research, a position that has been adopted by the Association for the Accreditation of Human Research Protection Programs.[12] However, the pilot studies that are in progress (see Institute of

---

[12]For more information, see http://www.aahrpp.org/principles.htm.

Medicine, 2001) do not encompass SBES research. For this reason, we consider it premature to determine whether accreditation of IRBs would improve protection for human participants in SBES studies.

> **Recommendation 10: Pilot testing that is currently under way for a voluntary system for IRB accreditation should be expanded to include social, behavioral, and economic science research settings. Only when the program has been shown to be effective in such settings should proposals be developed for expanding accreditation to review of social, behavioral, and economic science research.**

Training

The success of the system for protection of human research participants in SBES research depends on the proactive ethical behavior of all of the relevant actors—principal investigators and other researchers and their professional associations, institutions of higher education and other research organizations and their IRBs, federal regulators and funding agencies. With respect to universities, we agree with the assertion by the Association of American Universities (2000:4) that senior managers "should state clearly to their entire campus communities the importance of conducting human subjects research in accordance with the highest standards of ethical conduct." But more than the top managers can and should provide leadership. Academic departments must incorporate ethical principles into the education they provide, and professional associations must regularly review and update their codes of professional ethics with regard to human research participant protection. Thorough, continuing training for researchers and IRB members is critical for the effective operation of the human research participant protection system and its continued improvement. For long-run success, the ethics of protection must be woven into the fabric of the research preparation of all scientists.

> **Recommendation 11: Academic institutions, working with scientific and professional associations in the social, behavioral, and economic sciences, should develop in-depth training curricula and materials that are customized for social, behavioral, and economic scientists regarding the ethical involvement of human research participants. OHRP should similarly develop for IRBs customized training materials that focus on review of SBES research.**

CONCLUSION

Our panel looks forward to developing a full agenda for research and practice to improve the operation of the IRB system for social, behavioral, and economic science research. Such a system should provide full protection for human research participants and, at the same time, promote a level of review commensurate with the level of risk to facilitate the conduct of high-quality, ethical research.

Sincerely yours,

Cora Marrett, *Chair*
Panel on IRBs, Surveys, and Social
Science Research

REFERENCES

American Association of University Professors (AAUP)
    2001 Protecting human beings: Institutional review boards and social science research. *Academe* 87(3):55-67.
Association of American Universities (AAU)
    2000 *Report on University Protections of Human Beings Who Are the Subjects of Research.* Report and recommendations from AAU's Task Force on Research Accountability. Washington, DC: Association of American Universities (June 28).
Bell, J., J. Whiton, and S. Connelly
    1998 *Evaluation of NIH Implementation of Section 491 of the Public Health Service Act, Mandating a Program of Protection for Research Subjects.* Report prepared under a National Institutes of Health contract, N01-OD-2-2109. Washington, DC: U.S. Department of Health and Human Services.
Cooke, R.A., A.S. Tannenbaum, and B.H. Gray
    1978 A survey of institutional review boards and research involving human subjects. Pp. 293-302 in *Report and Recommendations on Institutional Review Boards, Appendix.* National Commission for the Protection of Human Subjects of Biomedical and Behavioral Research. Washington, DC: U.S. Government Printing Office (September).
Davis, T.C., R.F. Holcombe, H.J. Berkel, S. Pramanik, and S.G. Divers
    1998 Informed consent for clinical trials: A comparative study of standard versus simplified forms. *Journal of the National Cancer Institute* 90(9):668-674.
Goldstein, A.O., P. Frasier, P. Curtis, A. Reid, and N.E. Kreher
    1996 Consent form readability in university-sponsored research. *Journal of Family Practice* 42(6):606-611.
Gray, B.H., R.A. Cooke, and A.S. Tannenbaum
    1978 Research involving human subjects. *Science* 201(4361):1094-1101.
Institute of Medicine (IOM)
    2001 *Preserving Public Trust: Accreditation and Human Research Participant Protection Programs.* Committee on Assessing the System for Protecting Human Research Subjects, Board on Health Sciences Policy. Washington, DC: National Academy Press.
Keiger, D., and S. De Pasquale
    2002 Trials & tribulation. *The Johns Hopkins Magazine* 54(1):28-41.

National Commission for the Protection of Human Subjects of Biomedical and Behavioral
Research
    1979 *The Belmont Report: Ethical Principles and Guidelines for the Protection of
          Human Subjects of Research.* Washington, DC: U.S. Government Printing Office.
          Available: http://ohrp.osophs.dhhs.gov/humansubjects/guidance/45cfr46.htm.
National Research Council (NRC)
    1993 *Private Lives and Public Policies: Confidentiality and Accessibility of Govern-
          ment Statistics.* Panel on Confidentiality and Data Access. G.T. Duncan, T.B.
          Jabine, and V.A. de Wolf, eds. Committee on National Statistics and Social Sci-
          ence Research Council. Washington, DC: National Academy Press.
Sieber, J. E., and R.M. Baluyot
    1992 A survey of IRB concerns about social and behavioral research. *IRB: A Review of
          Human Subjects Research* 14(2):9-10.
Stout, D.
    1999 U.S., citing safety, suspends human research aid at Duke. *The New York Times,*
          May 12.
Taylor, K.M., A. Bejak, and R.H.S. Fraser
    1998 Informed consent for clinical trials: Is simpler better? *Journal of the National
          Cancer Institute* 90(9):644-645.
U.S. Department of Health and Human Services (DHHS)
    1998 *Institutional Review Boards: A Time for Reform.* Office of the Inspector General
          Publication No. OEI-01-97-00193. Washington, DC: U.S. Department of Health
          and Human Services. Available: http://www.dhhs.gov/progorg/oei/reports/
          a275.pdf.
U.S. General Accounting Office (GAO)
    1996 Scientific Research: Continued Vigilance Critical to Protecting Human Subjects.
          GAO/HEHS-96-72. Washington, DC: GAO.

Appendix C

Clarifying Protocol Accountability

Although research organizations and research sponsors will include a variety of offices and activities in their formal Human Research Participant Protection Programs (HRPPP, "program," or "protection program"), the functional units that work together to review and oversee a particular proposal are the system elements of greatest significance to individual participant protection. In this way, the HRPPP acts as a "virtual" entity, with the relevant actors coming together on a protocol-by-protocol basis, depending on the methodology utilized, the risks posed, the research setting and objectives (e.g., a drug study carried out through individual physicians' offices), and participant concerns, such as the involvement of vulnerable populations. A basic template that defines accountability throughout the life cycle of a research protocol can serve as a useful tool to facilitate the tracking of human research participant protection in the context of the protocol-specific program unit. Such a template can be adapted to suit various research paradigms and institutional needs and may be most useful as an electronic, Web-based application that guides investigators preparing Research Ethics Review Board[1] (Research ERB) submis-

---

[1]Recommendation 3.1 calls for "Institutional Review Boards" (IRBs) to be named and referred to within research organizations by a title reflective of their focus on the ethics underlying participant protection activities. The committee has adopted the term "Research Ethics Review Board" (Research ERB) for this purpose. Therefore, Research ERB refers herein to the committee's idealized protection program, and IRB to descriptions of the current system.

sions. Undoubtedly, within the confines of academic settings there are likely to be many instances for which the assignment of responsibilities would remain constant, and template forms could be standardized accordingly.

An example of one such template is included in this appendix to illustrate the committee's conception of such a document. This example is oriented toward clinical trials, and it presents several case scenarios to demonstrate the variety of partnerships that are possible within this one research domain. Because it is not possible to include all possible collaborative arrangements among clinical investigators, private industry, and federal or private funding sources, these scenarios attempt to embrace a range of illustrative potential collaborative relationships.

When an HRPPP is assembled to review and monitor any given protocol, accountability for the required participant protection functions must be clear. An individual representing the research organization must meet with the Principal Investigator (PI) or sponsor to identify all organizations potentially participating in study conduct that may play a role in the protection of research participants. Responsibilities for tasks ranging from protocol review to ongoing monitoring should be assigned before study initiation, and for every project conducted, an official with overall responsibility for the participant protection program should be identified. The template presented in this appendix is provided as an example of an internal tool that can be utilized by a program in establishing a hierarchy of accountability. Research organizations may or may not choose to make such documents available for public review (i.e., by participants already enrolled or considering enrollment in a study), although the document may also serve as a useful communication tool for external as well as internal purposes.

It should be emphasized that these templates are not intended to become an example of documentation without function. The potential utility of this tool lies in its explicit delineation of responsibilities in a consistent format that is accessible to all elements within a particular HRPPP. It also provides an instrument that may be useful to safety monitoring, auditing, and even HRPPP accreditation activities.

CASE SCENARIO #1 – A SINGLE-SITE, INVESTIGATOR-INITIATED, FEDERALLY FUNDED STUDY

A. Introduction

A clinical investigator on the faculty of the Medical University of America (MUA—the sample academic institution in this case scenario) receives funding from a federal agency (e.g., the National Institutes of Health [NIH]) to conduct a single-site study (at MUA) evaluating a new indication for an approved therapeutic agent. The pharmaceutical company that produces the agent has agreed to provide the oral drug and placebo free of charge. The investigator contacts the MUA HRPPP to develop a research participant protection accountability plan, although the official with overall ultimate responsibility for human protection of his protocol is the President of MUA. (The president's authority is likely to have been delegated to a subordinate official such as the dean for research).

B. Protocol Development

The protocol was designed by the PI and his collaborators, and because the drug is not approved for this indication, the PI is the holder of the investigational new drug application (IND). The pharmaceutical company is responsible for product manufacturing, packaging, labeling, and distribution; the PI, however, will be responsible for storage, usage, and disposal at his site, and he ensures that all study procedures are standardized with well-established protocols and that all co-investigators and research staff are properly credentialed and trained. The PI has found an accredited laboratory at MUA to perform the laboratory assays. The director of the laboratory has provided the PI with documentation that the laboratory is approved according to the Clinical Laboratory Improvement Act and Amendment and that it has normative values available.

C. Protocol Review Process

The study receives scientific review both from NIH and the General Clinical Research Center (GCRC) Advisory Committee (GAC). Conflict of interest review is performed by the MUA's Conflict of Interest Committee, if necessary, which assures that the investigator does not have a significant financial interest in the pharmaceutical company and that he or she is not receiving financial remuneration. An external oversight committee established by MUA carries out a similar review examining potential institutional conflicts of interest. The ethical research review is performed by the MUA's Research ERB. The protocol is also reviewed by MUA's Radiation Safety Committee because patients will undergo Magnetic Resonance Imaging procedures. The PI establishes a data and safety monitoring plan.

D. Ongoing Monitoring

Because the study involves young children, the Research ERB requests consent monitoring. Protocol amendments are submitted to MUA's Research ERB. The PI requests that NIH establish a Data and Safety Monitoring Board/Data Monitoring Committee (DSMB/DMC) for review of the protocol. The PI is responsible for all adverse event (AE) reporting with timely submission of reports to NIH, the Research ERB, and the Food and Drug Administration (FDA), based upon FDA guidelines. Safety monitoring for the study is provided by the GCRC through its research subject advocate (RSA) program. The DSMB/DMC has two scheduled interim reports that are forwarded to the Research ERB. Onsite monitoring is performed by MUA's GCRC compliance officer, who limits the review to key outcomes.

E. Other Protection Considerations

Security, privacy, and confidentiality of the data are the responsibility of the PI, who will have control of the data and be responsible for preparation of all presentations and manuscripts. He will also inform the participants of the results of the study.

Both NIH and the pharmaceutical company are providing financial support for the study. NIH funding will cover patient care and travel costs as well as the cost of the investigators and their research staff to conduct the trial; the company will provide the drug and placebo free of charge. The company also is providing medical coverage for unanticipated AEs related to study conduct (indemnification). No inducements are being provided beyond the cost of conducting the study.

Training of the investigators and personnel is the responsibility of MUA.

CASE SCENARIO #2 – A MULTISITE DRUG STUDY INVOLVING A CONTRACT RESEARCH ORGANIZATION

A. Introduction

A pharmaceutical company is sponsoring a trial to evaluate the safety and efficacy of a new therapeutic agent for which it plans to submit a new drug application to FDA. This is a large, multicenter Phase 3 trial involving 100 sites throughout the United States. The investigators at all of these sites are practicing physicians in community clinics or hospitals. The pharmaceutical company has contracted with a large contract research organization (CRO), as permitted under 21 CFR 312.52: "Transfer of Obligations to a Contract Research Organization." The duties of the CRO versus the sponsor have been delineated in the development of this contract.

The PI is a well-regarded physician with substantial expertise in caring for patients who have the medical condition of interest (e.g., coronary artery disease, rheumatoid arthritis) and who will potentially benefit from the proposed therapeutic intervention. She has a clinical faculty position with an academic institution, and her practice is 90 percent community based. She has been a consultant for the pharmaceutical company for many years, but is currently receiving no financial support from the company and has no equity interest in it. The official with daily responsibility for the protection program is the president/Chief Executive Officer (CEO) of the CRO based upon the terms of the contract. The committee does not imply in this instance that the contractual delegation of direct HRPPP authority relieves the CEO of the pharmaceutical sponsor from her overall responsibility for assuring that participant protections are in place for any study sponsored or conducted by the company.

B. Protocol Development

A research team within the pharmaceutical company develops the protocol. The PI reviewed the protocol, but had limited input. The pharmaceutical company holds the IND and is responsible for the manufacturing of the drug. Packaging, labeling, and distribution will be the responsibility of the CRO, which will also review storage, usage, and disposal at the clinical sites with the investigators. However, the investigators are ultimately responsible for the integrity of the product at the clinical site. The pharmaceutical company is also responsible for developing standardized operating procedures for all procedures conducted during the study and for ensuring, along with the CRO, that the individuals are credentialed or trained and have proper documentation to that effect. The pharmaceutical company will assure that all laboratory assays have been validated and that they are being conducted at accredited laboratories. The PI at each site will provide appropriate laboratory documentation.

C. Protocol Review Process

The sponsor has contracted with an independent Research ERB to assume responsibility for the review process and ongoing safety monitoring. The pharmaceutical company initially conducts the scientific review, and subsequently, the independent Research ERB establishes an ad hoc scientific review board. Financial conflict of interest review of the investigators and their institutions is provided by the Conflict of Interest Office of the CRO, which requests financial disclosure statements from all investigators and relevant research organizations (i.e., the clinic through which an investigator will conduct the research). Potential CRO conflicts will be assessed by an independent entity, and the determination will be forwarded to the Research ERB. The ethical review, including assurance of informed consent, is conducted by the independent Research ERB. Because it is a multicenter study, this Research ERB will conduct the initial review process and will modify the disclosure documents to be consistent with each of the individual site's institutional (hospital, clinic) guidelines. Each investigator must meet with his or her own institutional Research ERBs to ascertain whether he or she will accept the independent Research ERB review or will also conduct a subsequent review. Because the study involves computed tomography imaging, a separate Radiation Safety Committee is established by the independent Research ERB.

D. Ongoing Monitoring

Plans for ongoing monitoring during the study conduct are the responsibility of the sponsor, although it has contracted much of the day-to-day responsibilities to both the independent Research ERB and the CRO. This study does not involve pediatric or other vulnerable patients, and no consent monitoring is recommended by the independent Research ERB. All protocol amendments will be submitted to the independent Research ERB for review. If community Research ERBs are also involved, the CRO will distribute the protocol amendments to the PIs, who are responsible for submitting them to their community Research ERBs.

A DSMB/DMC is established by the sponsor specifically for this trial. The sponsor has chosen a group of scientists knowledgeable in the field who are not investigators in the study or employees of the company. A biostatistician, pharmacologist, and participant/public representative independent of the company also are chosen. These individuals submit financial disclosure statements to the independent Research ERBs to ensure that there are no financial conflicts of interest. Two interim safety reviews are planned during the study. AE reporting is the responsibility of the CRO. The PIs are responsible for reporting AEs at their clinical sites to the CRO, which forwards the AE reports to the sponsor, which will in turn report them to FDA. All serious AE (SAE) reports are sent to the independent Research ERB, and the DSMB/DMC will receive summary reports of the SAEs. Ideally, the DSMB/DMC will submit its interim review report to the Research ERBs, although this is not mandated. Onsite monitoring for safety and compliance as well as data integrity will be performed on all sites and on all data by the CRO.

E. Other Protection Considerations

Data management, including security, privacy, and confidentiality as well as electronic data collection, transfer, and maintenance are the responsibility of the CRO. The PIs will control the data at their sites until two years after the publication of the results. The interpretation and dissemination of study results are the responsibility of the sponsor. The PI may or may not be the first author on the paper. All financial support, including indemnification, is the responsibility of the sponsor, as is the training of all investigators and key research staff. The sponsor is also responsible for selecting the investigators and ensuring that they understand their responsibilities. The sponsor may contract with the CRO to help in these efforts.

CASE SCENARIO #3 – A MULTISITE, INVESTIGATOR-INITIATED, FEDERALLY FUNDED STUDY

A. Introduction

The third case scenario is an NIH-supported multicenter trial awarded to a PI based at an academic institution (again, known as MUA). The study involves gene transfer studies on a rare genetic disorder. The therapeutic vector was developed by a scientist at MUA who is not the PI. A small biotechnology company was formed to develop the vector. The scientist has equity in the company and has fully disclosed this to MUA, which does not have any financial interest in the company. The company is receiving a small business grant from NIH. All participating institutions have National Center for Research Resources-funded GCRCs. The official with overall responsibility for the HRPPP is the President of MUA (in this case, MUA is the research organization, because it has assumed responsibility for conducting the study by virtue of the investigator's employment).

B. Protocol Development

The PI and his collaborators developed the study design. The biotechnology company holds the IND and is responsible for manufacturing the vector. The company has contracted, as permitted under 21 CFR 312-52, with a CRO for the packaging, labeling, and distribution of the vector. The storage, usage, and disposal at the site are the responsibility of the investigators. The complex procedures for vector administration have been standardized by the PI, who is responsible for training the other investigators. Laboratory assays were established by the biotechnology company, which performed these assays in its own accredited laboratory following Good Laboratory Practice.

C. Protocol Review Process

Scientific review of the study was conducted by NIH and the GAC at each participating academic institution. Extensive conflict of interest review was undertaken by the Conflict of Interest Office at each academic institution to assure that neither the investigators nor the institution had financial or other conflicts.[2] The inventor scientist's financial interest has been disclosed to the participants in the course of the informed consent process. This individual is not involved in the clinical trial. The ethical review was initially conducted by the Research ERB of the PI's institution. Most other participating institutions followed the recommendations of the primary Research ERB, although some institutions conducted their own reviews

The investigator submitted the proposal to the Recombinant DNA Advisory Committee (RAC) of NIH as well as the Recombinant DNA Usage Committees at each institution. A radiation safety review was conducted at each institution, and MUA's technology transfer office reviewed the intellectual property issues between the inventor scientist and the biotechnology company.

D. Ongoing Monitoring

A plan for ongoing safety monitoring during the study is prepared by the PI and is reviewed and approved by both the primary Research ERB and the GAC at each participating site. The Research ERB at the PI's site and the RAC mandate that monitoring of consent be performed at all sites. This monitoring is provided by the GCRC RSA at each site. All protocol amendments have been reviewed by the PI's institutional Research ERB. A DSMB/DMC is established through NIH, and three interim safety reviews are proposed. AE reporting is the responsibility of the investigators at each site, who submit AE reports to the biotechnology company, which in turn submits them to FDA. The investigators also submit AE reports to their respective Research ERBs and GCRCs. The PI submits the SAEs to NIH. The biotechnology company contracts with a CRO for onsite monitoring of all sites and all data.

E. Other Protection Considerations

The CRO is contracted to perform data management services and is responsible for security, privacy, and confidentiality, as well as electronic data transfer and maintenance. The final data are submitted to the PI and to the biotechnology company. The PI and the company are jointly responsible for interpreting and disseminating study results and for informing the research participants of results.

Financial support for the trial was provided by both NIH and the company. NIH paid for patient care costs and travel, as well as all clinical trial procedures and also supported all safety monitoring and data manage-

---

[2]Institutional interests were assessed by an independent mechanism and the summary report forwarded to the Conflict of Interest Office for communication to the Research ERB.

ment expenses. The biotechnology company supported all vector production, laboratory assays, and indemnification of sites. The training of the investigators was the responsibility of each institution. Selection of investigators was the responsibility of the PI, who also conducted the initial training of the other investigators.

Federal review (e.g.,
Recombinant DNA
Advisory Committee)   Y / N   _____
Biosafety   Y / N   _____
Radiation safety   Y / N   _____
Intellectual property   Y / N   _____
Grants and Contracts   Y / N   _____
Other   Y / N   _____

RECRUITMENT AND ENROLLMENT

Applicable? If yes, please identify responsible party.

1. Informed Consent Process: Y / N   _____
   Consent from   Y / N   _____

2. Inclusion/Exclusion Criteria: Y / N   _____
   Please check appropriate box:
       Vulnerable population   ❏
       Normal (healthy) volunteer   ❏

ONGOING MONITORING DURING STUDY CONDUCT

Applicable? If yes, please identify responsible party.

1. Data Safety Monitoring Plan: Y / N   _____
   Data Safety Monitoring Board   Y / N   _____
       Are interim reviews
       planned?   Y / N   _____
       Stopping authority?   Y / N   _____
   Consent monitoring   Y / N   _____

2. Approval of Protocol
   Amendments: Y / N   _____
       Revisions to informed consent
       process and disclosure
       document   Y / N   _____

3. Reporting of Adverse Events: Y / N   _____
   Training of investigators/research staff
   in identification of adverse events   _____
   Adverse event reporting
      Research ERB(s)   _____
      Sponsor   _____
      FDA   _____
      Other agencies   _____

4. Reporting of Protocol Violations
   (e.g., ineligible patients enrolled):   _____

5. Onsite Monitoring for
   Safety and Compliance: Y / N   _____
   Please check appropriate box:
      All sites, all data?   ❑
      Limited review of key outcomes?   ❑
      For cause only?   ❑

DATA MANAGEMENT AND ANALYSES/
DISSEMINATION OF STUDY REPORTS

Please identify responsible party.

1. Who controls access to data?   _____

2. Security, Privacy, Confidentiality
   of Data Collected   _____

3. Electronic Data Collection, Transfer, and Maintenance: Y / N
      Compliance with FDA and HIPAA regulations
      for security, privacy, and confidentiality   _____

4. Interpretation and Dissemination of Study Results: _____

5. Informing Study Participants of Results: _____

TRAINING OF INVESTIGATORS AND HRPPP PERSONNEL

Please identify responsible party.

1. Training of Investigators and
    Key Research Staff in the Ethical
    Conduct of Human Research: _____

2. Training of HRPPP Personnel
    in the Ethical Conduct of
    Human Research: _____

SIGNATURES

I have reviewed this Accountability Template and attest that the correct individuals are identified in each category.

Signed,

HRPPP Official   Principal Investigator:
(Head of research organization
or sponsors, as applicable):

_____   _____
signature   *signature*

_____   _____
printed name   *printed name*

_____   _____
date   *date*

Appendix D

Committee Biographies

Daniel D. Federman, M.D., Chair, is senior dean for alumni relations and clinical teaching and the Carl W. Walter Distinguished Professor of Medicine and Medical Education at Harvard Medical School. He graduated from Harvard College and Harvard Medical School and completed his internship and residency at Massachusetts General Hospital. Dr. Federman conducted research and trained in endocrinology at the National Institutes of Health, the University College Hospital Medical School in London, and Massachusetts General Hospital, where he served as a physician, chief of the Endocrine Unit, and associate chief of medical services. During his 4-year tenure at Stanford University Medical School, he was physician-in-chief, the Arthur F. Bloomfield Professor of Medicine, and chair of the Department of Medicine. In 1977, Dr. Federman returned to Harvard Medical School, where he has held the posts of dean for students and alumni, dean for medical education, and professor of medicine. He has served as chair of the Board of Internal Medicine and president of the American College of Physicians. He is a member of the Institute of Medicine and served on the Committee on Understanding the Biology of Sex and Gender Differences. In 2001, Dr. Federman received the Abraham Flexner Award of the Association of American Medical Colleges.

Daniel L. Azarnoff, M.D., is president of D. L. Azarnoff Associates and senior vice president of Clinical and Regulatory Affairs of Cellegy Pharmaceuticals. He has more than 20 years of academic experience in research and clinical medicine. For 8 years Dr. Azarnoff served as president of

research and development for the Searle Pharmaceutical Company, and for
the past 14 years he has served as a consultant in drug development. Before
joining Searle he was Distinguished Professor of Medicine and Pharmacology and director of the Clinical Pharmacology Toxicology Center at the
University of Kansas Medical Center, a position he held for 16 years. He
has published more than 175 articles in scientific and medical journals. Dr.
Azarnoff is a member of the Institute of Medicine and a fellow of the
American Association of Pharmaceutical Scientists, the New York Academy of Sciences, and the American College of Physicians and is chair-elect
of the Pharmaceutical Section of the American Association for the Advancement of Science. He maintains a teaching appointment at the schools
of medicine of the University of Kansas and Stanford University. Dr.
Azarnoff has been on the editorial boards of several journals and on committees of the U.S. Food and Drug Administration, World Health Organization, American Medical Association, National Academy of Sciences, Institute of Medicine, and National Institutes of Health, advising them on
drugs and drug development.

Tom L. Beauchamp, Ph.D., is professor of philosophy and senior research
scholar at the Kennedy Institute of Ethics. He was born in Austin, Texas.
He received graduate degrees from Yale University and the Johns Hopkins
University, where he received a Ph.D. in 1970. He then joined the faculty of
the Philosophy Department at Georgetown University and in the mid-1970s
accepted a joint appointment at the Kennedy Institute of Ethics. In 1976, he
joined the staff of the National Commission for the Protection of Human
Subjects of Biomedical and Behavioral Research, where he drafted the bulk
of *The Belmont Report* (1978). Dr. Beauchamp's research interests are in
Hume and the history of modern philosophy and practical ethics, especially
biomedical ethics and business ethics. Publications include the following
coauthored works: *Hume and the Problem of Causation* (Oxford University Press, 1981), *Principles of Biomedical Ethics* (Oxford University Press,
1979; 4th ed., 1994), *A History and Theory of Informed Consent* (Oxford
University Press, 1986), and *Philosophical Ethics* (McGraw-Hill, 1982;
2nd ed., 1991). Publications also include a number of edited and coedited
anthologies and more than 100 scholarly articles in journals and books. Dr.
Beauchamp is the General Editor—with David Fate Norton and M. A.
Stewart—of *The Critical Edition of the Works of David Hume*, Clarendon
Press, Oxford University Press. He is also the editor of an electronic edition
called HUMETEXT (coeditor, David Fate Norton), a complete electronic
edition of Hume's philosophical, political, and literary works.

Timothy Stoltzfus Jost, J.D., holds the Robert L. Willett Family Professor-
ship at the Washington and Lee University School of Law. Prior to coming

to Washington and Lee in 2001, Professor Jost taught at the Ohio State University for twenty years in the Colleges of Law and of Medicine and Public Health. He is the author of a book on comparative health law and a coauthor of casebooks in health law and in property law and has published a number of articles concerning health care regulation and comparative health law. Professor Jost has served as a consultant to the Institute of Medicine, the Administrative Conference of the United States, and the American Bar Association's Commission of Legal Problems of the Elderly and was a member of the State of Ohio Medical Board. A recipient of a Western European Regional Research Fulbright Grant, Professor Jost spent the winter and spring of 1989 at the Oxford University Centre for Socio-Legal Studies. He was also a guest professor at the University of Goettingen in Germany on a Fulbright grant in 1996–1997. In 2000, Professor Jost received the Jay Healey Distinguished Health Law Teacher Award from the American Society of Law, Medicine, and Ethics. He earned a B.A. in history at the University of California, Santa Cruz, and a J.D. from the University of Chicago.

Patricia A. King, J.D., is the Carmack Waterhouse Professor of Law, Medicine, Ethics and Public Policy at Georgetown University Law Center. She is also an adjunct professor in the Department of Health Policy and Management, School of Hygiene and Public Health, Johns Hopkins University, and chair of the board of trustees of Wheaton College. She is the coauthor of *Cases and Materials on Law, Science, and Medicine* and an area editor of the *Encyclopedia of Bioethics* (MacMillan Publishing Company). A member of the Institute of Medicine and the American Law Institute, she is also a fellow of the Hastings Center. She has served on numerous committees of the Institute of Medicine. Her work in the field of bioethics has included service as cochair for policy of the Embryo Research Panel, National Institutes of Health; the U.S. Department of Health, Education, and Welfare, Recombinant DNA Advisory Committee; the President's Commission for the Study of Ethical Problems in Medicine and Biomedical and Behavioral Research; the National Commission for the Protection of Human Subjects of Biomedical and Behavioral Research; and the Ethics, Legal and Social Issues Working Group of the Human Genome Project. She is also a member of the boards of the Henry J. Kaiser Family Foundation, the National Partnership for Women and Families, and the Hospice Foundation. Before joining Georgetown University, she was the deputy director of the Office of Civil Rights at the U.S. Department of Health, Education, and Welfare and special assistant to the chair of the Equal Employment Opportunity Commission. She also served as a deputy assistant attorney general in the Civil Division of the U.S. Department of Justice. Ms. King received a B.A. from Wheaton College and a J.D. from Harvard Law School.

Roderick J. A. Little, Ph.D., is the Richard D. Remington Collegiate Professor of Biostatistics at the School of Public Health, University of Michigan. He has also been a professor in the Department of Biomathematics at the University of California, Los Angeles, School of Medicine and a scientific associate for the World Fertility Survey. Little has been an American Statistical Association/U.S. Bureau of the Census/National Science Foundation research fellow and has held faculty positions at the George Washington University and the University of Chicago. He is a fellow of the American Statistical Association and an elected member of the International Statistical Institute. He received a Ph.D. in statistics from London University's Imperial College. He is currently a member of the National Research Council's Committee on National Statistics. He has expertise in the areas of survey sampling and statistical analysis of incomplete data and has broad experience with applications of statistics to demography, the social sciences, and biomedical research.

James McNulty serves on the board and the Executive Committee of the National Alliance for the Mentally Ill (NAMI), Rhode Island, as well as the Mental Health Consumer Advocates of Rhode Island, a statewide organization for mental health consumers. Having experienced the full impact of mental illness personally, he has been active in involving patient and family advocates in all aspects of treatment of mental illness. Mr. McNulty is President of the Board of Directors of NAMI National and also serves as president of the Manic Depressive & Depressive Association of Rhode Island. He served on the Protection and Advocacy Program for Persons with Mental Illness advisory committee for Rhode Island, as well as the board of the Rhode Island Protection Advocacy Services Agency. For several years, Mr. McNulty served on the Institutional Review Board of Butler Hospital, a freestanding psychiatric teaching hospital affiliated with the Brown University School of Medicine. He began his service with the Human Subjects Research Council Workgroup of the National Advisory Mental Health Council in 1999. He is a member of the Executive Committee of the Clinical Antipsychotic Trials of Intervention Effectiveness Project, a National Institute of Mental Health-funded multisite research protocol evaluating the efficacy of atypical antipsychotics in schizophrenia and Alzheimer's disease. Mr. McNulty also serves on the Governor's Council on Mental Health in Rhode Island and the National Advisory Mental Health Council.

Anne C. Petersen, Ph.D., has been senior vice president for programs at the W. K. Kellogg Foundation since 1996. Dr. Petersen was deputy director and chief operating officer of the National Science Foundation from 1994 to 1996, the first woman in the agency's 45-year history to serve in that position. She served as the vice president for research, as well as dean of the Graduate School, at the University of Minnesota. Dr. Petersen has authored many books and articles on adolescence, gender, and research methods and is a fellow of the American Association for the Advancement of Science, the American Psychological Association, the Institute of Medicine, and is on the Executive Committee of the International Society for the Study of Behavioral Development, among other societies. In addition, she was a member of the Board of Trustees of the National Institute of Statistical Sciences, among other boards and councils. She holds a bachelor's degree in mathematics; a master's degree in statistics; and a doctorate in measurement, evaluation, and statistical analysis, all from the University of Chicago.

Bonnie W. Ramsey, M.D., is director of the Pediatric General Clinical Research Center and Cystic Fibrosis Research Center at Children's Hospital and Regional Medical Center in Seattle. She is a professor in the Department of Pediatrics and program director, Core Center for Gene Therapy, University of Washington School of Medicine. She also is the director of the Cystic Fibrosis Foundation's newly formed Therapeutics Development Network Coordinating Center. Dr. Ramsey is an active member of several national professional societies including the American Thoracic Society and the American Academy of Pediatrics, serves on the Board of Trustees of the Cystic Fibrosis Foundation, and is chair of the Medical Advisory Committee for the National Cystic Fibrosis Foundation. She also serves as an ad hoc reviewer for the *New England Journal of Medicine, Journal of Pediatrics, Human Gene Therapy, Pediatric Pulmonology*, and *American Journal of Respiratory and Critical Care Medicine*. Dr. Ramsey has served on several government agency advisory panels including the Pulmonary Advisory Board, U.S. Food and Drug Administration, and advisory review groups for the National Heart, Lung, Blood Institute, National Institute of Diabetes and Digestive and Kidney Diseases, and National Center for Research Resources. Dr. Ramsey earned an undergraduate degree from Stanford University and a medical degree from Harvard Medical School.

Lydia Villa-Komaroff, Ph.D., is professor of neurology and vice president for research at Northwestern University, where she is responsible for policy formulation, strategy design, and operational oversight of the research infrastructure. She received an A.B. in biology from Goucher College and a Ph.D. in cell biology from the Massachusetts Institute of Technology. During her research career, she gained international recognition as a molecular biologist and was a key member of the team that first demonstrated that bacterial cells could produce insulin. Dr. Villa-Komaroff was an associate professor of neurology at Harvard Medical School and Children's Hospital and associate director of the Division of Neuroscience at Children's Hospital in Boston. She has published more than 60 articles and reviews and has served on a number of review committees for the National Institutes of Health. She was a member of the Advisory Committee for the Biology Directorate of the National Science Foundation (chair from 1997 to 1998), was a member of the congressionally mandated National Science Foundation Committee on Equal Opportunity in Science and Engineering, and was an invited participant in the Forum on Science in the National Interest sponsored by the White House Office of Science and Technology Policy. She is currently a member of the National Advisory Neurological Disorders and Stroke Council and the Board of Directors of the American Association for the Advancement of Science. She is a founding member of the Society for the Advancement of Chicanos and Native Americans in Science and has served as a board member and vice president.

Frances M. Visco, J.D., has served as president of the National Breast Cancer Coalition (NBCC), an organization dedicated to eradicating breast cancer through action and advocacy, since its inception in 1991. NBCC is a coalition of 600 organizations and 60,000 individuals. Ms. Visco is a three-term member of the President's Cancer Panel, past chair of the National Action Plan on Breast Cancer and member of the National Cancer Policy Board, and immediate past chair of the Integration Panel of the U.S. Department of Defense Peer-Reviewed Breast Cancer Research Program. After her own successful battle with breast cancer, she began her crusade as a breast cancer activist with the Linda Creed Breast Cancer Foundation. She continues to serve on the board of that foundation and is active in many of its programs. Until April 1995, Ms. Visco was a commercial litigator and partner at the law firm of Cohen, Shapiro, Polisher, Shiekman & Cohen in Philadelphia. Ms. Visco graduated from St. Joseph's University and Villanova Law School.

EXPERT ADVISERS

Kay Dickersin, Ph.D., is associate professor, Department of Community Health, Brown University School of Medicine, and is codirector of the New England Cochrane Center within the Cochrane Collaboration, which aims to facilitate systematic reviews of randomized controlled trials across all areas of health care. Her primary academic interests are evidence-based medicine, clinical trial design, and meta-analysis. Dr. Dickersin directs the coordinating center for two federally funded, multicenter randomized trials: the Ischemic Optic Neuropathy Decompression Trial and the Surgical Treatments Outcomes Project for Dysfunctional Uterine Bleeding, and has served on a number of national and international data and safety monitoring boards. She is on the Board of Directors for the Society for Clinical

Trials (1997-2000) and has served on the Institutional Review Board at the Johns Hopkins School of Hygiene and Public Health. From 1994 to 2000 she served on the National Cancer Advisory Board. She received a B.A. and an M.A. in zoology at the University of California, Berkeley, and earned a Ph.D. in epidemiology at the Johns Hopkins University.

Alberto Grignolo, Ph.D., is Senior Vice President and General Manager of Worldwide Regulatory Affairs at PAREXEL International Corporation, a Contract Research Organization headquartered in the United States, with offices in 35 countries. He has held this position for nearly a decade and is responsible for PAREXEL's regulatory services, including worldwide registration strategies and submissions, regulatory compliance and clinical quality assurance for pharmaceuticals, biologicals and medical devices. He consults with clients in the areas of drug development strategy, regulatory negotiation and best regulatory practices. Prior to joining PAREXEL, Dr. Grignolo served as President of FIDIA Pharmaceutical Corporation and held regulatory positions at SmithKline & French Laboratories. Having completed his undergraduate degree at Duke University, he earned a doctorate in Experimental Psychology from the University of North Carolina and conducted postdoctoral research in neuropharmacology at Duke University Medical Center. He is a past Chairman of the Board of the Regulatory Affairs Professionals Society (RAPS), has been involved in the advancement of the regulatory profession for most of his career, and was the recipient of the 1995 Richard E. Greco Professional of the Year Award from RAPS. Dr. Grignolo is currently an elected member of the Board of Directors of the Drug Information Association (DIA). He is the Chair of the Regulatory Track of the 2001 and 2002 DIA Annual Meetings, and serves on the Steering Committee of the Americas, the Regulatory Special Interest Area Committee, the Marketing Committee and the Regulatory Training Faculty. A native European who has also lived in Latin America, Dr. Grignolo is a regular speaker, instructor and participant at international conferences, seminars and workshops on Regulatory Affairs and Good Clinical Practice.

Mary Faith Marshall, Ph.D., B.S.N., is professor of medicine and bioethics at Kansas University Medical Center, where she also holds joint appointments in the School of Nursing and Allied Health and the Department of History and Philosophy of Medicine. She is principal investigator of the Research Integrity Project at the Midwest Bioethics Center. At the U.S. Department of Health and Human Services she serves as chair of the National Human Research Protections Advisory Committee and as a special expert consultant to the Secretary on research involving children and prisoners. She has been a member of on-site evaluation teams for the Office for

Human Research Protections. She sits on the Council of Academic Societies of the Association of American Medical Colleges. At the National Institutes of Health, Dr. Marshall served on the first special research ethics review panel advisory to the director and sits on the Cardiology and Hematology Data Safety and Monitoring Boards of the National Heart, Lung, and Blood Institute. She has served on multiple special emphasis panels, review panels and study sections in the public and private sectors. She is a past president of the American Society for Bioethics and Humanities and the American Association for Bioethics. She is an elected fellow of the American College of Critical Care Medicine and a former fellow of the Kennedy Institute of Ethics. She received the Trailblazer Award from the NAACP (Charleston Chapter) in 1999 for her work in perinatal substance abuse and has testified on this subject before Congress and in US District Court. She serves on the Life Sciences Research Committee for the State of Missouri. Dr. Marshall received a B.S.N. and a Ph.D. in religious studies (applied ethics) from the University of Virginia. She is a coauthor of the best selling text *Introduction to Clinical Ethics*. She has published numerous books, chapters, and articles in the fields of research and clinical ethics as well as on perinatal substance abuse.

Carol Saunders, R.N., is president and chief executive officer of the Center for Clinical Research Practice, a corporation that produces and publishes educational and management resources for institutions, sponsors, and clinical research professionals. She is executive director of the New England Institutional Review Board, which provides ethical review services for sponsors and investigators of drug and device studies. Coeditor of *Research Practitioner*, she has published extensively and lectured on a broad range of research-related topics and has been recognized for excellence in medical communications by the American Medical Writers Association. She has coauthored several textbooks on clinical research and human subject protection, including standard operating procedures for both investigative sites and sponsors. She earned a B.S.N. from Boston College and was elected a community leader Alpha Chi Chapter, Sigma Theta Tau International.

Dennis Tolsma, M.P.H., is associate director of Clinical Affairs and director of research at Kaiser Permanente in Atlanta. He is chair (2001–2002) of the Board of HMO Research Network, chair of the Science Steering Committee for a Centers for Disease Control and Prevention research contract with the Alliance for Community Health Programs and America Association of Health Plans, and a member of Kaiser Permanente Research Advisory Council. From 1994 to 1998, he was director of prevention and practice analysis for Kaiser Permanente and chaired the company's Institutional Review Board from 1995 to 1999. Before joining Kaiser, he was associate director for public health practice at the Centers for Disease Control and Prevention. He received an A.B. in mathematics and English from Calvin College and an M.P.H. from Columbia University.

LIAISONS

Richard J. Bonnie, L.L.B., is John S. Battle Professor of Law at the University of Virginia School of Law and director of the University's Institute of Law, Psychiatry, and Public Policy. He previously served as associate director of the National Commission on Marijuana and Drug Abuse, a member of the National Advisory Council on Drug Abuse, chair of Virginia's State Human Rights Committee responsible for protecting the rights of persons with mental disabilities, adviser for the American Bar Association's Criminal Justice Mental Health Standards Project, and a member of the John D. and Catherine T. MacArthur Foundation Research Network on Mental Health and the Law. He was a member of a delegation of the U.S. State Department that assessed changes in the Soviet Union relating to political abuse of psychiatry and is a member of the Board of Directors of the Geneva Initiative on Psychiatry. Mr. Bonnie is a member of the Institute of Medicine and has also served on and chaired numerous Institute of Medicine committees. He recently chaired an NRC committee on research on elder abuse and neglect. In addition, he serves as an adviser to the American Psychiatric Association's Council on Psychiatry and Law and received the American Psychiatric Association's prestigious Isaac Ray Award in 1998 for contributions to forensic psychiatry and the psychiatric aspects of jurisprudence. Mr. Bonnie is a liaison from the IOM Board on Neuroscience and Behavioral Health.

Nancy Neveloff Dubler, L.L.B., is the director of the Division of Bioethics, Montefiore Medical Center, and Professor of Epidemiology and Social Medicine at the Albert Einstein College of Medicine. She received a B.A. from Barnard College and an L.L.B. from Harvard Law School. Ms. Dubler founded the Bioethics Consultation Service at Montefiore Medical Center in 1978. She lectures extensively and is the author of numerous articles and books on termination of care, home care and long-term care, geriatrics, prison and jail health care, and AIDS. She is codirector of the Certificate Program in Bioethics and the Medical Humanities, conducted with The Hartford Institute of Geriatric Nursing at New York University. Her most recent books are *Ethics on Call: Taking Charge of Life and Death Choices in Today's Health Care System* (Vintage Books, 1993), and *Mediating Bioethical Disputes* (The United Hospital Fund, 1994; Second Edition, 2002). She consults often with federal agencies, national working groups, and bioethics centers and served as co-chair of the Bioethics Working Group at the National Health Care Reform Task Force. Ms. Dubler is a liaison from the Board on Health Sciences Policy.

Elena Ottolenghi Nightingale, M.D., Ph.D., is a scholar-in-residence at the National Research Council and the Institute of Medicine (IOM) and adjunct professor of pediatrics at both Georgetown University Medical Center and George Washington University Medical Center. She is a member of the Institute of Medicine. Dr. Nightingale serves as liaison or adviser to several IOM activities and is a member emerita of the IOM Board on Health Promotion and Disease Prevention. For more than 11 years she was special adviser to the president and senior program officer at Carnegie Corporation of New York and lecturer in social medicine at Harvard University. She retired from both positions at the end of 1994. Dr. Nightingale earned an A.B. degree in zoology, summa cum laude, from Barnard College of Columbia University, a Ph.D. in microbial genetics from the Rockefeller University, and an M.D. from New York University School of Medicine. She is a fellow of the American Association for the Advancement of Science, the New York Academy of Sciences, and the Royal Society of Medicine. She has authored numerous book chapters and articles on microbial genetics, health (particularly child and adolescent health and well-being and health promotion and disease prevention), health policy, and human rights. Her current research interest is in improving the safety and security of young adolescents in the United States. Dr. Nightingale continues to be active in the protection of human rights, particularly those of children. She also continues to work on enhancing the participation of health professionals and health professional organizations in the protection of human rights. She has lectured and written widely on these topics, particularly on the role of physicians as perpetrators and protectors of human rights. Currently she serves on the Advisory Committee of the Children's Rights Division of Human Rights Watch. She has also served on the Board of the Children's Research Institute of the Children's National Medical Center in Washington, D.C., and is on the Institutional Review Board of that institution. Dr. Nightingale is a liaison from the IOM Board on Children, Youth, and Families and is a member of the joint IOM/NRC Committee on Adolescent Health and Development.

Pilar N. Ossorio, Ph.D., JD, is Assistant Professor of Law and Bioethics at the University of Wisconsin at Madison. She is also Associate Director at the Center for the Study of Cultural Diversity in Health Care. Prior to taking her position at UW, she was Director of the Genetics Section at the Institute for Ethics at the American Medical Association, and taught as an adjunct faculty member at the University of Chicago Law School. Dr. Ossorio received her Ph.D. in Microbiology and Immunology in 1990 from Stanford University. She went on to complete a post-doctoral fellowship in cell biology at Yale University School of Medicine. Throughout the early 1990s, Dr. Ossorio also worked as a consultant for the federal program on the Ethical, Legal, and Social Implications (ELSI) of the Human Genome Project, and in 1994 she took a full-time position with the Department of Energy's ELSI program. In 1993, she served on the Ethics Working Group for President Clinton's Health Care Reform Task Force. Dr. Ossorio received her JD from the University of California at Berkeley School of Law (Boalt Hall) in 1997. While at Boalt she was elected to the legal honor society Order of the Coif and received several awards for outstanding legal scholarship. Dr. Ossorio is a fellow of the American Association for the Advancement of Science (AAAS), a past member of AAAS's Committee on Scientific Freedom and Responsibility, a past member of the National Cancer Policy Board at the National Academy of Sciences, and has been a member or chair of several working groups on genetics and ethics. She has published scholarly articles in bioethics, law and molecular biology.

STUDY STAFF

Laura Lyman Rodriguez, Ph.D., is a senior program officer in the Board on Health Sciences Policy at the Institute of Medicine and is the study director for Assessing the System for Protecting Human Research Participants. She came to the Institute of Medicine from the Office of Public Affairs at the Federation of American Societies for Experimental Biology (FASEB), where she was a policy analyst covering human subjects research and institutional review board issues, bioethics, and federal funding priorities. Before her tenure at FASEB, Dr. Rodriguez was a congressional fellow in the office of Representative Vernon J. Ehlers (MI), where she focused on national science policy issues and K-12 math and science education. Dr. Rodriguez has expertise in cell biology and genetics and is particularly interested in clinical research issues and the policy implications of genomics.

Robert Cook-Deegan, M.D., is director of the Center for Genome Ethics, Law, and Policy at Duke University. Until June 2002, he directed the Robert Wood Johnson Health Policy Fellowship Program at the Institute of Medicine and was a senior program officer for IOM's Health Sciences Policy Board. Outside IOM, he is also a Robert Wood Johnson Health Policy Investigator at the Kennedy Institute of Ethics, Georgetown University, where he is writing a primer on how national policy decisions are made about health research. He is also a seminar leader for the Stanford-in-Washington program.

Jessica Aungst is a research assistant in the Division of Health Sciences Policy of the Institute of Medicine. She received a degree in English with a minor in sociology from the State University of New York, Geneseo. Previously, she worked for the Maldon Institute, researching and writing about international affairs.

Natasha S. Dickson is a senior project assistant with the National Academies' Institute of Medicine in Washington DC. She is a graduate of St. Augustine Senior Comprehensive Secondary School in Trinidad and Tobago. She gained most of her administrative experience while working as a clerical assistant at the University of the West Indies, St. Augustine, Trinidad. She also worked as an advertising sales representative and freelance reporter for the Trinidad Express Newspapers before moving to the U.S.A. in March 2000. She became an administrative receptionist for telecommunications lobbyists Simon Strategies LLC before joining the National Academies in March 2001.

IOM BOARD ON HEALTH SCIENCES POLICY STAFF

Andrew Pope, Ph.D., is director of the Board on Health Sciences Policy at the Institute of Medicine. With expertise in physiology and biochemistry, his primary interests focus on environmental and occupational influences on human health. Dr. Pope's previous research activities focused on the neuroendocrine and reproductive effects of various environmental substances on food-producing animals. During his tenure at the National Academy of Sciences, and since 1989 at the Institute of Medicine, Dr. Pope has directed numerous studies. The topics of these studies include injury control, disability prevention, biologic markers, neurotoxicology, indoor allergens, and the enhancement of environmental and occupational health content in medical and nursing school curricula. Most recently, Dr. Pope directed studies on priority-setting processes at the National Institutes of Health, fluid resuscitation practices in combat casualties, and organ procurement and transplantation.

Charles H. Evans, Jr., M.D., Ph.D., is a Scholar-in-Residence at the Institute of Medicine (IOM). During 1998-2001, he served as Head of the Health Sciences Section and as senior Adviser for Biomedical and Clinical Research at the IOM. He was the study director for the IOM-NAS-NAE National Town Meeting for Discussion of the Common Federal Definition of Research Misconduct, Procedures and Policies, and the IOM Committees on Creating a Vision for Space Medicine during Travel Beyond Earth Orbit and on Strategies for Small Number Participant Clinical Research Trials. A pediatrician and immunologist, Dr. Evans received his B.S. in biology from Union College, and his M.D. and Ph.D. from the University of Virginia. His advanced training in pediatrics was at the University of Virginia Medical Center. Following his postgraduate training he was appointed to the National Institutes of Health intramural staff as a principal investigator and during 1975-1998 he served as Chief of the Tumor Biology Section at the National Cancer Institute. Dr. Evans's research interests are carcinogenesis (the etiology of cancer) and the normal immune system defenses to the development of cancer. Dr. Evans is an author of more than 125 scientific articles and is the recipient of numerous scientific awards including the Outstanding Service Medal from the U.S. Public Health Service and the Wellcome Medal and Prize. He is a Fellow of the American Association for the Advancement of Science, the American Institute of Chemists and a credentialed Fellow in Health Systems Administration of the American Academy of Medical Administrators. An active advisor to community medicine and higher education, he has served on several health system and university Boards of Trustees.

CONSULTANT

Kathi E. Hanna, M.S., Ph.D., is a science and health policy consultant specializing in biomedical research policy and bioethics. She has served as research director and senior consultant to the National Bioethics Advisory Commission and as senior adviser to the President's Advisory Committee on Gulf War Veterans Illnesses. In the 1980s and early 1990s, Dr. Hanna was a senior analyst at the now defunct congressional Office of Technology Assessment, contributing to numerous science policy studies requested by committees of the U.S. House and U.S. Senate on science education, research funding, biotechnology, women's health, human genetics, bioethics, and reproductive technologies. In the past decade she has served as a consultant to the Howard Hughes Medical Institute, the National Institutes of Health, the Institute of Medicine, and several charitable foundations. In the early 1980s, Dr. Hanna staffed committees of the American Psychological Association that were responsible for oversight of policies related to the protection of human participants in research and animal research. Before coming to Washington, D.C., she was the genetics coordinator at Children's Memorial Hospital in Chicago, where she directed clinical counseling and coordinated an international research program investigating prenatal diagnosis of cystic fibrosis. Dr. Hanna received an A.B. in biology from Lafayette College, an M.S. in human genetics from Sarah Lawrence College, and a Ph.D. from the School of Business and Public Management, George Washington University.

Index